THE ACHIEVEMENT
OF KARL RAHNER

The Achievement of Karl Rahner

LOUIS ROBERTS

HERDER AND HERDER

1967

HERDER AND HERDER NEW YORK
232 Madison Avenue, New York 10016

Nihil obstat: Thomas J. Beary, Censor Librorum
Imprimatur: ✠ Robert F. Joyce, Bishop of Burlington
July 28, 1967

CONTENTS

FOREWORD

A theologian who publishes the fruits of his studies and reflections most certainly desires to have as wide a readership as possible. Particularly in the case of the Catholic theologian, who must always practice his art within the realm of faith of the Church, he must want above all to witness to that faith, to "think with the faith"; but it is precisely this witness which he cannot achieve except by making the Church's faith his own by allowing it to suffuse his person and temperament. This can never be done merely by passively accepting a doctrine, or by simply repeating what has been passed on to him. To this extent, therefore, a Catholic theologian might speak of "his (own) theology," for in the final analysis such a phrase does not necessarily signify originality and creativity on his part; rather it points up the limited, fragmentary nature of what he has done, how liable "his theology" is to the criticisms of his fellow theologians with whom he shares a common faith. Thus when a theologian's "own" theology is spoken of, what is implied is the hope that this will help others to find their "own" theology as their own comprehension of the faith of the Church.

I am grateful, therefore, that Dr. Louis Roberts has written this present "introduction" to "my" theology—all the more so in that it is a project which I myself have been unable to realize. It is one thing to distil a theologian's work into a kind of digest, as Otto Weber has done with Karl Barth's *Church Dogmatics*—that is a commendable and helpful service, but it is a much easier task than what Dr. Roberts has attempted: fashioning the *membra disiecta* of a theology into an organic whole. Happily, I believe that he came to solve many of the problems raised by this undertaking while he was still a student of mine in Innsbruck.

This is not the place to go into details regarding particulars of this presentation. The reader is constantly referred to my own writings, and if he wishes to have fuller understanding on any point he can easily locate the relevant passage. Of course, such an introduction cannot exceed a certain number of pages, or otherwise it perhaps becomes more profitable to read in the first place a number of the more significant works from which the material of this introduction is derived. The reader must also keep in mind that the theological environment is such that no theologian's "own" theology can be fully and precisely presented in all details, especially since he is so dependent on so many other theologians, and indeed far more reliant on them than Dr. Roberts indicates, with regard to me, in this first chapter, referring particularly to Maréchal, Blondel, and Heidegger. (Perhaps Dr. Roberts overestimates this latter influence somewhat.) A further consideration is that the "development" of a personal theology cannot be the perfect subject of an introduction. It goes without saying that today I would not always or necessarily say about certain subjects (and not only on the question of monogenism) what I said about them in previous years. This is not to say that the development of my theology was so radical, so full of "reversals" that any introduction to my thought would have to give a full account of them. Finally, of course, it ought to be pointed out that such a thoroughgoing introduction as Dr. Roberts has undertaken cannot at the same time be a critique of what I have written. (Perhaps Dr. Roberts has also—in order to do me honor —overemphasized the aporetic in my theology. Surely I do not raise a question simply to disquiet other theologians, but also to help elicit an answer to it. But of course, the theologian must answer with a question, and in such a way that he is dealing with the eternal mystery which is called God.)

In closing, I would like to express again my sincere gratitude to Dr. Roberts, and to wish his book success.

KARL RAHNER

THE ACHIEVEMENT
OF KARL RAHNER

INTRODUCTION

Karl Rahner is a nervous man. When he lectures, he paces up and down the platform or traverses the length of a side wall. His eyes seem to peer beyond his listeners and they squint a little bit through his glasses. He had the habit of playing with the long green drapes on the windows of his lecture hall in the theological faculty of the University of Innsbruck, where he taught so many years. While talking he may stop and stare several seconds at light patterns formed by the sun streaming through a windowpane. He cannot be motionless for any length of time. This constant activity perhaps overflows from the constant cerebration of this theologian, whose interests range over scientific and historical subjects and whose friendships number directors of the scientific Paulus Gesellschaft and literary people like novelist Luise Rinser.

Rahner's nervousness and tireless productivity partially explain the vast range of his published thought. He is not a scholar in the typical German sense of *Wissenschaftler*. He is professedly exploratory, even in his more thoroughly "scholastic" or "patristic" studies. His genius is not in the laborious effort of verification but in the more unique area of synthesis. His talent lies in asking the right questions. He pounces on important themes and these recur over and over again with ever so slight variations. The same insights are expanded and given new applications. Rahner at work has been likened to an intellectual spider spinning forth a splendid web, all points of which are directed ultimately at trying to clarify for modern man some of the exquisite insights of genuine theological method and what this method can disclose to man's inquiry.

Until recently any theologian could, like a well-rounded Cartesian, expound his set of clear and distinct ideas from shopworn theology manuals and demonstrate his points by means of a well-chosen string of Denzinger numbers. Whatever else might be happening in the intellectual climate would have little effect on theology. Today an eruption of earthquake proportions is taking place in theology. And everything happening in the intellectual climate is tempering the conduct of theology. Some view this as sheer chaos. Others think it a glorious chaos. No matter how history will interpret this chaotic situation, there is little doubt that the future will be different because of the work of a number of theologians today. Among the leaders stands out Karl Rahner.

Predicting the theology of the future is like predicting the weather. It is always subject to change. But evidence exists for making the educated "guess" that Rahner will become more influential rather than less, not because of what he has done but because of what he leaves undone. He asks the real questions and points to possible directions for their solution. This direction reveals the course of future theology. And all theologians work around this fundamental direction. Today there is no such thing as a "school" of theological thought in Catholicism or anything like the abortive *nouvelle théologie* movement of three decades ago. Among theologians there are differences. For example, Hans Küng and Karl Rahner have little in common except that they both teach at German universities (Küng at Tübingen and Rahner at Munich) and both desire to produce good theology. But Rahner cannot be understood without appreciating his considerable ability as a philosopher, whereas Küng might never have studied philosophy in his life for all the real difference it makes in what he writes. Bernard Lonergan, Hans Urs von Balthasar, and Karl Rahner all share a common philosophical vision, but Lonergan tends to be more "traditionally scholastic," Urs von Balthasar more patristic and historical, while Rahner tends to emphasize his transcendental method.

This emphasis accounts for not a little of Rahner's obscurity. His German tends to be opaque and his periodic style frustrating. His brother Hugo, professor of church history at Innsbruck, likes to joke that someday when he has time he will translate Karl into German. But just as it is nearly impossible to translate Kant or Hegel or Heidegger, so is it impossible to translate Rahner. When his work does appear in English, as is slowly the case, not a great deal of enlightenment about this theologian results. A number of works have already appeared about Karl Rahner's theology. Justification for another book must be in the form of a new approach. Such a book must offer new material.

I have tried in this book to focus on the question of Rahner's transcendental method, the source of so much obscurity in his thought. Hence the book must be a difficult book. One cannot treat of transcendental philosophy in simple terms without wrenching the context all out of proportion. I have tried whenever possible to let Rahner speak for himself, that is, follow the logical order of his reasoning process. But not everything is to be found formally in his thought. Some conclusions and some premises are my own, but I believe that they all follow upon or are conditions of what Rahner thinks. Not everything is based on published materials. Much of what is developed comes from notes taken over a three-year period of listening to Rahner lecture at Innsbruck and in the "free theological discussions" it was his habit to hold on Friday evenings.

I have annotated wherever I felt it was absolutely necessary. Otherwise the reference must be to his publications or doctrines found in hundreds of places, primarily his series of *Schriften* and his many contributions to the *Lexikon für Theologie und Kirche* edited by him and probably the most convenient source for a quick view of his thinking on most questions. The appendices contain brief notes and bibliographical references which will provide help in obtaining more detailed information. The bibliographical citations are not meant to be complete in any sense but are rather representative of those I found most helpful, either because they clarify some position or are themselves good bibliographical sources. When possible I have indicated English sources, though I have not meant to be complete in this respect either. Anyone interested enough can easily obtain further information from the brief sources indicated.

The order of the book both mirrors the tightness of Rahner's theological system and follows roughly his own plan for ordering the various theological tractates. A summary of this kind cannot expect to give more than a brief critical synopsis of Rahner's thought on any question. Because the emphasis of the book tends to be upon method, more traditional arguments from scripture and the magisterium—which in the long run do not differ a great deal from those of most theologians—have been largely neglected. Finally, I have not tried to examine critically many of the assumptions involved in Rahner's arguments. I agree with most of these, but I also disagree with a significant number, particularly in questions which Rahner himself would admit are still open. Despite the obvious defects a book of this kind must display, its careful reading should assist anyone who wishes to gain insight into the thought of one of Catholicism's most powerful thinkers, Karl Rahner.

CHAPTER ONE

PHILOSOPHICAL PROLEGOMENON

Theology is traditionally dogmatics, the positive science developed from the data of revelation, not a search—in scripture or reason or elsewhere—for answers to prior questions arising out of an analysis of the human situation. The scope of Karl Rahner's theology includes traditional dogmatics as well as biblical theology, patristics, and almost any other interest that bears on the life of man today. Yet the concern of theology with the data of revelation takes on in Rahner's thought an added dimension. For these data of revelation comprehend for Rahner not only the usual understanding of revelation found in theology manuals and texts but also and more importantly man in his existential dimensions. These focus primarily on man as questioner in his openness to the infinite. These existential dimensions of man's being structure Rahner's entire approach to theological method.

It is with Rahner's approach to theological method that this book is concerned. For this is a book about method. Perhaps the word *hermeneutics* should be used instead of *method*. The nature of theology as a whole is hermeneutical. Its method is hermeneutical, though not in the common meaning of hermeneutics as a general theory or "technique" of understanding. Theology lives as an understanding of certain specific contents of revelation and so is a continual effort to understand better. In a sense, asking about the program of Rahner's theology cannot avoid the problem of understanding, the hermeneutical problem. Every theologian must face up to the nature of understanding and of knowledge. More than most theologians today, Rahner not only faces it squarely but his very hermeneutics constitutes his method. This contrasts with other theologians who assume a method and work wholly from data given by history or the magisterium and scripture. Were Rahner not a brilliant metaphysician, his hermeneutics would not play such an important role in his theology, which depends on his method. And to understand Rahner's hermeneutics is to understand his theology. This is a book about Rahner's theology and so about his hermeneutics. It will not make for easy reading. But any reader should gain from the book some help in understanding Karl Rahner and some insight into his theological method.

Because Rahner's hermeneutics serve as the "open sesame" for understanding his sometimes convoluted thought and because they really do knit the scattered published works of this theologian into a tight system, a study of method becomes the logical starting point for any understanding of his work. But because of the very tightness of his system, it is almost impossible to separate philosophical principles from theological conclusions without first analyzing his philosophy and anthropology (understanding man as the *locus* of openness to the infinite, as receiver of revelation).

Yet it is with a number of reservations that I begin this book with an analysis of some basic ideas structuring Rahner's thought. His metaphysics contributes to his greatness as a theologian. But this means that without some familiarity with his philosophy, understanding Rahner's unique contributions to the theological enterprise is precluded. Ultimately, any theology will only be as valid as the philosophy that gives rise to it.

A philosophical paradigm of the one in the many and the many in the one models Rahner's hermeneutics. The more clearly this paradigm is perceived, the deeper one can peer into the vastness of his insight and the more orderly his work becomes. No summary account can give a fair treatment to philosophical questions of any sort, let alone those attempting clarifications of fundamentally transcendental positions. This is especially true of Rahner. The footnotes and bibliographical information in the appendices will supply the more philosophically oriented with directions for finding a fuller and more satisfying treatment.

PLAN OF CHAPTER

This first chapter, then, indicates in skeletal fashion the philosophical premises used by Rahner to draw conclusions in theological argument. What is of greater significance for his hermeneutics will be developed—sometimes at the expense of repetition—more fully than other questions. After noting something about the origins of Rahner's positions, the chapter discusses them in terms of his metaphysics (philosophy of being) and of his epistemology (philosophy of knowledge). Thirdly, the chapter singles out some important principles to be given contextual development in later chapters. Finally, the chapter finds its resolution in a brief but important discussion of the relation between philosophy and theology.

I. SOURCES OF KARL RAHNER'S PHILOSOPHY

George A. Lindbeck has stated that a rather Heideggerian interpretation of Aquinas's metaphysics of knowledge and an ontological anthropology constitute the philosophical prolegomenon to Rahner's systematic theology.[1] Lindbeck summarizes quite correctly but his summary suffers from understatement. Rahner does indeed draw heavily on traditional interpretations of St. Thomas, but his reading of the text has been filtered by a transcendental approach. In this Rahner admits his heavy debt to the work of Joseph Maréchal [2] and Pierre Rousselot.[3] Above and beyond this influence of Maréchalian Thomism, German transcendental philosophy as such has left its distinct mark on Rahner's method. Because transcendental philosophy is so little known in Anglo-Saxon countries, it may be worth digressing for a moment or two on its nature and development—particularly since this way of "doing" philosophy orders most of Rahner's system.

A. Transcendental Philosophy

What distinguishes transcendental philosophy from Greek cosmologism and its concern with the "irrational" is concern with the human person. Kant, German Idealism, and modern phenomenology have given transcendental philosophy a horizon [4] which distinguishes it from both empirical and certain neo-Thomistic approaches to metaphysics. In general, transcendental philosophy is the enterprise which asks about the inner conditions for the possibility of metaphysics. In this tradition metaphysics is defined—as by Baumgarten—as the science which contains the first principles of that which is within the comprehension of human knowledge. Asking about these first principles has been called the basic direction of modern philosophy in its attempt to dislodge a naïve realism and to explain and ground itself. Yet in a broader sense transcendental philosophy means pursuit of knowledge not ordered to knowing things themselves but to understanding the generally unknown presuppositions or principles underlying all knowledge. In this sense Karl Rahner's hermeneutics and transcendental philosophy dovetail. Both ask the questions about the internal conditions for the possibility of knowing and of being.

B. History of Transcendental Philosophy

A transcendental philosophy of the question about preconditions has a history. Its association today with names like
Emmerich Coreth, Rahner, Max Müller, J. B. Metz, and
Bernard Lonergan may disguise both its long development
and the unique turn these men have given it. Historically,
Kant called the demonstration of the *a priori* conditions of
human knowledge "transcendental philosophy." Kant's
metaphysics turned out honestly enough to be a metaphysics of subjectivity, so Kant saw that under his premises he
had to reject the possibility of metaphysics.

Asking about the possibility of metaphysics already implies some knowledge of what is in question. For some
kind of knowledge must already be present in the one
asking the question. Kant refused to consider this possibility and limited knowledge to experience of the sensible
world. German Idealism reacted against Kant by positing a
purely deductive method for philosophy which was to
achieve completion by utilizing various formulations for
the concept of substance. Fichte began with the "absolute
self-positing ego" as distinguished from the "non-ego"
from which he was able to deduce all experience. This
meant that while Kant had worked back from the manifold
given in the content of consciousness to the all-embracing
unity, Fichte adopted the converse order and started from
the original activity of the ego and attempted to deduce
from it the special forms of the manifold. And this involved an actual construction of empirical consciousness.[5]
It seemed to solve the question of the principles of knowledge. For if I fix my attention on ordinary consciousness, I
find that I can think both of myself (ego) and of something which is not myself (non-ego). But even when I
think of the non-ego I can only do so in virtue of a
spiritual act. The non-ego exists only in virtue of an act of
the ego, only because it is posited. Fichte was led to posit a

dualism between infinite and finite. So the step from formal role to actual performance of the subject in the act was taken by Fichte, who thereby goes decisively beyond Kant and supplies the authoritative starting point for all German Idealism: the self-performing (actuating) and self-mediating spirit which experiences itself (ego in itself).[6] Fichte then attained being subjectively in man's self-performance. But this meant that thought was wholly enclosed in subjectivity. Schelling moved a further step backward to an Absolute prior to ego and non-ego. He asked how the organism can become its own object, and so obtained being before reason as an absolute *prius*.

Idealism then freed itself from total dominance of the concept of substance (as represented, for example, by Absolute Ego) by winning from the tension between Kant's system and the ontology of substance a pure activity of act, an enduring power in which ego seems to progress in a series of self-appearances which lead to the Absolute. (This involved an identification of the transcendentals with the Absolute.)

It was at this stage that Edmund Husserl furthered the transcendental critique with his transcendental-reductionist phenomenology of "pure intuition." Kierkegaard had already reacted violently against the Hegelian synthesis and had injected the stream of modern subjectivism into the question about objective spirit. But Husserl saw the origin of understanding not just in the power of the act of knowing (the formal conditions), but in the systematic, *self-performed* examination of the area of the subjectivity of knowing itself in its constitutive performances. We must remember that metaphysics is to be the science containing the first principles of what is within the comprehension of human knowledge. Hence the temptation to see the study of phenomena as performed by the subject in a reductionist thesis in Husserl's phenomenology came as a wholly logical step. And Husserl argued that talk about the object or thing-in-itself could only be justified when its meaning had been demonstrated by a return to its primordial source in the constitutive, experienced performances of subjectivity. Now, since the intentionality of this act includes an unthematic element—among which the limits of time and history are especially important—a knower is forced to distinguish in the performance of his knowledge the mundane from the transcendental, the world from the spirit. Husserl, however, bracketed out being-in-itself, not only regarding objects but also regarding the subject's own performance. He restricted philosophy to a purely eidetic science, a philosophy of pure essences.

Husserl's student Martin Heidegger was the first to break open the union of idealist conceptualism (represented by Fichte and Schelling) and the concept of the subject as developed by Husserl. It was a step forward similar to Fichte's progress beyond Kant. For Heidegger went beyond Husserl to interpret the self-performance of the subject as the being of the existent. He did this by conducting a transcendental questioning of the human self-performance about the possibility of knowing.[7] Heidegger asked specifically about the very giveness of the *a priori,* about the manner of being and its constituents, about the *locus* or place of the transcendental, and about the essential correlation of these performances constituting the world. It was out of this development by Heidegger that attempts were made by Maurice Blondel and Joseph Maréchal to relate Christian philosophy to the tradition. Maréchal and Blondel took as unquestionably right from transcendental philosophy the insight that we always have being only in the medium of *consciousness.* But they added the proviso that any ontological analysis must be open to include God.

C. Joseph Maréchal

In Maréchal's philosophy the point of departure is intellectual knowledge taken as a fact, and especially the judgment of affirmation which is the consummation of knowledge. We ask ourselves what makes this affirmation possible? What is bound up in every affirmation—for example, "San Francisco is (or is not) the second largest city in California"? From all evidence, as Kant would admit, every such affirmation includes a knowledge of being. But just what is being? It is the absolute outside of which there is nothing. Hence every affirmation must involve some knowledge of this absolute. But then what can be said about contingent propositions like "Margaret is blushing"? When uttered they too bear a certain absolute value which gives them their consistency and truth. It will be up to the intellect to qualify each affirmation and so determine whether what it affirms is definitive or not.

Just what is in fact this absolute, the consciousness of which is included in every affirmation? And what makes it absolute? Is it a matter of the law of contradiction governing all thinking? If I say that Margaret is blushing I cannot at the same time deny that she is blushing. If the absolute is this law, then we simply have a convention for avoiding inconsistency and so the mind would fashion the absolute. Maréchal held that if every affirmation includes some absolute, then it can only be because there *is* an absolute Being. The intelligible world in its consistency and coherence necessarily implies the existence of a Being who *is* unconditionally. Otherwise everything would fall apart. This is why every affirmation affirms implicitly that God is, so that by its inner dynamism, its "natural appetite," the human intellect drives toward God.

Maréchal's fundamental issue is that the known (or intentional) being is some being that is, and so there is no need to go beyond ourselves to know being. For Maréchal this absolute character of our judgment reveals the existence of the Absolute; not that the being placed in the judgment is God—that would be Ontologism—but that it does point to God. And by reason of this ordination the mind can objectify, that is, it can affirm as existing certain contents of its thought. Here are introduced both the distinction between extramental and intentional being and the solution to the critical problem. Maréchal's originality consists in attempting to proceed from intentional to extramental being, whereas classical positions would rather begin by taking such a distinction for granted and then attempt to justify it by reflection on the act of knowing.

We will see that Karl Rahner's position is basically that of Maréchal as outlined above. It is for this reason that we have focused on Maréchal to this extent. But Rahner found another source of philosophical inspiration in Martin Heidegger.

D. Martin Heidegger

Paradoxically, the real figure dominating German theology at present and who will probably do so increasingly is not a theologian at all. He is what Germans call a *Denker* (thinker): Martin Heidegger. In 1934 Rahner was sent by his Jesuit superior to study philosophy at Freiburg under the supervision of Martin Honecker, a little known neo-scholastic (and not, as is commonly misunderstood, under Heidegger). Rahner did attend some of Heidegger's lectures where he picked up several common concerns. Of course, much of Heidegger agrees astonishingly well with Maréchal. But just how heavy Rahner's obligation to Heidegger is will only become apparent when we see how a Heideggerian doctrine of existentials determines Rahner's anthropology. In talking about Heidegger's influence philosophically, we are concerned now with the problem of hermeneutics and concepts.

In spite of some stark differences, scholars commonly agree that the fundamental positions of Sartre, Gabriel Marcel, Jaspers, Merleau-Ponty, and Heidegger are all elaborations of the same primitive fact, the intentionality of existence conceived as man's essential openness, as the encounter of subjectivity with given realities which are not this subjectivity. Yet Heidegger is not to be classed with

Sartre or Merleau-Ponty. Nor is Karl Rahner "existential" in the same sense as Heidegger. Yet should it appear that the philosophical vision of the existentialists is shared by Rahner, he would have to be classed with this group of "existential" thinkers.

It is particularly in Heideggerian themes that we find the strongest influence on Rahner—in themes of Being and Time, dread and fear, death and repetition, time and historicity. True, the influence of the later Heidegger, so strong at present in Protestant theology, is not profound in the case of Rahner. Yet the themes do remain constant. In addition, Rahner has adopted verbatim a number of concepts which require careful analysis. For Heidegger did with otherwise commonly accepted terms in German what Whitehead was forced to do in English, give these words entirely new significations in order that they might carry the burden of his original insights. Many of Rahner's arguments, like those of Heidegger, appeal to structures and concepts of the German language which cannot easily be rethought or understood in English.[8] A good illustration might be the term *Gelichtetheit* (luminosity). Rahner tells us in *Hörer des Wortes* that being is *an sich selbst gelichtet* (illuminated of itself). For Heidegger, being (*Sein*)—the process of lighting—is such as to manifest itself in every case *in* beings or existents (*Seiendes*)—that which is lighted. But it does this in such a way as to draw attention away from itself and to the illuminated beings upon which it has conferred its "is"—shed its light. To ground metaphysics is to think the Being-process (process of making luminous) in order to comprehend it in its positivity (capacity to reveal existents—which makes metaphysics possible as the study of beings in their being-ness) and its negativity (tendency to self-concealment, which brings about obliteration of the distinction between Being and beings and resultant confusion).[9]

Just as Maréchal had understood being as the *a priori* form making possible our knowledge, Heidegger speaks of the *a priori* understanding of being which signifies the existent, the being-in-the-world, making it an illumination of being, the *locus* of the truth of being which makes it possible to encounter an existent under the horizon of Being. It is the quality of being *gelichtet* (illuminated) which makes being present to itself. Given this understanding, we can come to see that Heidegger's influence on Rahner is nearly as great as Maréchal's.

Rahner brings Heidegger's stress on man's existential dimensions to its fullest development.[10] Rahner takes from Heidegger also his criticism of the convention of designating knowing man as a subject in opposition to the object as such. Defining man in this way suffers in much the same way as does defining God by contrast with creatures. Kierkegaard had first seen this difficulty and provided a missing element by referring to a kind of subjectivity logically prior to any distinction between subject and object. Heidegger attempted to capture some of the existential traits of human beings in asking about man. And just as Heidegger himself understood Kant's *Critique of Pure Reason* to be an answer to the question "What is man?", so Rahner has taken this as his fundamental issue. Man must know himself in himself as opposed to the world in order to be an existent. What Kant had referred to as the transcendental unity of apperception or the transcendental imagination is a stumbling approximation to that aspect of man wherein he is regarded precisely as an existent orientated to being as such. It is this aspect of orientation with which Rahner is primarily concerned.

Rahner found in St. Thomas a way to keep from accepting wholly Heidegger's answer to what is metaphysics. Rahner found an escape hatch in the Thomistic teaching that all knowledge must start from sense experience in the sense of a naïve realism. The theme of Rahner's first "philosophical" book, *Geist in Welt* (first published in 1939 and reëdited in 1957), dealt with this question of the relation between intellect and world. It asks about the possibility of metaphysics for an intellect whose knowledge must be derived entirely from the material beings of a spatio-temporal world presented to the intellect in what St. Thomas called the *phantasm*. Briefly, Rahner's philosophy encompasses a meditation upon consciousness (human knowledge) present to itself in the unfolding of its spiritual dynamics taking place in an encounter with the other.

II. RAHNER'S METAPHYSICS AND THEORY OF KNOWLEDGE

A. Transcendental Method

Rahner fits tightly into the tradition of transcendental philosophy. This is especially true of his hermeneutics. But before looking at this method, it is well to note something about the transcendental method in general. Rahner stands in a direct line of development. He considers Kantian any modern criticism of traditional metaphysics which focuses on the "objectivity" [11] of knowledge, the criticism which forced Kant to reject metaphysics. Transcendental philosophy has avoided Kant's criticism by placing the starting point of metaphysics in the very performance of the question of the possibility (as Fichte did in his analysis of consciousness), a question which Emmerich Coreth has carried one step further (in the performance of the question of the question of the possibility of metaphysics). Ultimately, the asking of questions must spring from the restless demands of critical intelligence. In its act intelligence grows, criticizes, and authenticates methods which meet its own standards. Hence the question is a rational and self-authenticating starting point for metaphysics. And metaphysics becomes truly the articulation of basic experience, the mediation—through reflection—of the immediate.[12]

Reflecting on the performance of the question reveals the conditions for the possibility of the question. These conditions are rendered as certain as is the performance of the question itself. Even though the question is asked in the context of man's experience of the world, there is an unthematic knowledge presupposed and necessarily involved in the question as the condition of its possibility. This *unthematic* knowledge means that it is not known in an express and reflexive manner but is what is present when something is known precisely as the condition for making the more reflexively known possible. Unthematic knowledge is that which is concomitantly present in the "performance" and so implies a necessary dialectic that strives to render thematic and reflexive what is contained unreflexively in the performance. In a sense the unthematic is what Heidegger means by his concept of "thinking" or Jaspers by his "clarification of existence." The reference is to a level of understanding different from immediate apprehension and yet not objectifying it in reflection. Modern philosophical analysis refers to something like this as "private language" and questions its possibility. At least at this important point there is a meeting place for linguistic analysis and Rahner-Maréchal metaphysics, each side having something to contribute. But how is this unthematic knowledge to be made thematic? Rahner accomplishes this in his use of the transcendental method.

As outlined by Kant and developed and rebuilt by philosophers of the tradition, the transcendental method is composed of a pendulum-like motion. The two extreme moments are reduction and deduction. The reductive moment consists in illuminating the data of consciousness out of what is presented immediately by indicating their transcendental *a priori* implications, the presuppositions of performing knowledge. It is grasping out of what is known or willed objectively and thematically to the pre-given, unthematic, non-objective content that is concomitant with the performance. In this moment transcendental philosophy has been called *a priori* by Heidegger.[13]

The deductive moment consists in the fact that out of the reductively obtained *prius* the objective performance in its essence and structure, its laws and limits are deduced. Reduction is the movement from *posterius* to *prius;* deduction, the movement from *prius* to *posterius*. Or reduction is like motion from below to above; and deduction, from above to below. Both moments in the transcendental method occur simultaneously with one moment being stressed at one time and another moment at another time.[14] Rahner develops this method as his hermeneutics and we will see it at work in later chapters where he is most original. The basic paradigm is the movement or dialectic between the one and the many, the constant metaphysical problem. Rahner specifically applies the method to a reflexion on human spirit made present to itself in response to the world of space and time grasped in sensation. He says that the validity of the method "is to be shown through the fact that what is shown is implicitly affirmed as valid there where it is only questioned or even where its validity is argued or put in doubt." [15] Following Heidegger, Rahner seems to be the first to have used this particular method as a strict hermeneutics.[16]

B. Geist in Welt: Spirit in the World

Rahner shows that the possibility of metaphysics for the human intellect can be grounded only in the unthematic knowledge of Absolute Being given in every objective judgment. Like Maréchal, Rahner maintains that such affirmation is only possible on the ground of an *a priori* drive of the intellect toward Absolute Being. Rahner holds that this realm is disclosed by application of the transcendental method to the conditions of the possibility of the judgment in which a universal quiddity is affirmed of a sensible, particular object.

Rahner demonstrates this in *Geist in Welt*—in terms of influence probably one of the most significant books of our time to use a transcendental hermeneutics. Although Rahner never explicitly discusses the method of metaphysics as such (a problem left for Coreth to handle, who relying on Rahner's original insight deduced a method of questioning the question), he dug his foundations in *Geist in Welt*. The superstructure of his theology rests firmly on these foundations. And once the transcendental method has been completely applied, the conditions for the possibility of metaphysics—and so for theology—have already been satisfied.

In the conduct of the transcendental method Rahner developed a number of themes which have attracted the attention of later authors. Among these themes are the perfect reflection in which the knowing subject becomes conscious of his own identity in the act of affirmation through which it posits an object over against itself, the identity of the abstraction of the intelligible species in the *conversio* to the phantasm as that one intellectual operation in which the intellect sees the abstract universal form in the one particular given in the phantasm, and infinite existence affirmed in the content of every objective judgment.

Rahner stresses the fact that he tried in *Geist in Welt* not to relate Thomas Aquinas's epistemology to the present, nor to do a historical study. Rather his intention was to further a linear development. *Geist in Welt* is his transcendental deduction of sensibility that belongs of necessity to a finite receptive intuition. To ward off criticism, he notes that his is in no way a Kantian critique of knowledge (*Erkenntniskritik*) but a critique of the metaphysics of knowledge (*Erkenntnismetaphysik*), and his concern as opposed to Kant focuses on a noetic hylomorphism (an analysis of the constituent principles of consciousness) corresponding to the ontological hylomorphism of the object. Were this understood in Aristotelian categories, Rahner could not be called an existentialist theologian. So we should remember that although many terms may sound traditional, transcendental philosophy tends to give them a meaning Cajetan could never have understood.

Geist (spirit) Rahner understands as the name for the power which knows the metaphysical (what is beyond the physical) in a "grasping" movement that reaches outside the physical world. *Welt* (world) is the name for the reality of the physical world available to immediate experience. It is the context of meaning that inheres in things. Rahner asks how according to St. Thomas human knowledge can be *Geist in Welt*. Here the meaning of the preposition *in* has an important connotation. For it indicates how a man is *in* the world. Heidegger had said man is in the world as a being who dwells with the things with which he is familiar and looks after them with care. Man is open to intentionality or directedness toward what is other than himself. In preserving the basic force of this preposition Heidegger thought he had brought into focus the phenomena (world) which are the structural ingredients of man's openness to or fundamental posture toward entities within his world.[17] Hence as one reads Rahner's frequent references to "world" it is important to think of *world* not only as what is presented by sensible experience and so rather like what Kant meant by "space," but also what is included when we say "He lives in a different world" or "She withdraws into her own private world." This should help clarify some points to be discussed in later chapters—particularly with reference to the pervasiveness of the *supernatural existential* and man's task of completing the "world."

C. Conversio ad phantasma: Conversion to the Phantasm

Rahner develops *Geist in Welt* as an elaboration of a statement of Aquinas and says the whole of the book can be summarized under the Thomistic phrase, *conversio ad phantasma*. A knowledge of the self and of the Absolute depends on knowledge of the *essentia rerum materialium* (essences of material things). Its possibility should be understood as depending on this knowledge. The corpus of *Geist in Welt* applies the transcendental method to *Quaestiones 84–86, pars prima,* of the *Summa Theologiae.* Rahner centers his discussion around answering the problem of knowledge. He says any satisfactory answer must include three basic directions:

> The answer must be concerned with intellectual knowledge, because this is the place of the appearance of a theological event.
> It must be concerned with knowledge of the world as the basic source of human knowledge (in its possibility).
> It must open up the possibility of an approach to an "other" than the world.

Sensation and intellection together form the one human objective intuition of the world in space and time. The real metaphysical question concerns the possibility of the question as a conscious act. This is *the* transcendental question which does not ask about the object alone but about the subject asking the question. In the second chapter of *Hörer des Wortes* Rahner develops this point and gives his reasons why it alone is the starting point of metaphysics and why it is the real question about man. Briefly, being is essentially knowing and being known in an original unity, a presence to self of the *Gelichtetheit* (luminosity) of being. The *conversio* involves this, for it asks about the possibility of metaphysics and shows that the question itself is metaphysical. The ability of metaphysics to question itself reveals that being is presence to self. To the extent that an existent is present to itself it has being.[18] The variation among the degrees of knowing is founded on the degree of immateriality of being. Rahner is careful to point out how the grade of a being's subjectivity indicates its "power" of being. Careful attention to his closely worked out argument guards against a possible idealist interpretation.[19] This particular section of *Geist in Welt* reads rather like Leibniz's *System des transzendentalen Idealismus,* where Leibniz observes that all the forces of Nature are powers of representation at different degrees. Elsewhere, in treating of angels, Rahner distances himself from any kind of monadology.[20] Schelling had carried this notion to an ultimate idealist conclusion, so Rahner's *caveat* is not out of place.

Any existent, then, enjoys interior illumination, that is, possesses itself by means of the object of logical truth in that degree in which it has being. Hence it can be known. So there is no *gap* to bridge between the knower and the known. The more man knows and wills, the more he draws back into himself and the more he becomes present to himself. The more he becomes present to himself, the more he places himself in the presence of Absolute Being. Stated differently, since being is primarily self-presence, the genuine and primordial object for a knower has to be himself. Hence the power of being of a knower and of that which is originally known must stand in a relation of identity.

Rahner sees the problem of the Thomistic theory of knowledge not in how the distance between knower and known can be bridged, since the "distance" is only apparent, but in the problem how the known which is originally identical with the knower can stand in a relation of otherness. The transcendental method must make provision for making this distinction between subject and object thematic, with the latter, the object, necessarily given independently of the subject. But such a distinction cannot be made unless it is previously and unthematically known in the question as one of the conditions of the possibility of the question. So the transcendental method renders as *a priori* that the object exists independently of the knowing performance of the subject. Just how a knowledge which recognizes the other as other is possible at all is really the existential question of the encounter of subjectivity with a given which is not this subjectivity. Hence Rahner's thought penetrates to the heart of the real problem of contemporary existentialism.

Man's attempt to understand himself implies the notion that he finds himself in the "world" in which the "other" is present and given as man's *objectum proprium*. Consequently, man's self-presence is given as his presence-to-another. On this basis man can understand himself in all his compossibilities. This point is most important in understanding Rahner's treatment of the theological virtues and will be repeated again in Chapter Four. Here we see how the question about knowledge becomes for Rahner an anthropological question. He summarizes by stating it in Aquinas's phrase as the *reditio completa in seipsum* (complete return to self). Yet Rahner understands by this what is usually meant by reflexivity or self-relatedness in the form of self-awareness. This is man's basic and ontologically indispensable structure, his true existential dimension. Man is only aware of himself (which is the same as saying he is only man) in so far as there exists a situation in which man has (is) this consciousness. Self-awareness is not immediate but is mediated; this is an ontological truth that enters into the constitution of man's *facticity*. It makes both knowledge and being a problem for man. At this point, then, Heidegger and Thomas Aquinas converge most closely in Rahner's thought. For the question about man can only be developed as the question about the *conversio ad phantasma*. This involves the return of the subject to himself in a knowledge that is self-presence.

1. MAN AS KNOWER

In developing this insight, Rahner asks about man as knower on three levels. These levels establish a transcendental dialectic: (1) the one knowing as sensation—*praesentia mundi;* (2) the one knowing as thought—*oppositio mundi;* (3) the one knowing in its very unity—*conversio ad phantasma.*

(1) If knowledge is self-presence and if there is to be a knowledge of another as a primary knowledge, and if the world is to be man's primary intuition, then it has to be of sensible, material being.[21] Since the intuition of sensible

things requires no *species expressa,* Thomas cannot be called a critical realist. Rahner holds that for Thomas space and time are the *a priori* forms of pure intuition.[22] He says this is true for time especially, because the *mobile* is a being the totality of whose realizations always lies ahead and so it always has "futurity." These pure forms are self-performed in the knowing act of sensation.

(2) Intellection is the ability of a human knower to question what is given him in sensation, to judge about it, and to objectify it. The judgment of affirmation is the consummation of knowledge. The possibility of a complete return to self is the distinctive mark of intellection.[23]

(3) The formula "Present-to-itself, set over against-another" expresses some notion of the more precise understanding of what knowledge is. Self-presence as really being-present-to-oneself, and this being-present-to-oneself as being-opposed-to-another, form one basic concept of the diadic character of the human intellect. Thomas called this the agent and possible intellect. The agent intellect is the *a priori* condition of knowing a form of matter. It involves a drive to the further possibility by means of which a form given in sensation is possessed both as limited and as abstracted. But the affirmation of real being as limited demands as its condition the reality of an unlimited Absolute. In this Rahner does not differ from Maréchal.

Rahner develops another statement of Aquinas.[24] Whatever is known intellectually is known only as illuminated by the light of the agent intellect and received in the possible intellect. Therefore, as in every color we see the material light, so in every intelligible object we see the light of the agent intellect, not however by way of an object, but by way of that by which we know (*in ratione medii cognoscendi*). Whatever is known intellectually contains data coming from within and data coming from without, that is, includes both *a priori* and *a posteriori* elements. The *a posteriori* elements are that which we know reflexively, the *a priori* elements are that by means of which we know whatever we know, the unthematic given. This notion goes to the heart of Rahner's method.

The *a priori* consciousness of the Absolute is wholly unthematic and non-objective. It cannot be made objective, so proofs for the existence of God are needed. Transcendental philosophy need not lead to Ontologism. Rather human knowledge is seen by Rahner as an ordered drive toward the Absolute. Man is distinctively spirit. Yet he possesses his unlimited drive only in the unlimited manner of his striving. Man only knows the Absolute to the extent that he experiences himself as open in the dynamism needed for each act of knowledge. In the excess of this drive man becomes *quodammodo omnia,* in a sense everything.[25]

Human understanding springs from the fact that man's actuality comprehends his ability to be known as self-presence. The agent intellect involves the spontaneity of man's drive, orientated to the totality of possible objects. As such it comprehends in its orientation all possible objects according to their most universal metaphysical structure (*sub ratione entis*). Still, the spirit needs the condition of sensibility in order to present to the possible intellect an object having this metaphysical structure. The excess of man's drive is the metaphysical *locus* or place where limited spirit recognizes its openness and its dependence on the Absolute.[26]

We shall now summarize briefly some chief points of *Geist in Welt* (and also of *Hörer des Wortes* as far as transcendental method is concerned). Every transcendental reflection on the performance of the question about being shows that it has as condition of its possibility an unthematic knowledge of being. The unthematic, non-reflexive knowledge is grounded in immediate awareness of this sensible. Man is aware of some identity between being and knowing in the performance. This identity between being and knowing, an identity in which being performs itself as knowing or in which knowing is realized as being, is the primordial knowledge on which all other knowledge is founded. Reflexion on the performance of the *conversio* makes it clear that being is different from and transcendent to the actual performance. This means that man knows being which is not identical with his performance and so the problem of objectivity finds a solution. Both subject and object are *a priori* conditions of man's questions about himself. They are *a priori* because the difference of subject and object does not have its ground in the performance, but the performance requires as the condition of its very possibility that subject and object be different.

Human presence to self must take place by means of sensation, and self-presence only becomes possible when man knows the *other*. The phantasm is the sensibly known as such. *Conversio ad phantasma* is the name for the act of sensible intuition which as united with an act of intellectual thought forms the one complete act of human knowledge. Because the sensible is apprehended in the dynamic tendency of the intellect, the particular is known as finite, that is, as incapable in its limitedness of satisfying the full extent of man's dynamism. Because of this act of comparing the particular with the absolute and ideal term of knowledge, the particular appears as existent (being) in relation to Being; and because of this, it appears as "such"—as a finite individual, corresponding to which, since it is finite, there are other possibles as objects of yet another possible experience. Since man knows the particular in this way, the universal is known simultaneously and vice versa. The judgment of affirmation is the completion of the knowledge act.

In this way transcendence relative to all possible objects of knowledge appears as a transcendental condition of the possibility of abstraction and consequently of judgment—that is, of comprehending something as *some thing*. This in turn is the condition for the complete return to self which characterizes human knowledge.

2. MAN AS FREEDOM

Since the human soul (*anima*) is something which does not have the power of becoming present to self, and since by itself it is not self-present, the soul enjoys the lowest degree of intellectual being. The precise determination of the human degree of being is *intellectivum in potentia*. We have seen how spirit is understood as drive (Hegelian "appetite"). This drive is toward the Absolute. Every being longs for its own perfection. The human spirit grasps its formal object in its drive toward the Absolute. Consequently, spirit has a perpetual orientation to its object, Absolute Being, the goal of man's total openness. In this sense Rahner defines man as *transcendental consciousness*.[27] All human activity can only be understood as a moment on the perpetual drive to satisfy its desire. This dynamic movement toward the Absolute is the *a priori* form under which the sensible must be apprehended. Aquinas calls this movement the *tendentia in objectum formale intellectus*.

For Rahner the performance in the drive involves a dialectic between the drive toward the Absolute (the source of the spring in every question) and the finite, conceptual expression in which the answer must be phrased on the objective level. All the various conceptual formulations are but stages through which the human spirit must pass in its drive toward that horizon already known unthematically. This insight of Rahner's into man's consciousness is the key to his understanding of human freedom.

The very ground of freedom is that abyss of mystery which can never be comprehended. It is not something not yet known but which could be known eventually. Rather it is the original datum of transcendental experience in knowledge and freedom which in its perpetual non-comprehensibility is the ground of the possibility of conceptualizing everything which comes under its horizon as a particular.[28] Freedom, then, means the *transcendence of the particular by means of the spirit*. This transcendence of sensation, the very return of spirit to self, is the freedom of the human spirit. By virtue of its dynamism spirit leaps toward its goal. In the course of this leap it frees itself from sensation, and in this way it is not sensible but "abstract"—involving a return to itself. So the very possibility of a return to self is grounded in freedom. We have already observed how the concept of a return to self is what distinguishes man from other beings.

Freedom, then, must be understood previous to objective experience as a *form* of transcendental experience. So freedom really is subjectivity. Man's freedom is a more original reality than any possible, factual objective choice. In other words, just as the ontological structure of any being determines its activity, so the freedom of man's spirit means that man is bound to be and become the person he is through exercise of his freedom. This insight gives Rahner an opening for a penetrating theological analysis of the meaning of sin as a misuse of human freedom. For freedom is self-responsibility. In the harsh reality of the terrible every day man must act continually for eternity, because every one of his decisions takes place under the horizon of the Absolute acting on a particular. Subjectivity, the very performance of the person, is accomplished in the natural order. And this is where the very createdness of human freedom becomes most clear.[29]

In a sense, freedom is really total power. It calls forth a determination of the whole man, whether to effect his salvation or his perdition, in the intermingling of his existential dimensions—his relations to self, the world, and to God. Freedom is always the self-performance of the spirit in choosing objectively with respect to total performance. So it implies total responsibility for man's existence. Of course, this performance may have a temporal extension lasting over a man's entire life span. (This will be discussed more fully in later chapters.)

D. Summary: Anthropological Considerations

Rahner's anthropology (in a sense, the real subject of his theological method) is a logical development upon his understanding of man as transcendental consciousness. In order that man attend to whether God speaks to him, man must know that God exists. The existence of God is demonstrated by unfolding the implications found in the givenness of limited existents. The transcendental method establishes the fact that every limited existent has a real and substantial relation to God. But only transcendental consciousness can become aware of this relation. Man's free spirit strives beyond this limit of his nature toward the Absolute. For man must realize his transcendence in freedom. And the more man transcends himself, the more he realizes himself. The drive toward the Absolute expresses itself in an orientation to the "world"—especially to other persons.

In order that God speak to man, God must find man where man is: in the *world* of the *conversio* with its openness to Being, where the knowledge of God is always "performed." Abstraction is the very act of opening up being and of placing man before God. The *conversio* is a penetration into the here and now of the finite world. *"Abstractio* and *conversio* are for Thomas the same thing: man."* So understood, man can attend to God. Man can learn whether He speaks. In other words, man is the *locus* of revelation. Rahner's philosophy, then, supplies him with a foundation for a theological anthropology which views man as the place of revelation. This will have a tremendous impact on Rahner's understanding of grace and of Christology.

III. SOME HERMENEUTICAL PRINCIPLES

A. Analogy of Being

Being, self-presence, luminosity of being—these are all *analogous* concepts. Rahner accepts the traditional interpretation of the analogy of being. According to this interpretation analogy means in general that aspect of a concept which in its application to different existents or areas of being undergoes an essential change in meaning and yet loses nothing of the unity of its conceptual content. What is analogous is neither univocal (same meaning for many things) nor equivocal (different meaning for different things). Still analogy is not, as might seem the case, a second level or subsequent form of thought. Rather it lives at the base of all univocal conception (in the categorial range) and is the condition of its possibility. The unity which both includes and founds the multiplicity of univocal, categorial concepts is the concept of being.

In particular, the analogy of being concerns the ontological basis for all non-univocal predication of metaphysical concepts to God, analogical or symbolic. The ontological basis cannot be ignored. There must be some natural resemblance between finite beings and the ultimate source of being. Otherwise we would have no way of justifying the use either of analogy or of symbol. With St. Thomas, Rahner understands being everywhere as somewhat discontinuous, so he can treat the difference between the finite and the infinite as one of degree, involving a greater or lesser degree of discontinuity. Theologians such as the late Paul Tillich who do not see this discontinuity within finite being itself are forced to treat the finite-infinite difference as one in kind, one that is wholly unique and uninterpretable in terms of other instances of ontological discontinuity. Although Rahner emphasizes the traditional understanding of the analogy of being, he is ready to admit that even within thought—itself analogical—there is a way of speaking about God as the "wholly other." So Rahner would stand somewhere half way between Karl Barth, who rejects the analogy of being, and Tillich, who argued that the finite can become the basis for an assertion about the infinite.

For Rahner, since the dynamic movement of spirit is grounded in true, though unthematic, knowledge of the unconditioned and infinite identity of being and spirit (knowing and willing), it can open out into the analogus knowledge of the infinite Person needed if it is to be a truly personal theism and not just a Heideggerian concept of being. Consequently, Rahner can stress the positive side of the analogy of being. He notes how knowledge is univocal of itself as form of the drive in the *conversio*. Analogy is the ground of univocity, and not vice versa.

B. Analogy of Faith

In contrast to the analogy of being, a formula grounded wholly in philosophy, the analogy of faith is a formula grounded in scripture—*Romans* 12, 6 (ἀναλογία τῆς πίστεως)—where it stands in the framework of the various charismata given the *many* members of the *one* body in Christ. Charismata—for example, prophecy, teaching, almsgiving, and so on—all have to do in this passage with "service" and ultimately and immediately lead to an analogy of faith.

Karl Barth wants to oppose this kind of analogy to the analogy of being (an analogy of a "similarity with a greater dissimilarity" between "human decision in faith and decision of the grace of God" [30]). Rahner, on the other hand, accepts the analogy of faith along with the analogy of being, and in his application the analogy of faith means that there can be no statement of revelation—taken in the wide sense—not even one spoken with the gift of prophecy, which is not analogous to the one objective faith. There is one Lord, one faith, one baptism, all constituting the one objective reality of the one church.

A direct development of the analogy of faith is Rahner's concept of a *theologoumenon*. Rahner says a theologoumenon is a principle which makes a theological statement which cannot be seen as direct official doctrine or as a teaching binding in faith. It results from and is an expression of the effort to understand the faith by making connections between binding principles of faith and the total experience and knowledge of man or of a definite period. Hence, properly understood, revelation always takes place in theologoumena.

C. Symbol

Paul Tillich believed that there had to be a "natural resemblance" between finite beings and the ultimate source of being. Otherwise we would have no way of justifying either the use of analogy or of symbols. Rahner takes a similar hard look at the nature of the symbol which occupies an important place in theology. For Karl Rahner, symbol does not mean artificial symbol—that to which convention gives meaning, as the color red symbolizes danger. Nor does it mean a specifically natural symbol—as smoke symbolizes fire. Rather these would serve to demonstrate the analogous character of symbol. Rahner's interest lies in the "real" symbol.

A *real symbol* is an "appearance" in which something proclaims itself to another, as in a crude illustration the symptoms of a disease proclaim the presence of the disease. Rahner begins his consideration of the real symbol with the givenness of the plurality of being which is analogously one. The one *of* the many can be an essential expression of the "other" in the manifold oneness. All finite beings, for example, manifest the stigma of limitedness, proclaiming the fact that finite being is not Being pure and simple but rather is a plurality within the unity of the one reality. Hence Rahner's first principle for understanding the concept of real symbol is: in its unity being is multiple. Being proclaims or expresses itself because it must perfect itself by means of multiplicity in unity, whereby the multiplicity is often the index of limitation and "ontological weakness." The precise measure of individuality (unity) is determined by the analogical possession of degrees of being. As we have seen, the degree of "power" of being, the ability of a being to return to itself, implies that it comes to self by positing the internal "other." By means of expressing itself, being comes to itself. To the extent that a being becomes present to itself, it is essentially symbolic. To the extent that a being is to be the reality in which an *other* comes to the knowledge of being—the extent to which it perfects itself—it proclaims itself. A real symbol, then, is the presence-to-self belonging to the essential constitution of a being-for-another. Where self-perfection is performed by means of the other (as a necessary precondition of its own development), there is the real symbol.[31]

The special importance of this understanding of real symbol will only become clear when we take up Rahner's theology of the Trinity, his Christology, and his sacramental theology. But to give some small indication, Logos theology for Rahner is really the supreme theology of the symbol and can be summarized in the scriptural quotation, "Who sees me sees the Father."

One illustration may be helpful. Man can learn what the soul is in terms of its performance of its own essence as it proclaims itself in the body. Body and soul are not two distinct entities but two principles of one being. Consider the following: in achieving or performing a specific attitude, say friendliness, by means of a definite gesture, for example a smile, man is successful or not depending on the performance of the gesture. To the extent that the attitude "proclaims" itself, it becomes more successful, more what it should be. In a similar sense, the body may be thought of as the symbol of man. This accords with the Thomistic teaching on the soul as the substantial form of the prime matter.[32] The body is the actuality of the soul itself in the *other*—the self-performed otherness of the soul. Hence the body is an expression, a real symbol. The body is a symbol of the soul to the extent that the body is formed as the soul's self-performance. The body lets the soul "appear" and become present to itself. The unity here of symbol and symbolized implies that the individual members of the body are not just quantitatively added pieces. Rather the members are parts, each of which includes the whole, even though the inclusion will vary in degree as far as individual members are concerned. For instance, man's speech proclaims the whole man, even though the form of the expression is situated in the mouth and vocal apparatus. Psychosomatic medicine has demonstrated that it is not just a part of man who is sick; it is the whole man, though various illnesses may make a greater claim on specific areas of the body. Rahner thinks such considerations give a more clearly defined meaning to the teaching that the completely simple soul is given in each and every part of the body. The substantial and informative presence of the soul means that it forms the part precisely as part of a whole. Yet the soul is the one liberating source of the whole man. It must not be thought of in any way as separate from the body.[33]

D. *Potentia Oboedientialis: Obediential Potency*

Another principle Rahner consistently calls upon is "obediential potency." By this he understands man's capacity for the supernatural. The very transcendence of spirit *is* the obediential potency for grace. By means of its condition of possibility of grasping a categorial object, spirit is freed for the possibility of immediacy to God Himself. Hence man's nature, by virtue of its transcendence, exists as openness for all Being and so for the self-communication of God. When God shares Himself with an existent, there is a danger that this sharing will wipe out the nature of the existent unless this nature already exists as a potency, a capacity to receive this sharing. Such a capacity is called "obediental" because what it actually is would still make good sense (making possible the personal existent) even if God did not communicate Himself to the nature. Obediential potency may be thought of as a transcendentality for another person in a relation of love. First and foremost this means love of one's fellow man.

God's sharing of Himself remains free despite the givenness of this potency. Man stands obediently only under God's disposition. Philosophically, Rahner situates this total openness for the Absolute in man's spontaneous drive, the condition of the possibility of objective knowledge and freedom. The openness is not something under man's control, but is the very condition of what man must become. Man exists only by virtue of the fact that he is always on his way to God, whether he knows it explicitly or not and whether he wills it or not.

Awareness of man's transcendence is the first principle in Rahner's ontology of the *potentia oboedientialis* for a possible revelation. To anticipate for a moment, a proper understanding of this obediential aspect of man's being, including his understanding of being as illuminated, will reveal how his being is potentially Logos and so can be revealed in the Word. Rahner's Christology makes capital of this insight.

IV. RELATION BETWEEN PHILOSOPHY
AND THEOLOGY

We have seen how Karl Rahner argues that being of itself is illuminated and how man of himself is capable, at least to the extent that he questions his transcendence, of comprehending all possible existents under the horizon of consciousness. True to his method, Rahner asks a further question: Does not this absolute transcendence of simply illuminated being already bypass possible revelation? Rahner answers by pointing to the fact that as far as factual knowledge goes, God always remains for the human intellect the Unknown. Using his rational faculties, man could never demonstrate that a direct vision of God could be his natural end. But just what does this question of *natural desire* for God (to be touched upon more fully in later chapters) have to do with the relation of philosophy to theology? Further, how is a question about the relationship of two sciences an anthropological question?

Applying the transcendental method, Rahner quickly finds a position. He argues that in discussing the relationship of any two sciences, one must see that the *plurality* of sciences springs from *one* common ground (the subject of metaphysics).[34] So a question about the relationship of any two sciences is not really a question about their own constitution, interrelations, and situation, but is really a question about their unity in the common metaphysical ground. And this is to reduce the problem to an existential question about man.

Rahner feels that the notion of a rather complete separation between philosophy and theology holds sway among Catholics. He thinks the stress on the double character of knowledge (reason and revelation) given by Vatican I may partly account for this.[35] Certainly, everyone admits that these "two" knowledges cannot be contraries, because they have the same ultimate source in God. Still, though Catholics may emphasize the importance of philosophy for theology, the situation holds pretty much true that philosophy and theology are considered to be two separate studies. Catholics tend to think this way and philosophers who have abandoned the tradition for the sake of pure history of philosophy or linguistic analysis certainly think so.

Rahner approaches the question of relating philosophy and theology by viewing the problem as an extension of the larger one of nature and grace. "When we make this determination, we must be sure to add immediately that little has been won by this indication, because the relationship of these two quantities has not become any clearer.

But it is still important that one not overlook the greater while considering the lesser problem." [36] In the same way that the reality of grace comprehends nature as an inner moment, theology comprehends philosophy.

To anticipate Chapter Four once again, grace must not be thought of as a "thing." Instead grace is a definite condition of an intellectual person (actually constituting the person himself, though not owed to him). As a determination of the subject, grace is formally independent and yet exists only as determination of the subject. So it is with the relation between theology and revelation on the one hand and philosophy and reason on the other. For revelation as received by man is already theology. It is perhaps a very rudimentary and primitive theology, but still theology. For revelation is heard by a man who already knows something in addition to what is here and now revealed. As listener, as recipient of revelation, man hears an announcement from someone who knows. Man can only understand what he hears through confrontation with whatever else he already knows, no matter how open his original encounter with revelation may be. It is in this sense that all revelation takes place in theologoumena. Only by transcending himself, by passing over into the "other," the world of sensation in order to return to himself in a dynamic relation of identity and opposition to the "other," can man realize himself and so become what he truly is—presence to himself. Hearing and receiving revelation thus must take place by means of categories obtained from the sensible world. *Receiving revelation under this previously given horizon means that it is already an active, conscious human act and so is already theology.* Thus Rahner reduces the problem to an anthropological moment on man's self-performance (and as we shall see this is why no man can really have nothing to do with God and Christ).

Such a theology—as a necessary and inevitable element in revelation—implies a previously given philosophy. Whoever admits that in the unity of the knower every bit of knowledge is also a function of every other bit of knowledge, and whoever does not assert that all knowledge is revelation, must admit that the knowledge of revelation itself is a function of philosophy.[37] If the independence of the sciences is not to become blurred, their relation must mean that revelation presupposes as the supreme entelechy and norm of the many different knowledges in the one subject a different "philosophical" knowledge precisely as "other," as the condition of its own possibility. Only under such a condition can the dilemma be avoided whereby man betrays revelation either by depending on another independent knowledge or making revelation simply independent of philosophy. Just as any existent can be thought of as composed of different constitutive principles, so philosophy can be considered a moment in theology—or better, a moment of theology can be called philosophy.

The real core of the problem of relating philosophy and theology, Rahner says, lies in the fact that philosophy, called the handmaid of theology, can only serve in this capacity if it is at the same time queen. To resolve this paradox, Rahner goes back to the original problem of nature and grace. He asks why it is that everything may not be considered an inner moment of a concrete relation to God—called the order of grace—and why if something is not given grace, it must be thought meaningless and sinful. He replies, because grace as the absolute self-communication of God must presuppose in every case as the condition of its possibility one addressed to whom the grace is not owed and who can be imagined as existing without grace.

Revelation as a moment in God's free self-communication presupposes as the condition of its possibility a *potentia oboedientialis*—man, to whom revelation comes as a gift. As a gnosis of man's adopted sonship in grace, revelation presupposes the servant. God created the servant to make him His son. God could have created a son formed in grace and still distinct from His only begotten Son. God

would have done this had he created man without any
claim at all to sonship. And God willed the truth of philosophy precisely in this sense—because He willed the
truth of His own self-revelation, the blessed truth that He
is for us *visio beatifica,* the very nearness and not the absence of absolute incomprehensibility.

Even this divine truth God willed as spoken in freedom
and love. So He had to create one before whom He could
hide. This meant creating the philosopher, who because he
experiences God as the silent one could perceive revelation
as grace. What we call revelation, then, is really not something tacked on to nature and presupposed by intellect.
Rather intellectual nature is the very condition for the
possibility which itself presupposes revelation and frees
itself to be revelation: grace, person, free self-
communication of God. In this sense, revelation presupposes free philosophy as the space of its possibility, since
only in one who comprehends himself and who can act
autonomously is revelation received as a personal sharing
and a free act of love.

This relation between philosophy and theology holds
even if philosophy exists prior in time to revelation. For
temporal distance is the precise historical method of manifesting the essential relationship. The temporally prior can
be and become, since it is the condition of the possibility
of the temporally later. Both moments come as carried by
the one God who desires one thing—to share Himself. He
posits both the constitution of the receiver who is to be
given both news-laden grace and the news itself. The two
elements must be separate if the news is to be the free act
of love. Autonomy of spirit is the condition of the possibility of that obedience in which alone revelation can be
received as it must be, as a free acceptance of grace.

Rahner states that whoever believes in God's supernatural saving will must see that the universal history of revelation includes human history and the history of religions.
Universal revelation does not take place at once in a
definite word or idea but by a gradual change in the

unthematic horizon of the person. This change takes place in accepting or refusing grace. Since every free act (which such acceptance or refusal must be) is always an ultimate concern, happening uniquely (because unforeseeable), revelation is not just the continuation of an act of unveiling being. Man is always open to God, forever prepared for a possible communication from Him. Because revelation in the metaphysical sense is necessary, and because man is always encountering it, revelation is free. In this theological sense revelation is not the free decision of God to manifest or disclose but the factual disclosure of His essence. In this sense revelation is given to man freely and not in virtue of man's nature as openness. This follows as an application of the transcendental deduction of the being of man as the *locus* of revelation. The Absolute which is in a thousand ways the theme of philosophy [38] is that abyss which the grace of God opened up for man.

Where Christian revelation presupposes philosophy as the condition of its own possibility, this does not happen by positing pure possibility but as determined Christian philosophy. And this is equally true of all philosophers. For all philosophers, like all other men who have not specifically attended to revelation, are "anonymous Christians." The proposition always remains true that in every philosophy there exists inevitably and unthematically a performed theology. For no man can be sure, even if he does not know this reflexively, whether or not he is being chased by God's revealing grace.

Rahner feels strongly that there is much more Christian philosophy in the history of philosophy than most Christians dream. The movement from the objective cosmos and nature-oriented philosophy of the Greeks into the anthropocentric, transcendental philosophy of the present is so thoroughly Christian in its approach that the so-called traditional philosophy of the schools has a lot to make up for and a lot to salvage.

From the close relationship between philosophy and

theology, Rahner draws some important conclusions. First, he thinks there is no need for the West to abandon its own synthesis of theology and philosophy in favor of an attempt to shake loose the dead weight of Western thought from the naked gospel. It is true that metaphysics is constantly in danger of being trapped by history, but it must be continually set free. There can be no preaching of revelation without theology; there can be no theology without philosophy. Non-philosophical theology would be very bad theology. And bad theology cannot perform its function in preaching the good news of revelation.

Secondly, Rahner admits that there is no need to propagate any particular system of philosophy developed in Western Europe as the only possible vehicle for theology. This statement concerns not only wholly alien cultures but also the more modern contexts of thought which emphasize pragmatic models and scientific constructs. It is quite true that any unit of symbolic thought can to some extent be transposed into the conceptual mode and its components partially broken down into concepts. Yet such translation can never be exhaustive; it must always leave behind, unanalyzed and unthematic, a certain living residue, an existential attitude which must be lived within the culture in order to be understood adequately. It can perhaps best be understood by what Max Scheler called "empathy" but cannot be expressed in abstract, analytic language.

No Western thinker has the philosophical equipment to think about cows in the way a Hindu mystic philosophizes; nor does the average American possess the "felt" background for appreciating the integrity of Hegel's doctrine on the Trinity. Yet all men share the same presuppositions so far as their ability to think at all is concerned.

Rahner formulates this thought as a statement of the widely accepted insight that the limits of the human intellect preclude the possibility, even in principle, of a single philosophical system—Greek, Thomist, or Eastern— which could adequately represent the many faces of reality. In a later chapter dealing with pluralism and with intellectual honesty we will have more to say with Rahner on this point.

Thirdly, philosophy and theology must continually meet the challenge of finding new formulations for old propositions. This is the subject of the next chapter. A listener always partially determines a speaker. Implied in this is the notion that there is a danger in Western Culture and in any industrialized society that the conceptual-analytical mode of thought become so predominant that its members almost lose the feel for the rich existential meaning and power of symbolic thought, language, and action. This is the philosophical point of the return to biblical theology, to patristics, and to a renewal of the liturgy—a restoration to vitality of the living core of the content of revelation, the unthematic element in Christian life, too long repressed by expressions of a language that does not speak to the present.[39]

Rahner's philosophical reflexions, often couched in Heideggerian terms, really are able to speak to his contemporaries in a way which many more traditional theologians tend to ignore. At least he has the courage to ask the questions that really need asking.

The nucleus of the problem of relating theology and philosophy, then, is how both can be basic disciplines at the same time so that a man is not put in the awkward position of having to chose to be either a philosopher or a theologian without mistaking the essence of one or the other science. Catholic theology recognizes an essential difference between nature and grace. This same difference obtains between natural knowledge about God and knowledge given in revelation. Hence Catholicism promotes philosophy as an independent discipline. History shows that theology has always thought in terms of philosophical concepts. But revelation and grace speak to the whole man—and consequently to man as *thinker*. The close relationship of the two sciences could not find a better working model than that of the hermeneutics of Karl Rahner.

APPENDIX TO CHAPTER ONE

1. George A. Lindbeck, "The Thought of Karl Rahner, S.J.," *Christianity and Crisis,* 25 (October 18, 1965), pp. 211–215. Lindbeck's article is a sound and fair appraisal and coming from a non-Catholic theologian and observer at the Vatican Council is doubly valuable. He calls Rahner a "man who in comprehensiveness and sheer intellectual quality can, alone among contemporary Catholics, be ranged alongside of Barth and Tillich, and who in terms of balance is perhaps the greatest of the three."

2. As opposed to the traditional approach to being, which Kant rejected and which is usually labelled "conceptualist," the Rahner-Maréchal school can be called "intellectualist." This school distrusts the concept as such, especially in the matter of knowing *being* and will have nothing to do with the concept as a representation or with the idea as an image of reality. It tries to describe the dynamic process of the intellect's activity and find therein the factors needed for its act, the conditions of its possibility. For Maréchal, see Joseph Maréchal, S.J. *Le Point de départ de la métaphysique,* 5 vols. 3rd ed., Paris, 1944–49; esp. vol. 5, *Le Thomisme devant la philosophie critique.* Also valuable is "Abstraction ou intuition," *Mélanges Joseph Maréchal,* vol. I, Paris, 1950, pp. 102–180. A good brief presentation of Maréchal's position is presented by G. Van Riet, *L'épistémologie thomiste,* Institut Supérieure de Philosophie, Louvain, 1946, pp. 263–301.

3. Pierre Rousselot, *L'intellectualisme de Saint Thomas,* Paris, 1908. The English translation, *The Intellectualism of Saint Thomas,* done by J. E. O'Mahony, London, 1935, is still useful. For a complete bibliography and some stimulating articles see the dedicatory issue of *Recherches de Science Religieuse,* LIII, July–September, 1965, no. 3.

4. As explained by Bernard Lonergan, a horizon is a maximum field of vision from a determinate standpoint. In a

45

generalized sense, it is specified by the two poles, one objective and the other subjective, with each pole conditioning the other. Hence the objective pole is taken, not materially but like the formal object *sub ratione sub qua attingitur;* similarly, the subjective pole is considered not materially but in relation to the objective pole. "Horizon is prior to the meaning of statements; every statement made by a realist denotes an object in a realist's world; every statement made by an idealist denotes an object in an idealist's world: the two sets of objects are disparate; and neither of the two sets of objective statements can prove the horizon within which each set has its meaning, simply because the statements can have their meaning only by presupposing their proper horizon." Bernard Lonergan, S.J., "Metaphysics as Horizon," *Gregorianum,* 44 (1963), p. 314. Reprinted in *Collection,* New York and London, 1967, p. 202.

5. For a more extensive account of the history of transcendental philosophy see Harald Höffding, *A History of Modern Philosophy,* vol. II, New York, 1955, pp. 147 ff.

6. Johann Gottlieb Fichte, *Erste Einleitung in die Wissenschaftslehre, Werke,* vol. I, pp. 427 f.

7. See Emmerich Coreth, S.J. "Dialectic of Performance and Concept," *Continuum,* 2 (Autumn 1964), pp. 447 f. Heidegger's transcendence of metaphysics is the real springboard for his relevance to contemporary theology. See *New Frontiers in Theology:* vol. I, *The Later Heidegger and Theology,* ed. by James M. Robinson and John B. Cobb, Jr., New York, 1963.

8. Rahner's distinction between something that is *mit-gesagt* and *mit-geteilt,* for example, baffles adequate translation. This is but one of the problems in trying to simplify Rahner's turgid German.

9. See S. A. Erickson, "Martin Heidegger," *Review of Metaphysics,* 19 (March 1966), pp. 472 ff.

10. It is important to recall that unless Heidegger specifically considers the being of a particular object such as man, he is talking about the formal characteristics of being wherever it is found. This same principle holds for Rahner. The question about being as Heidegger places it is different from the question as posed by Aristotle and the scholastics. For

being is not *a* being because it is that which enables beings to be manifest (unconcealed), illuminated to man and men to each other. It is nearest to man because it makes him to be what he is. Yet it is also farthest removed from man because it is not *a* being with which man, structured as he is to deal with beings, can comport himself. But such an analysis does not set limits on what can exist. As far as Heidegger's work is concerned, God may or may not exist. If God does exist, His presence or disclosure itself will be His being, since being is presence in any case.

11. "Objective" and "objectivity" are terms plagued with a certain ambiguity. Rahner customarily uses the term in its Kantian reference to the process of theoretical reasoning as such. But even Rahner gives it at times a different meaning. Sometimes it means what is objectively given as distinguishable from others by reflection and seen together with others. More often it is the *a priori* mental horizon of which we are conscious in being aware of ourselves, the context for all our knowing of *a posteriori* singular individuals.

12. The question is an absolute starting point because whatever other starting point is assumed, the beginning can still be questioned. But the question of this question itself cannot be meaningfully questioned.

13. See Martin Heidegger, *Sein und Zeit,* 5th ed., Halle, 1941, p. 50

14. For a fuller explanation see Emmerich Coreth, S.J., *Aufgaben der Philosophie,* Innsbruck, 1958. In particular see pp. 44 ff. In the same volume is a valuable essay by Otto Muck, S.J., "Methodologie und Metaphysik," which builds on the transcendental method.

15. Karl Rahner, *Das Problem der Hominisation,* Freiburg, 1961, p. 70.

16. See *Geist in Welt,* München, 1957, pp. 71–78; Emmerich Coreth, *Metaphysik; eine methodisch-systematische Grundlegung,* Innsbruck, 1961, pp. 99 ff.

17. Martin Heidegger, *Introduction to Metaphysics,* New Haven, 1959, p. 57.

18. Rahner takes St. Thomas's dictum, *"eadem est dispositio rerum in esse sicut in veritate,"* to mean precisely this point. He observes that differentiation among the de-

grees of knowing is based on the difference of degrees of immateriality of the beings. This element in his system is a stumbling block for many scholastic philosophers. For "ontological" knowledge derives from "ontic" knowledge and a real convertibility of being and intelligibility is involved.

19. How does this guard against idealism? Because for Rahner being and knowing do form a radical unity, paradoxically enough. And in the ultimate analysis, knowing can only consist in possessing an object present intentionally (being intentionally in the presence of an object). Thus knowing is the self-presence of the existent to itself, that is, the internal illuminatedness of being relative to itself. This is the identity in being between knowing and Being which primarily knows itself. Pure Being and Pure Knowing are identical and this we call God. But the ability of any being to be known is not primarily the possibility of being known by another but rather presence to itself, and only secondarily its ability to be present to another. The degree of presence to self will vary with the degree of potency of being belonging to any existent. Hence idealism is no longer a danger because of the radical difference of degree or disparateness. Rahner states that the scholastic dictum "cognoscens et actu cognoscibile" aptly expresses this notion.

20. See, for example, "Der einzelne in der Kirche," Sendung und Gnade, Innsbruck, 1959, pp. 91 f.

21. Rahner explains that according to St. Thomas the ontological unity of knower and known is not produced by the knowledge—as an intentional grasp—but is logically prior and so is not a consequence but the very cause of the knowledge, as actually and really consciousness. See Geist in Welt, pp. 95 f.

22. Imaginatio tempus et continuum non transcendit. See Geist in Welt, p. 128.

23. In the Thomist theory of knowledge the separation of the subject from the sensible is given by the abstractio and in a return to the world which becomes the object is the conversio ad phantasma. Abstraction always involves the formation of universal concepts, and the conversio is precisely the relating of the universal concept to the existent. Hence abstraction as the formation of the universal is the ultimate completion of the return of the subject to himself.

24. The text is *In I Sent.* d. 3, 4, 5. See *Geist in Welt,* pp. 150 ff.

25. In *Hörer des Wortes* Rahner calls this drive the condition for the possibility of universal concepts, for the act of abstraction, which makes possible the objectivization of the given sensible. It is an *a priori* potential in human nature of the dynamic movement of spirit over the extent of possible objects. In this drive the individual is known simultaneously under the horizon (formal object) of the Absolute. See Chapter Six *passim* of *Hörer des Wortes* for elaboration of this inner drive of man. See also *Schriften,* vol. VI, p. 486; and Joseph Donceel, "A Thomistic Misapprehension?", *Thought,* 32 (1957), pp. 189–198.

26. This is quite a different thing from the way all contingent being points to a necessary being. This is the recognition that in every act of the intellect there is in the judgment the affirmation of absolute existence (*esse absolutum*). See *Geist in Welt,* p. 232. Rahner quotes: *"omnis cognitio a lumine increato derivatur. Omnia cognoscientia cognoscunt implicite Deum in quolibet cognito."* Rahner gives a brief historical account of man's drive for the absolute. He says there are three typical ways of approaching the problem: (1) That of the *philosophia perennis,* extending from Plato to Hegel and which sets no outer limit on the drive, including the very being of God. (2) Kant's solution, which states that the horizon under which objects are presented as conceivable is a horizon of the ideal intuition limited by space and time. (3) Heidegger calls this horizon the transcendence found in the nature of man as it moves over nothingness. Rahner opts for the first solution, that of the *philosophia perennis,* but with borrowings from the other two. In a later formulation Rahner said Thomas did not consider such a principle in the line of Plato, Plotinus, Augustine, Bonaventure, and Malebranche in an objective *a priori* which is a second realm of objects immediately apprehended by the senses, but in the line of Aristotle, Kant, and Hegel, he sees it in a formal *a priori* of the spontaneous spirit itself.

27. See Chapter Five of *Hörer des Wortes.*

28. See *Schriften,* vol. VI, pp. 229, 230.

29. *Schriften,* vol. VI, p. 231.

30. For a discussion of this point see Hans Urs von Baltha-

sar, *Karl Barth, Darstellung und Deutung Seiner Theologie,* Köln, 1951, pp. 93–181. For Barth's own discussion consult the first volume of *Kirchliche Dogmatik,* pp. 252 f.

31. See *Schriften,* vol. IV, pp. 282 f. A different example of a real symbol might be Heidegger's understanding of language. For Heidegger the term *language* does not merely designate audible or verbal articulation. It is more basically related to the conveying of meaning. For example, a thing's identity with itself "speaks" this identity to us, calls upon our thinking to correspond and our speaking to respond. Rahner seems here to adopt a Kantian position that holds that only if a thing-in-itself manifests itself can it manifest itself other than it is in itself, and Rahner gives this notion a radical, existential twist. Hence for something to *be* a symbol is for it first to *be* an appearance and the concept of symbol is seen to presuppose the concept of something else—what is symbolized.

32. See *Schriften,* vol. IV, p. 305.

33. The act of the soul receives being and expression in what we call the body (which must exist as possessed by a soul). A part of the body may be symbolic of the whole under the particular relation it bears to the whole. Thus the Sacred Heart is the symbol of the whole under the particular relation of giving life and love.

34. What is said about the relation between theology and philosophy holds also for the relation of theology to any other science. See, for example, *Hominisation,* pp. 20 ff.

35. See *Schriften,* vol. VI, pp. 92, 93.

36. *Ibid.*

37. There must already be some understanding of the self when man "hears" revelation. Further, in so far as man must ask questions he affirms his own finitude. In so far as he questions, he admits the givenness of the question. And while he affirms it necessarily, he affirms as unconditional his nature in and in spite of its givenness. In other words, for Rahner, because affirmation of the contingent fact is necessary, an absolute is revealed in contingency itself: the inability to escape affirming the contingency; for its existence excludes the possibility of its denial, despite its possibility of not being. It does not matter that this fact remains unthematic for most men when they receive revelation. Nor does it matter that the

categories in which revelation are received would not constitute philosophical categories. Yet if one admits that philosophy itself is only the methodically exact and controlled presentation and articulation of the original and never wholly governed self-knowledge, the point Rahner is making becomes clearer.

38. Plotinus would be a classic example.

39. For a good discussion of this point see *Faith and the Philosophers*, ed. by John Hick, New York, 1964, esp. pp. 127 ff.

It is difficult to suggest sources in English which might help in gaining further understanding of Karl Rahner's philosophy. The brief remarks on Rahner in Gerald A. McCool, S.J., "Recent Trends in German Scholasticism: Brunner and Lotz," *International Philosophical Quarterly*, I (December 1961), pp. 668–682, might be good for an over-all indication of his importance in German philosophy today. Sten H. Stenson, "Prophecy, Theology, and Philosophy," *Journal of Religion*, 44 (January 1964), pp. 26, 27, gives some interesting conclusions on the relationship of the sciences. For Heidegger, see James Demske, *Sein, Mensch und Tod: Das Todesproblem bei Martin Heidegger*, Freiburg, 1963. Demske studied under Rahner at Innsbruck before going to study under Heidegger at Freiburg and gives some good insights into the relation between the two thinkers. William Richardson, S.J., "Heidegger and God—and Professor Jonas," *Thought*, 40 (Spring 1965), pp. 13–40, pulls together some major ideas from his larger book dealing with problems touched on in this chapter.

Also good is Fergus Kerr, O.P., "Heidegger among the Theologians," *New Blackfriars*, 46 (April 1965), pp. 396 ff.; Otto Muck, S.J., *Die transzendentale Methode in der scholastischen Philosophie der Gegenwart*, Innsbruck, 1964, and Klaus Hartmann, "On Taking the Transcendental Turn," *The Review of Metaphysics*, 20 (December 1966), pp. 223–249, are also useful.

CHAPTER TWO

THE DEVELOPMENT
OF DOGMA

The previous chapter took a somewhat stuffy view of Rahner's philosophical prolegomenon, the basic structuring of his method. But before seeing how he applies this method to specific theological problems a second and also thorny matter needs some attention. It involves the problem of development, of becoming, and the related question of authority. Having seen Rahner's hermeneutics in general, then, we still have to see this other side of the theologian's problem. This involves the question how a theologian's own work contributes to the development of theology. Since this includes the problem of development, before we can go on to consider Rahner's specific contributions we must see how he views the more general problem of development. Thus our concern here is how an individual's theological effort fits into the over-all progress of doctrine. Seeing how Karl Rahner treats the development of dogma will enable us to gain insight into how he himself fits into this development.

Man is a listener to the Word. What God reveals to man is not the broadcast of a number of propositions, a kind of platform whose content is fixed, to which addition or subtraction may be made at will. So the work of the theologian cannot be adding to or taking away in any sense at all. Revelation is a historical dialogue between God and man, a dialogue in the course of which something happens, an event in which the communication of God relates itself to history. This dialogue is a progression in which something first happens and is followed by an unsurpassable communication. So revelation is *the* saving event; only subsequently can it be a sharing of "truths." In Jesus Christ this event reaches its unsurpassable climax: God Himself has definitively given Himself to the world. Just how does the theologian's work enter into the problem of revelation? In what sense is this revelation definitive if there is question of development? The problem, then, is quite simple. How is the *new* really *new* in the sense of development and yet at the same time identical with the *old* definitive revelation in Christ? And how does the *new* possess the authority and authenticity of the *old?* This is the heart of the problem. Since this is the question of the permanence of identity in the face of change, it has to be reduced to a metaphysics of being and becoming. And as far as dogmatic theology is concerned, how can truth both manifest historicity and yet not fall into historical relativism? This chapter will begin to consider some aspects of this problem.

PLAN OF CHAPTER

This chapter can be divided roughly into four parts. The first part makes some distinctions Rahner stresses between law and doctrine and between laws which can be changed and laws which cannot. The second part discusses the actual problem of development, clarifying the question and giving Rahner's answer. The third part briefly touches upon the matter of development in moral theology. And the fourth part treats development of doctrine by giving some examples from the way church teaching develops and Rahner's reflexions on these.

I. DIVINE LAW VERSUS CHURCH LAW

A. Change in Law

Karl Rahner sees that the *aggorniamento* begun in the Second Vatican Council has caused many Catholics to become uneasy. One group tends to view the current situation of change as total catastrophe. Another and perhaps larger group tends to think of the present in terms of a glorious opportunity. Rahner is as thoroughly aware of the pastoral problem involved in this as any theologian today and this has motivated his efforts in helping to bring out a new series of pastoral theology texts. His concern is to alleviate the uneasiness by a practical approach. He shows where change occurs and why it must occur. He demonstrates that change always has an unsettling effect in any area. More importantly, he offers a theory of development of doctrine which explains the problem in a way calculated to clarify and so to alleviate unwarranted concern. Properly understood, his theory can calm both reactionary and ultra liberal, showing the former that change is inevitable and part of the Christian task in the world, and the latter that change must come by way of development and not replacement.

Rahner first makes a simple distinction between law and doctrine. A law is an ordination of some kind. It usually commands or forbids a specific act. For example, God's commandments and the commandments of the church are laws. A doctrine, on the other hand, is a general or a specific teaching about something—for example, that there are three persons in one God.

As far as laws are concerned there are in general two kinds, those given by God (divine laws) and those established by the church (ecclesiastical laws). It is changes in laws and not in doctrine that disturb Catholics most frequently. Rahner calls laws the positive rules of the game of Christian life. Random examples of such laws might be

fasting regulations, norms for eucharistic sobriety, laws
governing the form of marriage. Some laws change and
others cannot. Divine laws can never change. Divine law
springs from the changeless nature of God and man. And
because God's revealed divine will holds for all of salvation history, divine law is permanent. It is a question of
divine law, for example, that a marriage between a brother
and a sister can never be a valid union. Or a valid marriage between baptized Christians could never be dissolved
except by death. Nor could any of the sacraments be taken
away, because they are given by God's divine law. True,
there is question in some areas about what is a divine law
and what is not, but where this is clear, there can be no
question of change.

Church law is basically changeable. But it would be
folly to think that because ecclesiastical law bears some
resemblance to divine law, the church has the power to
change divine law. The church has the responsibility of
making such changes in its laws when new historical situations demand them. Quantitatively, ecclesiastical laws constitute what most Christians consider to be "law." And
were the church to fail to establish rules of this kind, the
church would fail in its pastoral obligation and would not
manifest genuine concern for the salvation of the individual. But when the church does establish or change laws, it
does so within the framework of that divine law which
gives it the right and duty to set up norms for the good of
the individual. Obviously, the church cannot think up such
rules at pleasure. And the justification for change will vary
from case to case. For example, Rahner observes how
extremely tardy the church was about changing the customary knee bend before the Eucharist to a deep bow for
the Japanese faithful. And the church should long ago
have given up the use of spittle in the baptismal rite. But
the church will think long and hard before changing the
obligation of going to confession once a year when serious
sin is involved, even though this law has only been on the
books since 1215. For a law of this kind is a legitimate

application of the church's obligation to care for the salvation of souls.

Rahner notes how in the practice of his faith the average Christian may view even necessary changes in laws way out of perspective. Confronted with change, this average Christian may be tempted to think that God or the eternal nature of the church has suddenly been overturned, that one can no longer rely on anything. If a change takes place in, say, the law governing Christian burial in consecrated ground, a Catholic may think the practice of his faith has somehow become "easier." Rahner counsels, "Here only patience and understanding will help and a realization that the church too stands necessarily and in an obligatory way under history's law: what was good yesterday must not be so today. New times . . . require of the church different actions than the past." Rahner notes, however, that such changes should respect the real needs of the people. Evening Mass may be a necessary practice in an industrial community but would probably be out of place in a small farming village in Bavaria. A large urban parish visited by people of vastly different cultural backgrounds must show greater respect for aesthetic taste and art than a country parish where the people find nothing wrong with painted plaster statues of the Little Flower.

B. Changes Must Occur

In an earlier age changes in church law could take place so slowly that the individual in the course of his lifetime scarcely noticed them. Today's rapid tempo of social change no longer abides such a pace. Changes must come ever more quickly in the future. New experiments must be tried, the ultimate outcome of which no man can prophesy. Rahner feels that judged in comparison with the lightning development of political and economic society, one has to say that the renovation of the church is happening at a turtle pace.

Changing times produce discomforts for everyone. It may look as though things are becoming easier. But one should reflect on how a change in the law concerning mixed marriage may in the long run, by emphasizing on the part of the Catholic partner a sense of personal, religious responsibility, produce an even more positive Christian result. Such changes do not make things "easier" but "harder" and are in greater accord with the gospel message. The new ecumenism, for example, may factually lead to a decline in the number of conversions—at least for a while. And some may even be led to indifferentism in matters of confessional faith. Yet this matter of the ecumenical movement Rahner calls a holy command of our day.[1]

Periods of transition in the church, Rahner counsels, must be lived with patience and courage. No one need become nervous because the problem of artificial birth control is openly debated. Everyone should be able to see that any remodeling operation involves a certain amount of discomfort and dust. All should be able to see that no church law, old or new, has only advantages and no disadvantages. Not every well-meant change in law (and also in the paracanonical style of Christian living which is often of greater importance than canon law) works out for the best. One might argue for hours on end over what is the right age for confirmation. Rahner wants the problem of change put in perspective. He says that in earlier times the possibilities of free and active molding of human existence were so narrow that man could not really be the creative draftsman and planner of himself and his environment. Today, however, he can do this, and Christians must take account of this new way of experiencing human existence. It cannot be directly and adequately dealt with by means of the New Testament because this experience of existence was not then to any great extent present. In the light of this fact of experience Christians must see how and why changes must occur.[2]

II. THE DEVELOPMENT OF DOCTRINE

A. The Fact

Having seen how changes in ecclesiastical law must take place, what about the question of change in church doctrine? Does this change also? The situation doubtless obtains that the church defines as revealed by God propositions which were not always so defined or taught as binding in faith. Further, the church propounds the content of previously defined propositions in concepts having quite different meanings from what they had in the earlier definitions. In this latter case the church usually calls attention to a heretical misinterpretation or stresses individual moments in the play of the dialectic of faith and reason in order to situate one of these moments in a more obvious light. In addition, the church defines as apostolic those propositions which cannot be presupposed as possessed in an earlier age with any degree of historical probability.

Consequently, not only theology but also revelation (in so far as it exists in preaching and accepting the faith) can be said to have a history, a real development and evolution after Christ, even if this history is essentially different from the epigenetic evolution of revelation given prior to Christ's coming.

Rahner cautions that this development is not a matter of the change within the church in the sense of historically greater or less involvement in socio-political society. Rather such change is the subject matter of ecclesiastical history and as such is only of peripheral concern for theology. And in a way, changes in positive ecclesiastical law usually follow closely upon problems of church history in the sense of its institutional involvement in society as a whole.

B. Actual Problem of Development

The real problem of dogma development does not involve such changes in law as we considered earlier or historically conditioned changes in church organization, though these may follow upon dogmatic developments. The real problem lies rather in the task of demonstrating the identity of propositions of the faith taught at a later period with the propositions revealed by Christ to the apostles. Such an identity must be shown to be possible. The difficulty lies in the fact that the "public" revelation binding all men was finished with the death of the last apostle. And this means that the church can only witness to what it heard in the actual apostolic times from Christ and His apostles. Any later "private" revelation must be just that, "private." [3]

Furthermore, this development of dogma cannot be understood to mean that the same thought is clothed in a new dress or that an older teaching is revived in newer words as conceptual fashions undergo change. The problem is rather how a genuine identity of doctrinal teaching can be united with an understanding of a real development. For example, how can the doctrine of papal infallibility or of the Assumption be shown to be identical with what Christ revealed to the apostles? This is the real problem, and its importance becomes clearer as more and more Catholics engage in ecumenical dialogue. Rahner says that because the answer has to be sought in the fact that the *new* is contained "implicitly" either in the older doctrines or in the entirety of what was once believed, the problem can be stated (1) by asking what kind of implication is involved and what is the process of its explication, and (2) in explaining the explication, asking what implications are sufficient and necessary to show that the explication is revealed (and not just something taught by the church with revealed authority).

The second question involves developing the implication in such a way that the *new* dogma not only testifies to itself as coming from an original revelation (and so appeals to the witness of God—purely objective implication) but also demonstrates that it has always been taught and held by the church (subjective implication). Only since the last century has this question been a real problem for the church. But from that time there has been a history of dogma which not only collects materials from an earlier period for the teaching of the present but also sees that the knowledge of the truth of revelation itself has a real history after Christ.[4]

To be viable, dogma must be capable not only of developing into the future but also of conserving the past. Cardinal Newman had declared that actual laws govern this development and that the chief law is that of the conservation of institutions, symbolically represented in the dogma itself. Hence Newman viewed dogma as a function of the preservation of the church. Rahner does not adopt wholly this way of seeing laws of development, and so he takes a positive step beyond Newman's position and makes the first real contribution to the problem of dogma development since the great Victorian.

The history of dogma should be carefully distinguished from the development of dogma. Dogmatic history sets forth the origin and development of dogma by using purely historical methods. It should be classed as a specialized sector of the history of ideas. Protestant theologians of the 19th-century professoriate first used this distinction for dogmatic purposes. Harnack, for example, believed that the history of dogma would offer the very best means of freeing the church from dogmatic Christianity and of hastening what he thought was an inevitable process of emancipation which began with Augustine.[5] The genuine development of dogma has been the very reverse of this process. It is the unfolding of the original revelation in terms of an ever richer and fuller penetration. True development vivifies rather than destroys.

C. Theories Regarding Development

Until recently, theologians considered only the manner
of explication which involved traditional formal logic as a
model (using the major and minor premises of the syllo-
gism). Accordingly, their solutions to the problem of development asked whether any new proposition could be
validated as revealed if it resulted by explicating it as
formally implicit in an immediately revealed proposition.[6]
More recently, theologians have started with the same kind
of argument but have tried to include elements of ecclesiology and a variety of epistemological theories. Hence an
analysis of the logical and psychological manner of implication has entered the discussion. Even now, Rahner
notes, new concepts are being developed and applied. For
example, the implicitness of a proposition is seen to lie in
the whole of revelation as such, since every proposition of
faith points to every other one (as the analogy of faith
demonstrates). Or a proposition may be thought of as
contained "reasonably" within an earlier doctrine. Or
again Christ's salvific will can be thought of as comprehending implicitly a multitude of propositions.

D. Directions for a Solution

This plurality of current theories regarding the development of dogma shows that theologians have not yet arrived
at a clear and understandable solution. Rahner feels that a
true solution probably does not lie in any one of the
directions already proposed. Rather he believes it lies in a
synthesis of all of them. And the total solution cannot be
simpler than the complexity of the faith as a whole. This
means that in the course of development of dogma many
constitutive moments must return to a unity. For every
later proposition implies the totality of what was earlier
believed. Previous solutions have emphasized one or an-

other moment. But a really satisfying solution must include all moments.

Without taking anything away from the eternal validity of a true proposition, a real historicity does exist, the knowledge of which partakes of the knowledge of revelation. This statement is an application of the transcendental method. Rahner argues that if a knowledge is to become faith (and not just theology), it must include the history of dogma. And this would be one of the moments in a solution. Another moment involves the authority that guarantees the consistency of the relation between old and new propositions. This authority is, of course, the church. But the authority may not constitute the relation between old and new, nor may it replace the relation. Even the very bearers of church authority (bishops and pope) enjoy no special prerogative as far as knowledge of the relation of new to old is concerned, and in this respect they are in the same capsule as are all other believers. Bishops and priests, however, do enjoy a certain prerogative regarding the certainty of what is taught. Yet what anyone at all knows about the relation of a new dogma to an old must display a structure of reason if it is not to constitute a new and so "private" revelation. The actual development of dogma does show a kind of reasonableness. For the process never takes place without the reasoning labor of theologians. (And it is here that the effort of the individual theologian fits into the over-all problem of development.) This would seem to testify to the universal validity of what is meant by an "instinct" or "sense" of faith.[7]

As often happens, only after questions have been properly distinguished may a problem be really understood. "The perfected law of dogmatic development . . . may only be given when the whole unique process has already reached its term. And because it is a genuinely historical process, under the impulse of the spirit of God, who never makes Himself accessible without remainder to laws which can be grasped by human minds, it is never just the development of a formula and an all-embracing law."

Definitive revelation came in Christ and will never be surpassed. Hence the affirmation that revelation was closed with the end of the apostolic period should be carefully understood. Before Christ it was not clear just how God's saving history was to unfold. Everything was still "open" and not closed. But with Christ the definitive event took place and can never be displaced. "It is because the definitive reality which resolves history proper has already come that revelation is closed." And that revelation is closed means that nothing of the divine plenitude has been left out.[8] Theological reflexion on revelation does not find its arena in a set of propositions but in what is heard through living contact with the revealed content itself. Knowledge in faith occurs in the power of the spirit of God and is at the same time the hard reality which is believed. The Holy Spirit is both object and principle. So development of doctrine happens in living contact with a "closed" plenitude of revealed truth. This contact includes the givenness of the object in the propositions together with the possibility of their logical development. The possibility of this development can never be exhausted. Nor is it a purely formal logic that powers the process.

Karl Rahner argues that theologians have explained the question in terms of the explication of an implicit cognition in an explicit one. He admits that there is an "explication" of a knowledge, the fullness of whose content is displayed in a more articulated manner. Formal logic and pure mathematics give excellent examples of this method, and propositions are related to each other precisely as implicit to explicit. However, in this sense neither mathematics nor dogmatic theology really adds new terms to knowledge or to their respective traditions. They both unfold the implicit meanings of old terms, though this too is a kind of intellectual accretion to their respective modes of discourse. As mathematicians illuminate other mathematicians, so dogmatic theologians illuminate the people of the Word by amplifying the word in its own terms.

This kind of explication is called analytic exposition of

the content of a proposition or the logical consequences of a number of related propositions with the help of logical principles like that of contradiction. The model used is the procedure of logic or mathematics. Thus a proposition that is true by virtue of its logical form (and so is an analytic sentence) may be "explicated"—and such instances do exist in theology. Rahner, however, is arguing that not a great deal is learned from all this. For example, if I explicate the proposition "No bachelor is married" by saying, "No unmarried man is married," I have not explained very much. So although tautologous axioms and their derivations may be useful in theology (and following Wittgenstein it is to be hoped that greater use will be made of this method), they do not provide really theological explanations. Furthermore, it is very difficult to distinguish between what is formally and what is virtually implicit in such an approach. What is formally implicit may be really just another tautology.

E. Rahner's Solution to the Problem of Development

Using the transcendental method, Rahner first illustrates the problem by drawing the portrait of a young man in love. This young man, he says, can only stammer and try to utter vaguely what he feels in the depths of his enamored soul. His emotional involvement, his love, represents a real knowledge which he has. The young man can try repeatedly to articulate this love, to communicate what he experiences. But he never will succeed in conveying the richness and power of his love as he really experiences it. True, his articulation is a kind of explication. For the knowledge the lover has of himself forms an essential element in his love. And this knowledge is infinitely richer, simpler, and more intense than any set of propositions about it could ever be. Yet even this knowledge is never without some degree of reflexive expression. For the lover states something to himself at least about his love. But the love does not alter thereby, no matter how poor or inadequate his statement of it. Reflexion in propositions is part of the progressive realization of his love and is not just something which happens to get involved in the act.

Recalling the model of the transcendental method of the interplay of unthematic and thematic elements, of the multiplicity involved in an unthematic unity, we can see how an original, non-propositional, unthematic possession of a reality (in Rahner's illustration, love) and a reflexive, thematic, articulated awareness of the love are not opposites but interacting moments of one unified experience which unfolds necessarily in historical succession. The problem in the development of doctrine, we saw, is to stand with the apostolic age and be wholly grasped by the same experience, the same vision of reality. By sharing this experience the theologian can proceed to articulate, like the young man, in contemporary terms the love which grasps him. As applied to the faith, then, the nonpropositional, unthematic basic awareness is the knowledge received in revelation.

Rahner holds that the apostles themselves had a global experience (analogous to the love of the young man in the illustration) which is the fountain for all later streams of propositions and which forms an inexhaustible source of articulation and expressions of the faith in ever fresher forms. Living contact with Christ preceded any kind of propositional statement of the faith. Even in scripture we find a model of doctrinal development and this provides a pattern for the real evolution of dogma. For scripture represents the attempt of the early church to articulate in propositional form the experience it had of Christ.

Such explication is not simply a formal deduction from given premises. It does not take a proposition as a conceptual expression of an experience and in measuring it against the original experience find it to be correct. Yet the experience depends for its correctness on stating what is actually known. Hence any individual proposition will be at the same time both more and less than its predecessor.

It is more because as formulated upon reflexion it clarifies the original, simpler possession and so enriches it. It is less because it never can do other than articulate a small part of what is wholly possessed from the very beginning. Understood in this way it is possible to draw upon a full consciousness of the apostolic faith existing today and still avoid anachronism.

The apostles passed on their propositions, poorly formulated when judged against what they had experienced. But they also passed along something more, the Spirit, the very reality they had experienced. And this original experience the church preserves and has ever present. The apostles handed on the Spirit with the Word. Spirit and Word belong together and build the permanent dynamism of the experience which in principles is the same experience of Christ which the apostles had. So the original possession of the whole truth exists in the post-apostolic period in an unthematic but conscious way. The church continually strives toward an ever more successful articulation of this experience. And this striving constitutes the development of doctrine. Each new attempt is really new and yet is identical with the old because every attempt is but a deeper penetration of the original, global experience. Rahner thinks that individual statements of the faith are rather like windows through which a panoramic view may be obtained out onto the vastness of reality. Statements of the faith are in no way like packages having a clearly attached list of contents.

Rahner provides a summary of the *a priori* limits needed for the development of dogma. He lists them briefly: (1) The development of dogma is ultimately a unique process which cannot be captured in formal laws.[9] (2) Revelation in Christ is definitive and unsurpassable. It is complete with the end of the apostolic period. This means that nothing of the divine plenitude has been excluded. (3) The development of dogma involves necessarily a unity of all the elements constituting its development as revelation. Such elements are, for example, spirit and grace, the church, tradition,and the nature of the concept. Some of Rahner's thoughts on these elements may clarify their respective roles in the process of his explanation.

(a) *Spirit and grace*: If revelation did not occur within the inner light of grace it would simply fall under the limited *a priori* of the human intellect and would be nothing more than an additional bit of self-knowledge. For whatever is received is received according to the manner of the recipient, as the scholastic dictum has it. This dictum applies to revelation. Knowledge which is essentially the coming to self of the knower is illuminated presence-to-self in such a way that everything which is received is understood as a moment of man's self-performance. Without grace, revelation would be but another moment on this self-performance, even though man would still be open to the infinite. Hence the word of revelation includes a supernatural communication, not only as the guarantee of its genuineness, but also as the source of its effectiveness and unsurpassability.[10] In this way the word and the content are given together. This will be clearer after the problem of grace is discussed more fully in Chapter Four.

(b) *Teaching office*: The individual recipient of revelation cannot be responsible by himself for handing on the word. So the development must take place within an ongoing dialogue with authority. The non-official elements (charismata and the Spirit, the work of theologians) always cooperate before the magistracy of ecclesiastical authority. For example, the labor of each theologian constitutes his contribution to the whole, but it is performed before the guidance of the magisterium and the scholarly surveillance of his colleagues.

(c) *Concept and Word*: Revelation (and dogma development) is given in the human word and concept. In so far as the word is spoken by spirit, it has a necessary openness toward the mystery of truth which is one with the reality of God. And in so far as this word is spoken by the teaching office of the church, it has an internal validity greater than the actual content of the word itself. For it points to the total understanding of the church and thereby surpasses the light of any individual human word. (As we shall see in the case of Rahner's Christology, the divinity grows in direct and not in inverse proportion to Christ's humanity. The assumption of human reality to the appearance of God brings it to its highest actuality.) So the development of dogma has to take place in the dimension of the human word. It is a development similar to what always happens in human thought. To answer new questions arising out of new insights, new and more refined concepts must be conceived. This requires a thorough recasting of older concepts. Sometimes this may cause crises to arise. These are not explained simply by a polemical attitude. They can also result from the difficulty of deciding at what moment and in what measure certain answers are no longer satisfactory. Theologians involved in such conflicts do not usually realize the significance of the crisis and only later may the full import be grasped.[11]

(d) *Tradition*: A revealed proposition essentially is something which happens in a communication among persons. Since God's revelation is a supernatural self-communication, the propositions of revelation have to be spoken by someone. This would seem to imply that the light of faith carried by the spirit and ultimately identical with the spirit is the *a priori* horizon under which individual objects of revelation are grasped, just as in the natural order being as such is the *a priori* horizon under which the spirit in its transcendence grasps individual objects and only then really makes them understood. Rahner says a double movement can be expected within the evolution of dogma. The infinite dimensions and intensity of the supernatural *a priori* must lead to an ever more articulate development of the objects grasped under its horizon.[12] This dynamic of development moves in the direction of an ever more express fullness of individual propositions. It is extensive. An application of the analogy of faith does not lead to continually different combinations and cross-relationships, but points up the relatedness between an understanding and penetration of one truth with that of another.

In contrast to the natural *a priori* drive of man's transcendence, the formal *a priori* of faith is not one of possibility but rather is the actual plenitude of what is implied in each individual object of faith. This means that not only what is in the concept itself but also in the reality (namely, the Triune God in His real self-communication) is given in revelation. So if in the act of faith—in speaking and hearing the Word of God—a synthesis of individual objects of faith with this *a priori* of faith takes place, then such a synthesis must release a dynamism toward progressive concentration of the multiplicity of all that is shared in revelation into the *a priori* unity implied or signified by the multiplicity.

We observe here Rahner's hermeneutics working toward a metaphysical reduction. His use of the transcendental method, his concept of symbol, his application of the analogy of faith all are at work in arriving at his solution to the problem of dogma development. He sees that this development must really lead to an ever greater degree of simplification and ultimately into the blessed darkness of the one mystery of God. And a development of this kind need not be in the direction of more individual propositions. More importantly, it leads to a deeper penetration of what is really meant all along: *mystery,* as well as an intensification of the original experience of the infinitely simple. The clearer this fundamental leitmotiv of faith is developed by the manifold of propositions of faith, the more genuine is the development of dogma. Rahner's transcendental method leads to the core of his solution to the problem.

(e) *Givenness of Dogma as Revealed*: The church was not always aware that it comprehended a truth of faith as revealed by God. In general, this is the problem of the transition from a state of non-belief or not-yet-believing to a state of faith. Rahner says it is possible to state that all the problems, theories, differences of opinion, and open questions regarding the development of the faith in the individual return again to the problem of the development of doctrine. In both cases the leap from the necessary presuppositions of faith to faith is the same.

Decision is not just the simple execution of insight. It is always a sublimation of illumination which alone justifies it as it must be justified, though one may not simply declare on this basis that all reasoning processes leading up to it are superfluous. Rahner holds that a real metaphysics of freedom and love would clarify this matter. We would then have a piece of general existential ontology which could be applied to this question which is much in need of an existential ontology.

(f) *Papacy*: Finally, the papacy is the point at which the total consciousness of the church effectively comes to itself authoritatively for the individual. Development of dogma means there is a genuine history of dogma. Vatican II has furthered this unfolding process. It has helped clarify the relation between the papacy and the college of bishops so that their respective roles in the development of dogma can be seen more clearly. Just as changes in church laws may disturb some Catholics, so it is possible that the development of dogma may give rise to crisis situations. The papacy is an instance in point. Rahner cites the case of a Catholic who had understood the church teaching on the primacy of the pope in such a way that the bishops were considered as subordinate provincial officials. The man who thought this way learned a hard lesson from Vatican II.[13] But such a previous understanding of the papacy was a misunderstanding and so not a matter of dogma at all. In such a case there is no question of change, of one teaching being replaced by another.

Further real changes involving dogma development have tremendous ecumenical importance, since even Catholic theology cannot foresee all that can be done in this direction. Otherwise the whole slice of future dogmatic history would already be cut. Nor should anyone say that such future changes in dogma cannot be sufficient to effect the ultimate unity in faith of all Christians. For changes within the validity of the same teaching can be astonishingly great, can explain *old* dogma from a wholly *new* aspect. It can change the crystallized form of the church to its very foundations. For example, Rahner says that we proclaim with St. Augustine the dogma of original sin, but what a change this dogma has undergone since Augustine's time! Rahner believes the history of this teaching would demonstrate to anyone how greatly a teaching can change and still remain the same. For God's truth is always the same. It is vital. It has a history which finds its end only in the vision of God. The way to this blessed vision is marked by parables and images for the pilgrim wandering into the future.

III. CHANGE IN MORAL THEOLOGY

The church claims to teach infallibly in matters of faith and morals. We have seen what is implied in change in matters of doctrine. But how is it with moral questions? Rahner thinks this is a greater stumbling block for the faithful than dogma development. Catholics are not so much disturbed by the problem of apparent change in defined dogma as by changes in the common teaching of the church on moral matters, questions which are not defined doctrine at all.

A. Not Defined Teaching

A teaching authority which strives to encompass the multiplicity of the divine mystery, having cross-relationships and analogical predications, which develops in time, cannot be put before the alternative of being either the last word on everything or of saying nothing. The very propositions of dogma cannot be preached without explaining and clarifying the concepts expressing the proposition. For without such explanation dogma would have no meaning. Yet the explanation itself is not the dogma. These explanations may vary in degree of clarity, certainty, and usefulness. They can always be improved upon. They are in no sense definitive. And an effort at greater clarification claims the attention of all theologians.

Rahner thinks that the area of moral theology is one place where attempts are continually made to explain doctrine. Indeed, he thinks that moral theology is made up of such attempts. For it is concerned with applying the basic attitudes and teaching of the gospel to the human situation. Since this human situation is one of perpetual change, we must expect the same thing to happen in the area of moral theology. At one time, for example, money did not simply represent one of the factors of production as it does today. So the implications for church teaching on interest and interest rates are obvious. Again, a moralist must give some kind of answer to such questions as: What forms may warfare take when soldiers armed with nuclear weapons march out to do battle? What is to be done in the face of a real population explosion? Previous history did not have to worry about such problems. The moralist must also take a closer look at the position of women. This position has changed drastically in society as a whole. What was unimaginable in the church two hundred years ago is a reality today. What does this fact of change in woman's status say about her role in the church, her rights and duties? Answers to such questions and to many others cannot be deduced from scripture or previous teaching. Nor can the church simply leave it up to individuals to find their own answers. "The church has to find such answers in many (I do not say in all) cases; she must search for them; and for this development, a history of reflexion and time is needed." [14]

The church has come a long way from the time of Gregory XVI to the decree on religious toleration of Vatican II. Church-state relations have improved tremendously. The church has had to change many of its teachings in this area along with changing its form. The state is still in the process of change and probably will always be changing. It is the same with the church. Only a child could be disturbed and cry out when confronted with the problem of the historicity of the church teaching in the area of morals, thinking that today the church says one thing and tomorrow something else. Such a reaction misses completely the nature of the church and its teaching authority.

There is and must be a teaching church which makes a claim on the belief of the individual, even though no claim to absolute assent may be made. The church could not make any such claim. Still, even teachings that are subject to change can imply an obligation on the part of the faithful, especially when in the judgment of the church a particular teaching is here and now the safest position. Just as a mother obliged to care for her children who is told by her physician that she needs a surgical operation is obliged to undergo the operation, even though she knows that the judgment of her doctor could be wrong, so too the Christian is obliged to defer to the teaching of the church, in the normal case. Of course, it is possible that after careful scrutiny of his conscience a Christian can come to the conviction that he is not bound by a specific teaching. A paleontologist, for example, could have come to the conviction that a theory of anthropological evolution was in accord with dogmatic theology twenty years before Pius XII's explanation confirmed his opinion, despite the fact that the church earlier tried to hinder such a conviction. The area of moral theology is full of such instances. Although Rahner does not specifically make the point, the example of the paleontologist and evolution might shed some light on the question of population control today.

B. Direction of the Future

Rahner believes that the future will see an even greater degree of responsibility given the individual for such decisions. Life is no longer simple. The social structure no longer revolves around a simple parish life as it did at one time. Problems have grown too great for small solutions. So just as in the area of moral theology today, so in the field of the dogmatic theology of the future we will see that the direction of development will be toward more precise explanation, toward a more vital, original penetration and expression of basic dogmas. In short, the direction of the future will be more toward liberty, toward "leaving open" rather than binding down. But such "leaving open" must not be interpreted as "doing whatever one wants," but rather as the imposition of an ever greater degree of individual responsibility, an opportunity to become more the persons we are meant to be.

IV. PROJECTIONS

Karl Rahner asks us to perform a small experiment. He asks us to project ahead into the future, the exact number of years does not matter. We are to see that the over-all Catholic population has dwindled. The church lives in a state of total diaspora. What will seem important to the future Catholic living in this state of diaspora when he reads, say, the constitution of Vatican II on the church? Rahner thinks that asking this question of a future Catholic should give us some insight into the problem of change and development.

Rahner cites from the introduction of the *Dogmatic Constitution on the Church* a sentence which he says will definitely strike home for this future Catholic. The sentence reads: *"The church is the sacrament of the salvation of the world."* Now living as a member of a small flock in the coming world of non-Christians, what is this future Catholic to think of this sentence? How will he understand his small and seemingly unimportant band of Christians as the only true and valid church, especially when for him the day when everyone will be a Christian has receded even further than it now appears to us? In the future the power of a homogeneous society will no longer fight for the church. How will the future Christian be able to understand his church? He will only be able to do this if he understands the church as the *sacrament* of the salvation of the *world.*[15]

The once and future Catholic will read and ponder the history of Vatican II. He will be astonished that these words were expressed without a shadow of contradiction, without even arousing any particular attention. It will seem that what was said was not really noticed or understood: *sacramentum salutis totius mundi.* Prior to this the church was always considered the plank of salvation held out to a capsizing world, a small boat, the bark of Peter, in which alone one could be saved, while *extra ecclesiam nulla salus* was understood in a most exclusive manner. Suddenly with Vatican II the church is to become the sign of the salvation of those who do not belong to it in the dimension of history and society.

This sentence from the constitution on the church will give the furture Catholic a *new* and deeper understanding of the theology of the church and its mission. He will not question nervously whether or not statistics show the church to be the largest numerically among religious bodies or whether it has the greatest impact on current philosophical science. For the church is a real symbol, a sign that must be rejected—sociologically, this means that as an institution the church will always be one among many, but as a *sign* it is the very symbol of the salvation offered to all.

Centuries ago when an inquisitive Japanese elder asked St. Francis Xavier whether his own Japanese ancestors were in hell, Xavier answered with an unequivocal *yes.* The man then in a cool and collected reply told Xavier that no one should look for a better lot than that had by one's ancestors. Rahner thinks this little scene contains in itself the whole problem of the development of doctrine for the church. It shows the point which the consciousness of the faith had reached in the 16th century (and illustrates its advantages and disadvantages for the mission of the church). Progress is always in the direction of greater determinateness and precision. Compared to our sharper understanding of the church following Vatican II, it would seem that a great improvement in precision has been made regarding the salvation of the world since the time of Xavier.

The same constitution on the church of Vatican II contains another sentence Rahner stresses: "The salvific will of God embraces those also who (without having received the gospel already) recognize the creator. . . . God is not far even from those who seek in shadows and images the unknown God, since He gives to *all* life and breath (Acts 17, 25–28) and wills as savior that all men be saved (1 Timothy 2, 4)." Even today's Catholic looks at this statement as a more or less common teaching. Xavier did not. And theology still has the job of explaining how the grace given the non-Christian is *eo ipso* revelation as the determination of the *a priori* horizon under which man comprehends his existence and performs the act of his freedom, a revelation which everywhere, even in the heart of error, streams its light.

The necessary and holy self-reflexion of the church emanating from Vatican II will not be the final period of theology. Another and more important period of dogma development will come for which this council was only a forerunner: the period in which the last truth and hope of the church, God and Christ, will be newly stated as though man had only really understood for the first time what had always been preached.

If we were to search for a patristic comparison for Rahner's use of method in determining his theology, it would be hard to improve on St. Irenaeus. For the nature of Irenaeus's method in his use of "hypothesis" of truth and its effectiveness as authority for his work becomes clear only as one observes him using it as a theological method. We find this same kind of effectiveness in Rahner. For Irenaeus the one supreme authority is the "hypothesis" of the faith, whose substance is comprised in God's redemptive dispensation in man's behalf. And Irenaeus's total theological effort works toward an ever clearer establishment of the truth. Anyone tempted to think Karl Rahner too "avant-garde" would do well to compare some considerable sample of his work with, say, the first book of the *Adversus Haeresis,* where Irenaeus sets forth the basic question of his treatise and in doing so clarifies the problem of authority.

We have seen how Rahner "does" theology by applying his method to the questions he asks. He does not always find answers, though he always seems to ask the right questions. In the case of the problem of dogma development his contribution is perhaps the most original since Newman.

APPENDIX TO CHAPTER TWO

1. See Rahner's article, "Kirche im Wandel" (*Schriften,* vol. VI, esp. pp. 463 ff.), for more of his observations on change and why the church must change. He brings out the importance for the ecumenical movement with great clarity.

2. See *Catholica,* 17 (1963), pp. 127, 128. Rahner says Christians must take an interest in the future world, not simply as providing neutral material for the practice of Christian virtues but precisely in its profane secularity and without religiously sublimating this secularity.

3. See Denzinger, nos. 2020, 2054, 2094, 2313, and Rahner's *Visions and Prophecies.*

4. In the shadows of this problem lurks as a natural condition the further problem of the historicity of the recognition of truth—and with this the added question of the union of vital revelation (necessarily new in each historical period), and yet this is preached as present kerygma of a historical past. Rahner thinks that such a development has to exist. God's revealing word is directed through the very medium of historical process at the total history of mankind. See, for example, *Schriften,* vol. I, pp. 40 ff.

5. Adolf Harnack, *Outlines of the History of Dogma,* Boston, 1957, p. 503.

6. Allied to this there existed another argument about whether what was deduced syllogistically and then defined was to be believed only *fide ecclesiastica* or whether it could be taught as revealed and so believed *fide divina.* Such theories which involved formal logical solutions failed for the most part to prove what was needed.

7. This implies the living impulse of the spirit as present, the light of faith in the instinct of faith. Secondly, there must be a rational, conceptual formulation which shows the relation to the whole of faith and revelation (the analogy of faith), to the teaching office and tradition so that it goes back ultimately

to the perpetually new event of the kerygma. In his solution Rahner strives to take account of all these factors. See "Dogmenentwicklung," *Lexikon für Theologie und Kirche,* cols. 459–462; *Zeitschrift für katholische Theologie,* 80 (1958), pp. 585–596, and the same article reprinted in *Schriften,* vol. I.

8. "This statement of course only acquires its full significance on the assumption that the actual support given to faith under grace of the Holy Spirit is not merely an ontological modality of the act of faith beyond conscious apprehension, but also has a specific effect in consciousness (which is not necessarily to say that it is reflexively distinguishable). This effect makes it possible to apprehend the objects of faith given through the hearing of the external announcement under a 'light,' a subjective a priori under grace (the formal object) which is not available to someone without grace. As is well known, this assumption is a controversial topic in Catholic theology. Nevertheless the Thomist view, which does make this assumption, seems to us to be true. . . . But if we do make this assumption, we cannot allow that the unfolding of the church's consciousness in faith is supported merely by an insight of a conceptual and logical kind and an assistentia per se negativa." *Theological Investigations,* vol. I, tr. by Cornelius Ernst, O.P., Baltimore and Dublin, 1961, p. 51.

9. It is clear that its history has a unique course and cannot be a repetition of the same laws. In this sense, Rahner changes Newman's position. The development follows upon the historicity of the knowledge of truth. Revelation has a history not because the speaker, God, can act freely in history but because the listener, man, is an historical being. Man and only man as spirit has a history. And as long as man furthers his own history there must be a history of dogma, even though revelation is complete. Man's historicity is the connection between the development of doctrine and revelation. Hence from still another vantage point we see how theology is anthropology. This is the matter we take up in Chapter Three.

10. With this is given that infinite openness in the perfected revelation and dynamism of self-development, which has itself a limit only in the beatific vision.

11. See Henri Niel, S.J., "The Old and the New in Theology," *Continuum,* 2 (Autumn 1964), pp. 486 f.

12. Again and again we will see this sort of reduction to the hermeneutical model of data coming both from within and without consciousness, the thematic and unthematic elements working together in man's spontaneous drive toward the Absolute.

13. See *Schriften,* vol. VI, p. 467.

14. *Ibid.,* p. 470.

15. *Ibid.,* pp. 482 ff.

For additional interesting insights on the question of the development of doctrine and Rahner's method see Herbert Vorgrimler, *Karl Rahner: Life, Thought, and Works,* tr. by Edward Quinn, Glen Rock and London, 1965; this is a good if somewhat sketchy source. A French edition has been enlarged upon with the collaboration of Charles Muller, *Karl Rahner,* Paris, 1965. This might be a good place to mention *Gott in Welt: Festgabe für Karl Rahner,* ed. by J. B. Metz and Herbert Vorgrimler, Freiburg, 1964. There is really no substitute, however, for trying to grapple with Rahner's lengthy periodicity, and once it is understood how his method proceeds, this should not be quite so difficult.

Rahner in a recent article explaining the third chapter of article 25 of the Vatican II *Constitution on the Church* takes pains to point out that the development of dogma in no way removes the past history of the faith of the church but is also never completely finished. So it always remains in this sense "reformable." See *Lexikon für Theologie und Kirche,* Supp. 1, p. 239. For the whole problem of the development of dogma see K. Rahner–K. Lehmann; J. Feiner–M. Löhrer (eds.), *Mysterium Salutis,* vol. I, Einsiedlen, 1965, pp. 727–787.

A good brief summary of Rahner's most recent thoughts on the work of the theologian in the church and the relation between bishop and theologian is given in a recent article in which he discusses the now "notorious" letter of Cardinal Ottaviani on July 24, 1966. Rahner does not discuss the issues in detail but remarks on many of Ottaviani's points and in so doing clarifies some positions and indicates a modified stand on such issues as polygenism. See "Kirchliches Lehramt und Theologie nach dem Konzil," *Stimmen der Zeit,* 178 (December 1966), pp. 404–420.

CHAPTER THREE

GOD'S SAVING PURPOSE

The previous chapter on the development of dogma indicated how for Rahner all development moved toward the simplicity that leads into *mystery*. God is the ineffable mystery. But man, too, is mysterious analogously. Since man's orientation to God by means of his transcendence is constitutive of his being, only God can express man "adequately." Man's real transcendence cannot be indicated otherwise. Its perfect expression came with the Incarnation. This chapter begins Rahner's interpretation of this "adequate expression of man," the heart of the matter of God's dealings with creation. Since the Incarnation came at a definite point in time, the question of the "adequate" expression of man must include an historical existential. This means that we are concerned in this chapter with salvation history.

PLAN OF CHAPTER

We consider first of all God's saving will in general. Then we take up the problem of salvation history, looking first at man's historicity and the question of the theology of history. The chapter makes a distinction between salvation and profane history, and the relationships of these are discussed from Rahner's special interests. A second major division of the chapter takes up the "adequate" expression of man, the center and crown of salvation history—the mediation of God's saving will in Christ. This final section considers the Incarnation and some soteriological issues.

I. GOD'S GENERAL SALVIFIC WILL

God is and forever remains a mystery, even in the *visio beatifica*. And even in the vision man remains the eternal acceptance of this loving mystery. Man's entire history witnesses to this fact. Rahner thinks theological anthropology simply represents the breakthrough of all other limited anthropologies into the mystery of God and the incarnate Logos.

According to Rahner, scripture does not illustrate God's saving will as something willed only once, a static kind of necessary attribute or property. Instead, scripture envisions God's saving will as a personal, free *relationship* which Christ revealed definitely. But Christ did more than just reveal this; he actually completed the relation. Church teaching on God's saving will focuses on man's situation after the fall of Adam, asking in general whether despite this fall God has an active, saving will, made objective in the offer of sufficient grace for salvation—a divine saving will implying man's obligation to strive after this possible salvation—or whether certain men, prior to their use of freedom, are already lost.

Traditional theology has attempted to solve this question by distinguishing between a conditioned and an unconditioned, a previous and a subsequent divine will, so that the *universality* of God's saving will comes to mean God's previous and conditioned will, not his absolute and subsequent will. But Rahner observes that proponents of these theories about predestination argue even among themselves about how these two "wills" really differ, one group stressing a human aspect (man's lack of merit) and the other, the divine (the revelation of God's justice). All theologians agree that in carrying out the universality of

God's saving will sufficient grace is always given the hardest sinner to achieve salvation. But the question *how* God's will can really be saving in certain problem areas (for example, in the case of unbaptized children and "good" pagans) has not been given a clear answer. It is Rahner's contribution to have spelled out the direction such an answer can take.[1] This contribution grows out of his methodological consideration of several problems, all of which find an anthropological solution. This means that it becomes a question of man's nature and his supernatural destiny. Now one of the most evident facts about man is that he strives for this destiny in time and space—in the world. Man is spirit in the world.

A. Historicity

Man is a historical being. Rahner says that he exists first in his own individual history, that temporal span bridging birth and death. But because he is factually ordered to an *other,* his dependence is not simply on his natural environment (as is the case with animals), but on the environment which he himself creates, his culture. Further, man's history is not just the condition and manner of his physical being, but is his history as a person and partner of God. He not only lives in history, but his history is an inner constitutive moment, an *existential* of himself, a condition of the possibility of the performance of knowing and of freely returning to self. History becomes the medium for making his personal self-performance objective, giving him the very possibility of being. Because man is transcendental consciousness, he necessarily has a history. The return to self must take place in the world. This means it must take place in time. So Rahner's hermeneutics derives historicity as a necessary existential of man. Because God is experienced in the space-time of increasing possibilities, as a reality always given, man in his history is the place, the locus, of a possible free encounter with God. Hence man is

obliged to reckon with the possibility of supernatural revelation.

Theological anthropology, however, cannot peer into
man's history as it is given in revelation. This history
presents an essential knowledge of man, but it has to be
educed gradually. And so it has itself a history. In the
course of the eduction it becomes clear that man is *the*
being whose essence is totally influenced by his history.
For in history he is either saved or lost. It is true, Rahner
notes, that theological anthropology has always stressed
some individual moments of this history, even though the
selection has been incomplete. For instance, the moments
of paradise and original sin have been considered historically, but the important elements such as eschatology,
grace, ecclesiology have been divorced from their real
historical situation. Rahner feels that part of the reason for
this is the quasi-Aristotelian conceptual framework which
influenced the development of late medieval theology
(which tended to overlook the dynamic aspect of unfolding truth and of the event-character of truth). Without
stressing truth as event, it is difficult to appreciate the fact
that revelation is not just a broadcast of new propositional
knowledge, but a personal meeting between Christ and
man. To understand this encounter, we need to learn the
historicity of truth itself. For truth as event is meaningful.
Man's birth, for example, is a meaningful event. So is his
death. That man can be in a lasting state of desire or
hunger or that man loves—all these are truths that are
events. They involve something more than just "knowing."

For Rahner, man falls under God's saving will in terms
of *historicity*. Rahner defines historicity as that unique
basic determination of man by means of which he is situated in a time which allows him freely to accept his world.
Historicity means further that man not only has to conquer
his own nature while changing his world (making physical
time into his own time), but also while integrating the
environment into his world and so becoming present to

himself as an existent. This task man never wholly finishes. It breaks on the rocks of his finitude. But his lack of completion does not change the fact that man's historicity is unique. It is transcended in his free decision to determine himself. Out of this task results the fact that man's historicity needs a salvation beyond the scope of his own historical dynamics. Rahner thinks that this fact makes it clear why only revelation can point to the real end of history as the definitive completion of man's historicity and of the world.

For Rahner, then, the concept of man's historicity is a refinement of and a conclusion from theological anthropology using the transcendental method. As a theological concept, man's historicity states that man is so open to the sovereign action of God that he may expect a historical-personal event which saves himself, his world, and history. Further, the anamnesis of this saving event can have the power of actual re-presentation (for example, eucharist, tradition). Included in historicity is the matter of preserving historically the saving event as communicative. This latter point will become clearer when we focus in Chapter Seven on Rahner's understanding of the church as the abiding presence of Christ.

B. Salvation History

In some contemporary Protestant thought history is man existing in his acts, not simply a description of them.[2] This means that the concept of saving history will have many meanings which depend on the particular account given of salvation. Hence the concept can include whatever happens to man, win or lose. Or it can mean simply what follows for man's salvation from God's historical dealings with him. Rahner feels that the negative moment of salvation history is so important that despite the radical difference between being saved and being lost, both positive and negative moments should be considered together. Rahner considers them methodologically as separate moments of a single action (in terms of possibilities).

Saving history in general means that God on account of his universal salvific will includes the history of mankind as a whole in his grace, and in this all men are offered salvation. It means further that some men have actually received grace and justification and that the history of this experience happens within the historical world. It implies that the experience of salvation prior to and outside of formal Christianity is ordered dynamically to the *kairos*,[3] the time of salvation in Jesus Christ. This comes in epochal ways which the *history of theology* tries to illustrate and clarify. The epochal ways we will see more clearly when we take up Rahner's view of the theological virtues.[4]

More precisely, saving history means that history of the experience of salvation within which it moves reflexively and in ever clearer stages toward the moment of the actual experience of salvation as such. So the real story of God's dealings with the world must begin salvation history with God's covenant with Israel. Saving history moves forward in the sense that wherever man encounters the saving event he can adopt a self-determining attitude toward it. As the structure of saving history develops, this attitude finds repeated expression, usually in terms of opposition and hostility.

Rahner says that we can distinguish within special salvation history a collective and an individual salvation history. Common to both is a visible historical structure (covenant and church). A specific moment of individual salvation history is the structure of dialogue: God's call to man wherein grace becomes realized, depending on man's acceptance or rejection.

Rahner admits that the Catholic theology of saving history is still in its primitive stages.[5] He says that the pre-conditions for saving history include an express knowledge of history and historicity as categories, a knowledge of the universal importance of historical events and of man's "facticity," a consciousness of the transcendent, monogenetic, and historically developed unity of man, and man's anthropological understanding of himself in terms of his historical dimensions.[6] Rahner's method, then, posits the conditions necessary for salvation history and questions them. Salvation history means God's historical action appropriating its object (effect) in a qualitatively higher fashion than any other of his works. This in turn implies that the "works" of specifically salvation history are God's in a "higher" sense than are the works of nature (in the non-theological sense). In the latter works God acts upon the "historical" world; in salvation history God enacts his own history within the world.

C. *Theology of History*

The study of *how* God enacts his own history belongs to the theology of history, the theological interpretation of history. To this study alone is given knowledge of the beginning and end of history; for here it is given as revealed. Both beginning and end share the character of *event*. And as with beginning and end, so also underlying the entire historical process of God's action there is developed a progressively clearer outline by a theological analysis of the course of this action. According to the plan of this outline God freely and supernaturally enters into a *historicity*—in Jesus Christ and his grace the world becomes the history of God. The internal differentiation of all history into saving and profane history can only be understood from the point of view of Jesus Christ. Rahner states that the revealed plan makes this clear. The word of the Old Testament in so far as it already contains the tidings of the gospel is necessarily obscure. For it only contains a prophetic anticipation of the New Testament. So the word of the Old Testament is historical with respect to contemporary events and prophetic with respect to the future. Clarity regarding the divine plan can only come with Christ.

The theology of history works with the inner-worldly data of history, interpreting problems such as sin, death, and the law. For in realizing His plan God calls man as a free partner. In interpreting the plan, primitive revelation and revelation as such both play important roles. The actual history of man's *no* to God's call—sin—is not an equally important theme. Rahner says that the theology of history sees man's rejection of God as the limit which has to be overcome, as a necessary refusal of the free gift. But out of the mutual action of God and man spring historically new epochs of saving history. And these epochs are elevated and interpreted by the theology of history with the aid of aetiology (reaching out of the withdrawn past), kerygma, anamnesis (in the sense of intertwining both past and future saving history), and the hermeneutics of eschatological statements.

Rahner states that the theology of the epochs of God's plan of salvation constitutes the real task of a methodical systematic theology of history. At two important points the results of this study require further development: as the foundation for a genuinely theological church history and as data for pastoral theology.

D. World History and Saving History

We can consider the interrelationships between saving history and profane history by examining some of Rahner's propositions on the matter.

(1) Salvation as the absolutely transcendental mystery clearly belongs to the basic determinations of Christianity. Salvation is not just an historical moment but rather its promotion, not an object to be possessed but actively to be sought in faith, hope, and prayer. This is the *space* in

which saving history occurs, the locus of revelation. In the first place, Christian salvation is not something which is yet to come and which when it comes will assume world history. Instead, salvation is happening right now. God's grace is being shared with men. So salvation history within world history means: the self-communication of God takes place in the free participation in God through faith, hope, and love. But accepting or rejecting salvation always happens in terms of an encounter with the world, as we have already noted. This does not happen usually in formal religion but in man's everyday meeting his neighbor, his historical task, in his confronting the terrible humdrum of every day—in what we call the history of man and of society. All this will become more evident when we come to see the importance of man's death as the summary event of life. Since saving history always takes place within history, everything in the whole of world history becomes pregnant with eternity.

We may note that salvation history participates in the element of mystery which surrounds man's death. It cannot be explained in its double character (being either saved or lost); for what happens within history does not reveal whether it leads to salvation or perdition. But the hiddenness of saving history does not mean just a kind of super-history, a history of faith. Profane history as a whole, because it is branched, cannot be interpreted clearly, but will become clear in what we call the last judgment, which itself is not a moment of history but its transformation. Rahner thinks that here and there profane history does become transparent in signs which call attention to salvific matters. For God calls man in the prophets and their social appeals, in opportunities to help and serve the world. But He does this especially in the event of Christ. In other words, a man as an individual confronted with a personal decision has ultimately only *one* history, so that within his one history there can be no dark corners which are overlooked by grace. It is man who joins together salvation and profane history.

(2) Salvation history is different from profane history.

(a) Saving history differs from secular history because the latter as a whole cannot be interpreted clearly as being either saving or damning. Man's free historical decision always remains hidden. Actions only become historical when they become the object of a human intercommunication. Their ultimate free quality cannot be made reflexive and thematic. Man's action always springs from the ground of his freedom which is unthematic. The contents of his consciousness are always greater and deeper than the boundary of what he knows reflexively. And if man cannot reflect on this fundamental fact, he cannot explain it and so the essentially saving character of all his actions remains hidden.[7]

In addition, being saved is not so much the finalization of man's freedom that he thereby saves himself. Rather, God is his salvation, but God's free self-communication must be freely accepted, even though this acceptance is still a free gift. God cannot be experienced. So for both of these reasons, man's freedom and the gratuity of God's saving grace, the saving event takes place in profane history. But as such it is not given historically in its genuinely salvific quality.

(b) If only the previous point were to be considered, then saving history would always be co-extensive with profane history. For this would be then simply unspecified salvation history. The two would only be formally, not materially, distinguished. Rahner says there is a concept of salvation and revelation history which is not formally identical but is materially co-extensive with profane history. But before noticing the material difference between saving (and revelation history in the narrowest sense) and profane history, the material identity of revelation history in general with profane history should be stressed. For God's saving will includes all historical spaces and all men. The possibility of being saved (because of God's saving will) comprehends the total history of human freedom. And this co-extensive space is called, as we have observed, universal salvation history.

(c) Saving and profane history differ because God in His Word is a constitutive moment of salvation history. A real piece of the double-branched profane history is actually God. Rahner thinks that this explanation may come as a surprise. He says that one would normally expect that where God appears within history to save mankind, we would have salvation history in the strictest sense. Yet when we ask what it is that allows God's action to slip into the dimension of the genuinely historical, we have to reply: It is the Word.

God's saving actions are present in the dimension of human history and become historical when the Word appears to speak and to interpret them. This word is not external and subsequent, but is an inner constitutive moment of God's saving action. It is *the* event of history. This determination of saving history (as apart from profane history) has itself a history. The two were not always so distinguished. Salvation history is the foundation of profane history, continually erupting into profane history. The concept of the *religious* is the meaning and root of history; and the religious element is never just the sublimest bloom on an otherwise humanly nourished culture. It is always fed by the grace of God. (And here we can gain insight into what Rahner means when he speaks of man's task of integrating his culture.) We will recall this point in the last chapter on the philosophy of religion.

Where saving history is crystallized, made objective in the Word, saving history spills over into particular salvation history. We do not know whether this takes place in this or that religious thinker, in this or that religious experience, in this mystic or that social reform. Just as it was difficult for the Hebrew to distinguish between the true and the false prophet, since there was no abiding institutional element which could decide infallibly for him, so only in the appearance of Jesus do we find the perfect union

between divine and human, between salvation and profane
history. This union is present historically, so that saving
history is distinguished from profane. Whatever follows
upon the Christ-event participates in this distinction
(church, sacraments, scripture, and so on). Yet paradoxically enough this special saving history exists for all men
of all times.

(3) Saving history explains profane history.

Saving history is the explanation of all profane history.
This is true because a universal salvation history founds
the deepest insight into the reality of history. It shows that
salvation takes place historically. And it shows that the
salvation of the Word is the explanation of profane history.

(a) Salvation history removes itself from profane history and demythologizes it. Creation and history are not
already salvation. Rahner points out that the world is not
just theogony and so cannot be pantheistic. It cannot
explain itself; nor is it a world court. It is a creature
ordered to mystery. Salvation history creates the necessary
conditions for man, the profane climate required for faith.
The silence of saving history about profane history, its
leaving the question open, lets man be free. But in reality
the dualism so often manifested (for example, between
church and state, science and theology, Christian and
pagan) has another side. God lets the world be delivered
up to itself. Salvation history sends man seeking his salvation out into profane history and tells him to hold fast. The
world he has to integrate and make use of in becoming
present to himself is not so much a realm governed by
demons as the actual material of man's self-performance.
As *homo faber,* man has not yet won his salvation, but he
receives it as God's free gift.

(b) Salvation history explains world history as veiled
and hostile. Because salvation is not an immanent fruit of
profane history, skeptical men look askance at salvation.

The task for the Christian is never finished and always ends in failure, since the absolute limit is always present for mortal man. This explains why death is immanent in universal history. The forms under which the hostility between man and woman, rich and poor, war and peace, and so forth, may change historically, may be made more endurable. Indeed, such a process of humanization is part of that integration of the world that is man's task. But the oppositions will always remain and will always beget man's melancholy. Rahner thinks that Christianity must even expect a sharpening in world conflict, an intensification of the struggle between light and darkness.

(c) World history is existentially powerless to explain Christianity. Rahner states that we must exercise care in estimating the real meaning of profane history. Yet life is not so private that the Christian can settle down in a forgotten corner of world history in order to look for his salvation undisturbed. The Christian lives under a metaphysical obligation to the world. What happens in the life of each man, how he uses his historicity, is eternally important. The Christian must take the world seriously. Because Christianity knows that the world has been redeemed, Christianity deflates the powers of world history. For even confronted by the most hostile opposition, salvation can still happen.

(d) World history is explained Christocentrically. This is really just a summary of what has been said. Christ is the center and crown of the universe. The world is the world created by and for the Logos. From the beginning the world was ordered to the Incarnation. Because God wished to express himself, because He is love, the world exists. The difference between nature and grace demands both saving and profane history. This means that this difference must be perfect in Christ. Just as natural history in its material vitality is the place which God posits as the condition of the possibility of limited spirit (the condition which allows spirit by the dynamism of its orientation to the Absolute transcends itself), so is world history the condition which God created for salvation history which transcends itself (in the place of the prehistory of history) in Christ: God's own history.

To summarize some of these themes as developed in Rahner's thought, we can note how he stresses as the precondition of salvation history (as the necessary determination of its unity) the fact that the relation of different moments in one world is not a static relation. Rather, the differences are varied in their degree of completion. Hence history as such is possible. Man in all his existentials is one being and yet still has to bring to a unity all the various existentials of his being (physical, sensible, intellectual, and spiritual) in history. Man must find himself in his relation to the world, where all the various elements mutually condition one another. It is the same with the unity of created and redeemed reality. It is one in God's original creative will, and yet the world must strive to become one. Saving history is the history of this process which has yet to be realized. In the Incarnation the history of this process has entered upon its eschatological phase. For God has summoned the world in an irrevocable unity into his own life in terms of one of its moments which He has personally assumed. The drama is decided in Christ. But even in this eschatological phase the Christian still must believe and live as though the ultimate unity were still an open question. Nevertheless, since he lives after Christ he has reason to be more optimistic than those who lived before.

Before Christ, the historical dialogue between God and man was still open. Mankind as a whole could be lost (though that does not imply any clear decision one way or another regarding the individual). Everything was still unsettled. What God would do could not be inferred from the previous course of the dialogue. Now in the Word, God's last statement is uttered, a word of grace and reconciliation: Jesus Christ. As Rahner puts it, the grace of God no longer comes (when it does come) steeply down from on high, from a God absolutely beyond the world and in unhistorical ways. Now it is permanently in the world in tangible, historical form, in that piece of the world and its history that is Jesus of Nazareth.

This is what Rahner means by saying that Christ is the actual historical presence in the world of the eschatologically triumphant mercy of God. It is possible to point to a historical man and say: Because of that man, God is reconciled to the world. There the grace of God appears in history. There is the real symbol that effects what it symbolizes. Christ is both reality and sign of God's redeeming grace. And so we arrive at Rahner's answer to the problem set at the start of the chapter, a wholly different approach to the question of predestination.

Rahner says that it would be totally to misapprehend the message of Christianity (yet how often this happens in preaching) if one were to think of God's plan of salvation as opening out onto two roads, on one of which man has to travel, one leading to salvation and the other to perdition. Each man has to decide freely. But God did not just build the roads for man's journey. God Himself has come part of the way and given the drama of life's journey the *dénouement* He Himself wanted: salvation, grace, eternal life. No individual as long as he is a pilgrim faced with the decision of which road to take can predict how the journey will end for him. But just because he cannot say that about himself, he should not get the impression that history as a whole is still at the crossroads, still under the disposition of mankind with God nervously awaiting the decision. In Christ, God has decided the free consent of mankind as a whole.

Just as there is a difference between public history and private history, between the history of a nation which is not the sum total of the history of the individual citizens, so there is in the history of salvation and perdition a "public" history. There is a private history for each individual and a public history of humanity. God has willed definitively a salvation for humanity. There is no question of distinguishing his will in this regard. It is to this public history that Christ belongs. In the dimension of salvation Christ is the primal sacramental word of God, uttered in the one history of mankind. Since the time of Christ, the "last days" have come. The ultimate "transformation" of history will be the salvation of the whole, including matter and the corporeal body, into the mystery of God.[8] But the high point, the crown of history, is not the "unworlding" of man as spirit in order to come to God, but the descent and irreversible worldliness of God, the coming of the divine Logos into creation, his assumption of the material. In this sense, Christianity is primarily Christ. The presence of this event in history is the foundation of Christianity. Since this salvation must be *present* for man as a saving reality which makes it possible to transcend human experience without having to appear in itself—that being which makes present for us existence as such. And such a real sign for man can only be the *word*. It is the word that mediates this salvation.

II. MEDIATION
OF GOD'S SALVIFIC WILL

A. Christology

In Rahner's system, mediation involves the real symbol. And Jesus Christ is the personal self-expression of God to the world, the abiding mediation of all creation to the immediacy of God. The event of Christ is not one which is historically neutral. We have seen that it is God's own history, so that the completion of the world can only come in the parousia of Christ which has already begun with his resurrection and ascension. The question about the exact point of time of the Incarnation was a real question for the theology of the early church. The early Christians experienced the coming of Christ on the one hand as the end, the event of the last age of the world, the final hour before the end. On the other hand, the Incarnation appeared as the start of a new epoch, the founding of the church which is to develop and constitute the leaven of the matter of world history.

Rahner thinks that under both aspects the view of the early church was shortsighted. For we know today that man's history before the Incarnation was a relatively long one and we also now have the impression that mankind stands on the threshold of a future whose innerworldly development has just begun to move away from a rather stagnant beginning. Thus the original impression of the early church that God set the Incarnation of the Logos at the evening of world history is being replaced by a realization that man's governance of history has really only just begun, so that properly situated, the Incarnation came very early in the course of history and that relatively very few men lived before Christ.

However, Rahner is careful to stress that as far as the beginning of the end is concerned (no matter how long human history lasts and what events yet transpire), Christ exists as the event of the radical self-transcendence of man in God. This event can never be surpassed and no greater self-transcendence of history can be given.

On the other hand, in the light of the eschatological understanding of salvation history, the Incarnation should be seen as founding an inner-worldly epoch. This means that we can look at Western history after Christ and the coming of interplanetary history whose beginning we are just now experiencing as something which will add to our control of nature (and need not fall into a communistic utopianism), as something moving toward the proper destiny of man, wherein man and his life achieve actively, not just contemplatively, self-presence, allowing the world to become present to itself really and aesthetically. Rahner says that we can view this new space epoch as wholly grounded in Christianity, because only through Christ can the ultimate transcendence of spirit in grace be formed into an absolute difference. Rahner and Friedrich Gogarten come to identical conclusions regarding the matter of the secularization of history. From such a viewpoint it is perfectly reasonable to consider the Incarnation as the real start of the wholly human epoch.

The Incarnation transcends all categorial events by giving to the world immediacy to God. So world history has already been overcome, since of its very nature immediacy to the absolute and infinite mystery surpasses whatever man can accomplish and so whatever science may perform in the future. Christology offers no competition to world planning. Rather, it sets this free, since the event of Christ does not deny but rather comprehends the fact that man achieves his transcendental future (his attaining his end) by means of the material world and its history. Space and time are the real dimensions out of which eternity is fashioned.

1. THE INCARNATION

In his handling of Christological problems Rahner repeatedly affirms that he has no intention of practicing biblical theology as such. He says that his intention is much more modest. "We propose to show by means of a kind of transcendental hermeneutics starting from dogma that the church's Christological teaching never claims to be an adequate condensation of biblical doctrine; so there does remain for dogma room for more biblical theology in Christology." [9] For situating the Incarnation Rahner takes as his conceptual framework an evolutionary understanding of the cosmos. Creation moves toward its perfection in the absolute self-communication of God. God wills the whole of creation for the sake of its highest moment. For Rahner this statement is not just an application of the principle that in the one world, in order to be one, everything must exist for the sake of everything else, but rather that it expresses the truth following on the action of God which orders the world hierarchically. God so creates out of nothing that he orders his creation to enable the Word of God to assume created reality as his own in the "hypostatic union." If by creation we understand everything that is not God, then God's self-expression in the Incarnation is the supreme creative act of God. In a hierarchically ordered universe the lower always depends on the higher. Because of the highest, everything else exists. So everything exists because of the Incarnation.[10]

Rahner argues that on the basis of such a viewpoint we can say that created reality belongs to redeemed reality in the same way that the self-communication of God in the Incarnation belongs to humanity, the very condition for created being to be itself. All creation, then, must be something more than a mere obediential potency for grace. Nature only finds itself in the real order, only becomes complete, when it understands itself as a moment in the grace of redeemed reality. We shall recall this point again when discussing the theology of grace.

Rahner, then, puts the old question about Christ's predestination under the norm of a cosmic view of creation in which the entire cosmos (spirit and matter) finds itself in Christ in the hypostatic union. This means the supreme unity of created spirituality and God, the goal and consequently the support of the entire cosmos and its evolution. It follows from this that one must consider the hypostatic union as the perfection of the cosmos, uniting spirit and its history into the immediacy of God, and as doing so in such a way that the hypostatic union and the order of grace are thought together.

Rahner thus gives the unending discussion about the metaphysical explanation of the hypostatic union the subjective turn of his anthropology. He says man is considered *as* obediential potency for an assumption by God (as God's Word expressing Himself). If man's nature is understood in this existential sense as open to the absolute reality of God (and so not having defined limits but still not *per se* demanding an absolute measure of fulfillment) to be performed personally, then the Incarnation can appear as the supreme fulfillment of what *man* expresses.

This is why only God can "adequately" express man.[11] Rahner feels that it is easier in this way to ward off from the Incarnation a false appearancy of mythology. The "humanity" of Christ appears as the place where God's Word is expressed positively, as that which *becomes* when God in His Word empties Himself into the (created) *other*. Christ's humanity is not seen as some kind of instrument or uniform of God. Theologically, Rahner opts for the Augustinian *ipsa assumptione creatur* (created by the very assumption) explanation. The act of creation ordered to the "humanity" is considered, then, from the very start as a moment of God's self-communication to the other. And Christ's humanity appears in the process of this assumption as achieving the highest possible human perfection.

To appreciate this fact fully, says Rahner, we need to observe how from the time of Chalcedon the propositions of Christology rest on but a very few concepts—those of the two natures in Christ, of one hypostasis and assumption of human nature by the person of the Logos.[12] Still, Christology is not forever packaged in these concepts. Its openness for further interpretation is a result of the tension between a Christology "from above" and a Christology "from below"—the basic paradigm of Rahner's transcendental method. A Christology *from above* would have to demonstrate both the possibility and the importance of the fact that God becomes the *other* (and basing this not just on an adequate theology of the Trinity but also on a genuine theological anthropology). This would mean developing the concepts *son* and *verbum*. A Christology *from below* would present the real history of Jesus, the mysteries of His life as given by scripture, and so demonstrate that the historical Jesus is the presence of God in the world and that the works done by this man constitute the world's salvation. A combination of both approaches, Rahner thinks, would show that the Incarnation is God's supreme historical communication and that Christology and soteriology may not be conceived other than as having an internal unity.

Rahner situates the real Christological problem in this way: Is the formula of Chalcedon to be so understood that the unmixed human nature (of the Logos) has a relation to the creator no different from that which any other creature has (so that what is "predicated" of the subject does not really "express" *itself*)? [13] Rahner argues that between Logos and human nature there obtains an inner, more essential relation than just human nature as the possible object of God's knowledge and power. This is seen in the fact that the Logos is the Word of the Father expressable into the world, so that when this expression happens precisely that becomes which we call human nature. In other words human nature is not the mask under which the Logos hides while gesticulating through the world, but from its very origin human nature is the real symbol of the Logos. Hence we can say that man is only possible because the expression of self of the Logos into the *other* is possible.[14] Here we have the primary use of Rahner's concept of real symbol.

Rahner would like to see the formula of Chalcedon understood as an historical attempt at formulating in all its onto*logical* dimensions the general relation obtaining between the spiritual creature and God as seen in its most complete realization in the hypostatic union. And it is precisely this relation that Rahner intends by calling our salvation a *relationship* which Christ founded definitively. This is an application of the analogy of being. In the dimension of spiritual reality the concepts *nature* and *hypostasis* could be contained in their difference and consequently not be explained negatively. The unity of the hypostasis as the *a priori* principle of union could be determined more precisely. The usual doctrine on the two natures is insufficient by itself as a starting point for deriving real insight into Christ's mediation (as something stemming from an inner dynamism of the doctrine). If one says that a human nature has a free will and this is all that is necessary, the real point is not seen that another question must be then answered: How can freedom belong to someone with whom it is not identical, whose intrinsic core it does not constitute? Only a divine person can possess as its own a freedom really distinct from itself in such a way that this freedom does not stop being truly free—even with regard to the divine person possessing it—(Christ's merit as man before God) while still qualifying this person as the ontological subject.[15]

B. Consequences of the Hypostatic Union for Christ's Human Nature

In accordance with Rahner's anthropological thought, the question about the "consciousness" of Christ plays a large role in his Christology. For modern theology the question of Christ's human self-consciousness is really actual. Paul Galtier holds that the knowledge of the hypostatic union in Christ's human consciousness is mediated by means of the *visio beatifica* and Christ has his *ego* in this way. But this makes God a simple object of "knowledge" and not of *human* self-consciousness. Such a view hinges on the thesis that supreme ontic reality (in this case, that belonging to the human nature of the Logos) is not necessarily the highest ont*ological* reality. Since this question is much discussed and Rahner often misinterpreted,[16] it may be worthwhile to develop this matter somewhat fully—both because it is a central concern and because, representing Rahner's method at its best, it may clarify some other issues.

In attempting an answer to the problem of Christ's self-consciousness, Rahner goes in the direction of Parente, stating that the human reality of Jesus *is* in its presence-to-self (belonging to the essence of spirit) present to its total being-given-over to the Logos. *This* experience of being-given-over (*Ubereignetsein*) is the immediacy of

the *visio*. The non-confusion of the human nature (and so
of its internal vision) does not oppose a subjective, human
experience if this nature experiences itself as that absolute
being-given-over as the real perfection of free human nature (and not as something known objectively). What
Rahner wants to offer is a dogmatic interpretation of
Jesus' consciousness of self and knowledge which the
exegete can accept more readily than the usual explanation. Rahner says that we have to recognize how knowledge is a many-sided thing, that it is possible both to
know something and not know it at the same time. In the
course of the discussion about Christ's knowledge it has
been customary to begin with the presupposition that
man's consciousness is a *tabula rasa,* and so far as anything being written on it or not is concerned, only a simple
disjunction is possible. But this is not the case. Human
consciousness is tremendously varied. We have reflexively
known elements and only dimly known elements, an objective and an unthematic element, an active conceptual
knowledge and a transcendental knowledge situated at the
most subjective pole. As far as reflexive knowledge goes
there is no problem. But non-objective knowledge involving the horizon under which a knowledge of objects occurs, the *a priori* condition for what is grasped *a posteriori,*
is most important. All this is usually neglected in discussing Christ's knowledge.

Rahner makes two points based on his philosophical
prolegomenon. First he says that under the forms of
knowledge we have the *a priori* non-objective knowledge
of the self as the basic disposition of the intellectual subject in which he is present to self and in which at the same
time exists his transcendental orientation to the range of
knowable objects and his freedom. Rahner says that we
need only recall that in every *human* act a multiplicity of
levels is found (intellectual, sensible, freedom, transcendence). Even our most ordinary acts include an unthematic
element which is in a sense still "known," the primary data
of consciousness—transcendental necessity and compre-

hensiveness. Still, these data can only be understood with a great deal of effort. Secondly, Rahner questions the philosophical ideal which considers whatever is not known as a lack of that perfection which belongs to man. It is curious that in this Rahner is satisfied to say that a philosophy of personal freedom would make this point more clearly! He does state this, it seems, to emphasize the element of mystery in man's nature. He recalls that even in the *visio beatifica* this element of mystery that is God will not be taken away. So whatever we say about man, we have said nothing unless we have included a reference to God's incomprehensibility.

Coming to the problem of the knowledge of Christ, Rahner asks on what grounds we must grant to Jesus an *immediate vision* of God in his earthly life and how this is the core of the vision of perfection. Rahner does not ask about a *visio beata* in Christ's earthly life. Instead, he speaks only of an immediate vision. And he does this on ontological grounds. The scriptural facts telling of Christ's suffering and anxiety, his passion and feeling of being forsaken, have to be accounted for. So Rahner asks what reasons might justify attributing an immediate vision of God to Jesus without qualifying it as beatific. The first group of usual answers centers around the fact that all perfections must be attributed to Jesus. But this suffers from the Neoplatonic complex of seeing a lack of knowledge as an imperfection. A second group of answers sees the *visio immediata* as an inner moment of the hypostatic union.

Rahner says the second group of answers is preferable because from the nature of the hypostatic union it is possible to determine what would result for a *visio immediata* and what would not. This would explain Christ's real suffering. Rahner starts with the Thomist axiom that being and self-presence are mutually conditioning moments of a single reality. So an existent which is self-present in the same measure in which it exists [17] enjoys its own degree of being. In the hypostatic union we have the supreme onto-

logical realization of created being. This Rahner considers
under the concept of a quasi-formal causality (and not
efficient causality) because it is a question of the uncreated being of God shared with a creature. However
much the hypostatic union means an ontological assumption of the human nature by the Logos, it also means a
determination of human reality in the person of the Logos
and so is at least an act of obediential potency, of the
radical ability of the creature to be assumed. In the assumption the Logos does not undergo change. Since only
man can exist to the degree in which he abandons himself,
the Incarnation is presented as the supreme achievement
of human reality. Traditional theology says that the moments of becoming and change are on the side of the
created reality which has been assumed. The affirmation of
the immutability of the Logos, however, must not cause us
to forget that what happens in the case of Jesus is God's
history. And if we view this in total perspective, we see
that God can become in another, be changeable in another. So the ontologically higher, according to the Thomist axiom, cannot be consciously inferior to the ontologically lower. Hence if there is a self-consciousness in the
human reality, then God's ontological self-communication
is a moment in the self-presence of Christ's human subjectivity. In other words, a purely *ontic* hypostatic union is a
metaphysical contradiction. And so a *visio immediata* must
belong to the hypostatic union.[18]

Immediacy to God as a basic determination of the spirit
of Jesus must be seen from the substantial root of created
intellectuality. It is the simple presence to self of the
substantial unity with the person of the Logos. It is this
and nothing else. But this implies that the immediate vision is no different from that original, non-objective, unthematic consciousness of Jesus that is given in the hypostatic union, since this consciousness of the Son of God is
the internal, ontological luminosity of the Sonship, the
subjectivity given in the objective order of things. For this
reason, awareness of Sonship, which is of the essence of

the Logos whose immediacy is an inner moment, should
not be considered as establishing an intentional relation as
a reflex "object." Jesus' consciousness of Sonship and
immediacy to God should be situated at the subjective pole
of consciousness where it is unthematic. We can understand this consciousness best if we compare it with the
basic disposition of all human spirituality, involving both
thematic and unthematic elements.[19] To this innermost
ground of all knowledge and actions belongs the immediacy of Jesus to God as an inner subjective moment of the
hypostatic assumption of human spirituality by means of
the Logos. The conscious immediacy to God participates
in the qualities of human intellectual disposition, since it is
an ontological moment of that person whose self-presence
is its basic determination. Hence immediacy to God belongs to the nature of a spiritual person as an unthematic
determination, as the given horizon which determines everything else.[20]

Such an immediacy to God is not only compatible with
real human intellectual history and growth (Jesus grew in
age and wisdom and grace), but is even demanded by it.
Just as any man despite his basic condition as spirit has to
come to himself by means of experiential contact with the
world, must learn to express what he is as a self, an ego, so
it is in the case of Jesus' self-consciousness. A history of
growth of spirit and awareness is what happens in the
process of making the world our own, in integrating ourselves and our culture. In terms of the given material and
of what is always present unthematically, we become ourselves. Jesus came to comprehend more and more clearly
what he already was and knew unthematically. Transcendence to God—whether in the case of Jesus or in our
own—is the condition of the possibility of our freedom,
the transcendental anticipation of all possible choices. An
objective individual perception of these in their individuality would remove freedom. So in this sense it is really
better that some things remain unthematic and "unknown."

Rahner argues that the eschatological consciousness of Jesus can be clarified even more precisely from the viewpoint of his immediate vision of God. It is not the anticipated removal of the eschata but their being sketched on the basis of his knowledge and Sonship. Christ knows these eschata and knows them to the same extent that he knows himself as Son and so in absolute immediacy of the objective mediation of his basic determination. Rahner closes his remarks on Christ's self-consciousness with the thesis: The dogmatic theologian and the exegete cannot question the immediate vision of God in the human soul of Jesus during his earthly life. But this fact does not say that the exegete must or even can consider this vision. Positively, one can think that a theologically correct interpretation of the immediate vision (as inner moment on the hypostatic union) can make it understandable, can bring it into agreement with the real human experience of that original immediacy which becomes thematic in terms of its encounter with environment and experience.[21]

C. Participation of Mankind in the Mediator

Christ brings salvation. This salvation is God's self-communication in grace. Being saved involves participation in God's self-communication. Obviously, this involves becoming present to Christ for participating in the divine life. So any consideration of man's participation in Christ, Rahner says, must include a consideration of the one who was closest physically to Christ, the one who as a consequence was most perfectly redeemed, Mary.

1. MARY AS THE REPRESENTATIVE OF HUMANITY

Rahner tries to integrate Mary's position into his scheme. He shows how the *de fide* proposition concerning the Immaculate Conception allows of being made intelligible in terms of Christ. Rahner says that it is a touchstone of

whether Christology is being taken seriously. For Christ is
true man and yet consubstantial with the Father. So Mary
is in truth the Mother of God. Belief in this motherhood is
necessary for understanding any other teaching about
Mary.[22]

Rahner feels that Mariology needs to be ordered within
the context of salvation history which is centered in Christ.
Mary's consent to be Christ's mother is an event of
"official" salvation history as such and is not just an epi-
sode in the private life of an ordinary Jewish girl. This is
why Luke was so careful to relate it. Applying his thought
pattern, Rahner argues that Mary's consent should not be
considered an external condition for an event which as
human would be what it is even had her consent not been
given. Rather, Mary is mother personally, not just biologi-
cally. "Looked at in this way, her personal divine motherhood precedes—admittedly, this is a rather bold way of
putting it—her son's divine Sonship." It was not just a
question of a biological process occurring within her and
terminating in a divine person. The official aspect (the
essential function of public saving history) and personal
individual sanctity always coincide at decisive points of
salvation history, where universal and particular saving
history combine, each supporting and making the other
possible.

In this sense, Mary's divine maternity belongs to the
ultimate decisive event of saving history that is the Incarnation. "In fact, so far as such an act of saving history can
be performed by a human being, it is the decisive event of
saving history, and an eschatological one." [23] The dialogue
between God and man is no longer open, because in
answer to Mary's assent, God spoke His Word of salvation
(and not of judgment). This event of public salvation
history in which Mary acted as representative of mankind
is at the same time her personal act of faith. So at this
point there coincide most clearly office and person, position in the church and situation before God, dignity and
sanctity.

Rahner summarizes by calling Mary the "most perfectly

redeemed." He explains this paradoxically by saying that redemption as the grace of one person is always the blessing of another. Redemption occurs as the reception of Christ in faith—which is itself grace and (for faith) thus establishes itself as something historically tangible. So the most perfect redemption is actual conception of Christ in faith and in body for the salvation of all. This takes place in the holiest act of freedom which is grace. Because Mary stands at that point of saving history at which by her freedom the world's salvation is accomplished, she is the most perfectly redeemed. Rahner cautions that we must keep in mind how Christ's descent into the flesh is the beginning of the descent into death, because the flesh he assumed is flesh dedicated to mortality. Hence the Incarnation is not just a precondition for an open redemption but the start of what really happens.[24]

A redemptive preservation from original sin is the most radical form of redemption. And this must have been the lot of her who is most perfectly redeemed, because by reason of Mary's office and person she stands at that point of history where Christ begins the redemption of the world. Thus Rahner explains the Immaculate Conception as a necessary consequence of Mary's position in universal salvation history.

The fact that the eschatological event for the world's salvation happened in the free and holy assent of Mary, where God's grace achieved its most incomprehensible and unsurpassable effect, grasping the world in the most "fleshly" way, cannot be underestimated. Christ's Incarnation is the beginning of the "descent into the kingdom of death" and of the resurrection. By Christ's death, salvation has come definitively. So there is in principle nothing to prevent man from finding this definitive salvation. Everything depends on the fact that our own reality is transformed and not replaced by another which could not be us or our world. We can note that the parousia will not be the introduction of just a new heaven and a new earth, but rather will be the earth as the perfection of the "heaven" which will have wholly transformed itself and its mode of being, the completion of the reality of our world. So we must see that the new heaven and the old earth are radically connected and that the notion of death does not involve a migration out of the world. So the reality beyond (in so far as it already exists in the glorified Christ) cannot be thought of as lacking all objective ties with the present world. Rahner argues, then, that reflecting on this fact will show why it makes sense to say that one man has "already" risen while another has "not yet" done so—since this does not involve application of limited categories to an object wholly transcending them. Eternity in glory of the creature is not identical with God's eternity (which is equally immediate and equally near every point in time and to which temporal statements cannot be applied). The eternity of what is created is a product of time and history. Salvation history transforms the temporal into the eternal by means of the process which on the one hand does not run its course simultaneously and on the other hand does not lose the connection of its parts with the process as a whole. So the part can be really determined temporally from the point of view of the whole.

We can see from this how Rahner urges that his concept of "perfectly redeemed" be understood dynamically, as a concept the contents of which cannot be defined or listed in a fixed order. It has a life of its own, obedient to the process of the evolution of dogma seen in the last chapter. It implies that Mary as the ideal representation of exhaustive redemption (because of her place in salvation history) must "even now" have achieved that perfect communion with God in the glorified totality of her real being—body and soul—which certainly exists now. This is what we mean, Rahner thinks, when we talk about her assumption.

2. UNITY OF ALL CREATION IN CHRIST

Rahner sees man as the creature in whom the basic tendency of matter to find itself in spirit through self-transcendence comes to a definitive breakthrough. This is most perfectly realized in Christ—so that man's nature can be viewed within the total comprehension of the world. The completion of self-transcendence into God by means of His self-communication is grace and glory. The Incarnation is the first step and the lasting guarantee of ultimate self-transcendence. It was taken in the hypostatic union. Rahner believes that we should not look upon this so much from the point of view of what makes us different from Jesus as Lord, but rather as something which only had to happen once, at the point when the world began its final phase. Here the Incarnation enters as the necessary start of the divinization of the world as a whole. And here the paradox occurs which we see so clearly today. For we are starting to see that the secularization of the world is really another stage of the world's ultimate divinization. And as man assumes more and more responsibility for the development of the world, its ultimate destiny comes closer. The future can be said to be already present in a much truer sense. And it is in terms of this cosmic evolutionism, which we will later examine more closely, that Rahner thinks Christology must be ordered, so that we see the unity of all creation in Christ, the one absolute transcendence of creation in God's absolute self-communication.

IV. SOTERIOLOGY

Rahner's contributions to the theology of redemption have not been in specifically soteriological terms. As noted earlier, his framework and methodology force him to consider Christology and soteriology as two moments of a unified action. The theology of redemption is really an outgrowth of what is implied in Rahner's understanding of Christ as mediator of God's saving will. It might be well, however, to review the fact that Rahner's approach is not a new one. The Scotistic theologians stressed for centuries that the basic motive of the Incarnation was not the wiping out of guilt, but rather that it was the fact that the Incarnation even prior to divine knowledge of man's sin was to be the free crown of the self-expression and self-emptying of God into the other of the creature—as the most original act of God in creating, so that (under the presupposition of sin) a redemption also occurs. From this Scotistic point of view one cannot say that Rahner's interpretation could arouse real ecclesiastical second thoughts. For it is quite Catholic to view the Incarnation primarily in the first intention of God as the crown and plan of creation and not just as an act of restoring a world disturbed and upset by man's sin but a world still wholly conceivable apart from the Incarnation. In light of this background it is not surprising that Rahner has not stressed what are usually called soteriological problems.

He does indicate, however, that it would be heretical to deny that the reality and performance of the incarnate Logos also means the actual victory over sin. But the actual work of redemption should not be separated from Christ's being.

The usual foundation for the scholastic teaching on satisfaction, the formal divine worth of the person of Christ, should only be considered an outline that needs filling in. Christ is His work (ontologically and functionally). Properly understood, Christology and soteriology are one. In Christ, God has assumed the world ontologically. And in the hypostatic union He has assumed the world and become man, so that in this assumption there is an expression of God and an appropriation of the expression by means of the world. This is especially true when Jesus fulfills Himself in freedom and death and so assumes Himself.

Fitted into the transcendental method, redemption is seen "functionally" (meritoriously) as an internal, essential moment, the high point of that salvation established by the Incarnation. This would be without meaning (merely ontic and ultimately mythological) if it were not seen as a condition of the possibility of actual Christology. This means understanding soteriology as Christ's obedient self-expression of God and loving acceptance of this expression. Just as the life and death of all men form a unity in a total acceptance of freedom, so the determining moment of the free acceptance of what God Himself has expressed—the Verbum as man—consists not in the *manner* of this acceptance in death, but simply in itself, in the course of accepting the fortunes of everyday human life. This acceptance on Christ's part began existentially with the first hour of his human life. For this reason, Augustine stressed the fact that Jesus would have died even if the Jews had not put him to death and that his "natural" death would have been equally redemptive.

Current theories on satisfaction (including the teaching on redemption involving a theory of a double moral subject in Christ) understand a redeeming act directed to all three divine persons equally. Rahner feels that such an approach suffers from the fact that it does not reflect on why satisfaction is offered by the *Verbum incarnatum* and not by another divine person. One might just as well imagine that any other divine person as man could have offered a *satisfactio condigna* to God. Rahner argues that this would be just as conceivable without having presupposed the Trinity as a condition of possibility at all.[25] And the theory of a double moral person in a substantial personality once presupposed, an absolutely one-person God could enter a hypostatic union with a human nature and so offer satisfaction to Himself.[26] Rahner thinks that this fact needs to be brought out more clearly in exposing the inadequacy of some current theories on satisfaction.

The Catholic position on the redemption and justification is not just that of a moral or juridical transaction, a simple declaration of freedom from guilt or a Protestant blanketing of sin. Rather, it involves participation in God's self-communication. Hence in every instance it is the continuation of that existential historical process of founding the relationship of divinized humanity. Such an understanding of the redemption is only possible because we have factual knowledge of the Incarnation. Rahner believes that such a metaphysical reflexion always involves bringing into clearer focus what has been vaguely perceived. Just as a transcendental sketch of man as free, for example, is transcendentally *a priori* and still factually dependent on its performance in the living experience of freedom, so it is in the matter of our redemption from sin. We depend on our knowledge of the Incarnation and so we can make explicit what it means to participate in Christ. Through the Incarnation the whole of redemption was accomplished, even if it was only finished on the cross because Christ had assumed the "flesh of sin" (Romans 8, 3). The Logos redeemed by really identifying Himself with the sinner.

The full meaning of the redemption only becomes clear when we discuss what is implied in living a life of Christ's grace. If Christ is the determining existential of man's natural existence, then the dynamism of the unlimited horizon of the future is already present. Its possible extension is unlimited. Among the consequences should be peace, because the real ultimate salvation is already at hand in the act of faith given and accepted.

The unity of mankind is confirmed, increased, and made definitive in the Incarnation. After Christ, human nature is divinized by means of the hypostatic union. Through the sanctifying grace that follows necessarily upon that union man shares in the immediate presence of God.[27] The unity of all creation in a true and real sense means that there cannot be any world separate from this unity, since it is grounded in God's decision of his own self-expression in the Incarnation. But this unity is willed as the condition of a created reality which has to *become* historically. The positive aspect of creation is complete in its beginning, because the humanity of Christ is the necessary doorway through which all other creatures must pass if they are to find completion before God.

Rahner notes how people who want to reject the orthodox expressions of Christology (usually because they misunderstand them) may yet perform existentially a genuine and believing faith in the Incarnation. Someone, for instance, who believes in Jesus and His cross believes what is true and real. What he does not confess is not necessarily what is denied. The grace of Christ allows any individual to accept his own existence, his own humanity, in silent patience, with respect for mystery. And any man who does this says "yes" to something that is true. Whoever lets go and does not wholly accept himself (and just who does this is uncertain) falls into the depths of rejection. Who accepts himself, also accepts Jesus, because in Jesus God has accepted man. Rahner notes that if scripture says that the man who loves his neighbor fulfills the law, then this is ultimate truth, because God Himself has become his neighbor, and so what is both nearest and transcendent at once is accepted and loved in every neighbor. We shall clarify this point in the next chapter.[28]

APPENDIX TO CHAPTER THREE

1. See *Schriften,* vol. III, pp. 419–439.

2. See, for example, *The Later Heidegger and Theology: New Frontiers in Theology,* ed. by James M. Robinson and John B. Cobb, Jr., New York, 1965, pp. 146 ff. Volume Three of this series is also helpful.

3. The word connotes more than just a temporal notion. It highlights the aspect of the proper, fitting, or critical time, that moment most apt for the insertion into the world of God's Son. Rahner likes to select words from classical civilization when he thinks they illustrate better what he is trying to say.

4. Following his method, Rahner finds the theological preconditions for this concept by arguing that it must be in the fact that man has to expect and accept grace not only within history but that grace itself is historical and history itself is grace and that all the data given (unity of mankind, revelation, and so on) are grace.

5. Biblical theology has progressed rather further. For example, in the matter of demythologizing, biblical theology could demonstrate that salvation history is not the metahistorical experience of faith but is real history which is coextensive with profane history.

6. See *Lexikon für Theologie und Kirche,* vol. 5, cols. 147–156.

7. This point needs the added clarification of Rahner's doctrine of grace which may be found in the next chapter.

8. See *Schriften,* vol. VI, p. 177.

9. See *Theological Investigations,* vol. I, p. 154.

10. Rahner explains this hierarchy of being in the following way. "At the lowest end of the scale is the merely individuated single being which must pay for being 'in itself' by being enclosed within itself, excluding everything else, and which cannot go out from itself without ceasing to possess even its own action, making it into something outside itself

116

which it acts *upon*. At the highest is the greatest mystery of our Faith, the most perfect individuality, who, in the fullest sense, exists for his own sake and is immutable, but nevertheless excludes nothing of the perfection of any other being, having all reality within himself; who gives himself totally and yet for this very reason possesses himself most completely; in whom perfect individuality and perfect community do not conflict but *are* each other. Between the two extremes, the one the "death" of lifeless matter and the other the infinite life of the Blessed Trinity, is man. He is rooted in earth, individuated, and thus separated from others, by matter, in which there is neither true individuality nor true community, because the individuality is the same kind as every other man's and the community merely the sum total of all its component individuals." "The Individual in the Church," *Nature and Grace*, tr. by Dinah Wharton, New York and London, 1964, pp. 13, 14.

11. Provided, of course, that this is so understood that the grade of being and the fulfillment of transcendence present to self grow in the same proportion.

12. What "supposit" expresses in Christ cannot be identically what "nature" expresses, and this amounts to saying that supposit and nature are not the same. Christ does not exist in and through himself but in and through the Word of God: His human nature, complete and perfect though it is in its humanity, does not subsist. With reference to existence, Christ differs from and is independent of all other existents not as man but as a divine supposit, as the Son of God. Thomists usually state the cause of individuality in natures to be the quantified matter within such natures; that of individuality in supposits, the act of existing proper to and actualizing each supposit. The problem as far as Rahner is concerned lies in the fact that subjectivity is not identical with supposit (which for most Thomists is to deny that subjectivity immediately springs from the act of existing). One result has been that some Thomists have argued that the problem of subject/object does not belong to metaphysics in an "authentic" existentialism, because they refuse to consider the real meaning of existence for a philosopher of subjectivity as "to be human." For a characteristic example see Leo Sweeney, S.J., "Existentialism: Authentic and Unauthentic," *New Scholasticism*, 41 (January 1966), pp. 60 ff. We do not intend to go

into this problem, but merely wish to indicate where the real rub is felt and point out the source of the objection of many scholastic theologians regarding Rahner's Christology.

13. Rahner states that the slightest of discussions of the problems of the fomula of Chalcedon has shown that the attempt to advance our understanding of what this unity (unconfused and undivided) is which makes the human nature that of the Logos itself, would also further our understanding of who man is. We see that Christology is at once beginning and end of anthropology and that such an anthropology is really theo-logy, so the less we think of the humanity as something added on to God and the more we understand it as God's presence in the world, the more intelligible the faith becomes. It turns out to be an expression of our very own existence. See *Theological Investigations,* vol. I, p. 185.

14. See *Schriften,* vol. IV, pp. 122, 123.

15. Rahner continually drives home the fact that God wanted to be the God who is near to us, who gives Himself as a gift in love, who communicates Himself and who realizes our freedom in His freedom. He is the freedom of our freedom by the grace of His self-communication, without which free will could only choose slavery no matter what choice it might make. God is the freedom of our freedom by way of communication. The divine *pneuma* is the liberating freedom of our freedom, saving our freedom from the dilemma of being either a freedom lost in finitude or preserved by starving by reason of its own emptiness. See *Theological Investigations,* vol. II, pp. 93 ff.

16. For example: "It becomes obvious, then, that Rahner's final contention (which proves to be a *philosophical* one) is far from plausible. We are asked to accept a God who is partly mutable and partly immutable on the ground that his freedom in creation must be interrupted in a way which would lead to this result. It is certainly not clear that it must be so interpreted. To say that this account of the Incarnation is the only one which is theologically legitimate is plainly indefensible. And the account is in fact unthinkable." Dom Illtyd Trethowan, "A Changing God," *Downside Review,* 84 (July 1966), p. 258. Such criticism is helpful, but since it is based on a set of different philosophical premises misses the point. If one is unwilling to accept the starting point of any particular

system then criticism should be confined to the consistency of the argument in question, unless it is plainly a matter of starting from obviously mistaken principles. And because a transcendental system may not be clear to a metaphysican of a different school, there is no basis for attacking conclusions which derive from principles one may not clearly understand or assent to. Rahner would be the first to admit to a problem if his argument were shown to be weak in itself or deriving from false premises.

17. This means that the internal analogousness and applicability of being is related to the possibility of self-presence and self-possession—and so of consciousness.

18. Rahner observes how this same knowledge can be reached by a different argument. He cites Bernard Welte who in an ontology of limited spirit shows the hypostatic union to be the most radical actualization of what limited spirit means. From this it is easy to see that such a hypostatic union cannot be considered a mere ontic connection between two realities but as the absolute perfection of limited spirit necessarily implies an ontology of consciousness. In other words, in such a subjectively unique unity of human consciousness of Jesus with the Logos of the most radical nearness, uniqueness, and ultimacy, the hypostatic union is given in its complete essence. See Bernard Welte, *Chalkedon*, vol. III, "homoousios hemin."

19. This basic disposition of man (intellect, freedom, transcendence) is given without reflexion. It is conscious and yet unthematic, an illuminatedness of itself that is not seen reflexively. It cannot really be separated from consciousness nor may it be interpreted in a false conceptual manner. It should be viewed from the most diverse viewpoints and in wholly opposite conceptual systems, so that man may say thematically what he has always known unthematically.

20. It is the reflexively incomprehensible ground which carries all other spiritual performances because as ground is always more and more non-objective as everything else "is there"—as silent self-understanding which orders and explains but cannot be explained itself, because as basic ground it is always unthematic. See *Schriften*, vol. V, pp. 238, 239.

21. Observe that if to-be-human in the real order always means self-transcendence to the mystery of God until it finally

becomes vision, having come absolutely near by reason of grace so that to-be-human in this sense implies a God-humanity, then this God-humanity of Christ must be seen as the qualitatively unique point, so that man obtains from God an understanding of Christ's humanity without becoming involved in empty formulae. On the other hand man obtains from the experience of Christ the courage of faith in being gifted with God's grace.

22. "And if anyone protests against further Marian dogmas, either explicitly or by passive indifference, he must expect to be asked whether he believes and confesses what the Church solemnly confessed at Ephesus in 431 as the faith of the one and undivided church, and what the Reformed Church of the sixteenth century believed too, though it did not really raise the question whether this was necessary in order that one could as sinner be consoled by faith in a gracious God." *Theological Investigations,* vol. I, p. 203. Rahner may not be quite so sure of this point now and would not want any more definitions, Marian or otherwise, at the present time. The climate of post-Vatican II has helped this situation considerably.

23. *Theological Investigations,* vol. I, p. 205.

24. If in the final resort God's grace is the cause and not the effect of man's act; if consequently man's redemption follows upon God's saving purpose; if according to this purpose, which arises from God's free yet absolute initiative, redemption by means of the Incarnation was to occur by the assumption of an Adamitic human nature and its destiny, then it is clear that in God's predetermining will for this Christ an earthly mother was likewise predestined, that is, was willed absolutely and prior to any human decision, like the Incarnation itself. So Mary's free consent is already given. Human motherhood must be free, if it is not to injure the dignity of the human person.

25. See *Schriften,* vol. IV, p. 107.

26. *Ibid.,* p. 107, n. 8.

27. See *The Church and the Sacraments,* New York and London, 1963, pp. 12, 13.

28. Only the heretic can say it is possible to deny *a priori* that one can still believe in Christ when he rejects the proper formulas of Christology. In the performance of existence one cannot adopt just any thinkable position.

For further illumination on some of the questions treated in this chapter see P. Galtier, S.J., "Saint Athanase et l'âme humaine du Christ," *Gregorianum*, 36 (1955), pp. 553–589; F. Malmberg, "Ipsa assumptione creatur," *Een paging tot scholastick theologische geloofsinterpretatie*, Jubileum bundel Prof. Mag. G. Kreling (1953), pp. 63–84; A Grillmeier, S.J., "Der Gottessohn im Totenreich," *Zeitschrift für katholische Theologie*, 71 (1949), pp. 50 ff.; P. Descoqs, S.J., *Le Mystère de notre élévation surnaturelle*, Paris, 1938, pp. 94–103; A. Durand, S.J., "La science du Christ," *Nouvelle Revue Théologique*, 71 (1949), pp. 497–503. See in addition Rahner's notes to his articles, especially "Current Problems in Christology," *Theological Investigations*, vol. I, pp. 149–201; "Zur Theologie der Menschwerdung," *Schriften*, vol. III, pp. 137–157; "Dogmatische Fragen zur Osterfrömmigkeit," *Schriften*, vol. III, pp. 157–173; "Die Christologie innerhalb einer evolutiven Weltanschauung," *Schriften*, vol. V, pp. 183–221; "Dogmatische Erwägungen über das Wissen und Selbstbewusstsein Christi," *Schriften*, vol. V, pp. 222–248.

For historical questions see *Schriften*, vol. V, "Weltgeschichte und Heilsgeschichte," pp. 115–135; and *Lexikon für Theologie und Kirche*, "Heilsgeschichte." And for Mariology in addition to *Theological Investigations*, vol. I, pp. 201–228, see *Schriften*, vol. IV, "Virginitas in Partu," pp. 173–208; *Schriften*, vol. III, "Das Dogma von der Unbefleckten Empfängnis Mariens und unsere Frömmigkeit," pp. 155–164.

For the most recent Protestant thought on Christology see Peter C. Hodgson, "The Death of God and the Crisis in Christology," *The Journal of Religion*, 46 (October, 1966), pp. 446–462.

CHAPTER FOUR

THE SUPERNATURAL EXISTENTIAL DIMENSION OF MAN

Having considered something of Rahner's philosophical prolegomenon, the development of dogma, and man's historical dimension in saving history, we can now focus on the specifically supernatural dimension of theological anthropology. This involves looking at what grace is for man, the supernatural life that is the self-communication of God. The Christological considerations of the previous chapter should lead us on to specifically Trinitarian questions. Rahner believes that Christology must have a most intimate connection with the theology of the Trinity and thereby clarify how the economic Trinity (God in respect to us) is the immanent Trinity (God in His relatedness to Himself) and vice versa. No matter how freely we consider the Incarnation, we must come to see that according to revelation it is the Son in whom God assumes another reality than He already is and that God lets this assumption be His real symbol: the appearance of His really signifying presence. The real place of the Christian world and the interpretation of its history consists in being bound up with the theology of the Trinity and Christology. This place is man's supernatural existential dimension. It is with Rahner's development of such considerations that this chapter is concerned.

122

PLAN OF CHAPTER

In the first section we take up some of Rahner's Trinitarian speculation. Then the different modes of man's relatedness to the Trinity come up for consideration, and the Trinity of persons as immanently constituting the absoluteness of the supernatural will be discussed from Rahner's viewpoint. The second major section takes up the question of our participation in the Trinitarian life of God. This means giving a somewhat formal consideration to the many-sided problems connected with the doctrine of grace.

I. THE GOD OF THE ORDER OF SUPERNATURAL LIFE AND REVELATION

A. Historical Situation of the Problem of God

In the 19th century in many specific formulations, but all representing a community of interest, there appeared in theology a Socratic turn to the self, an "existentialist" understanding of religious truth. This means that theology has to start from, to articulate and interpret a subjective view of the religious object. Hence any meaningful talk about God has to be talk in which the self is concerned. It is about God as the object of concern. Kierkegaard is the real milestone of this turn. The point could hardly be put more sharply than in his insistence that, religiously speaking, "truth is subjectivity," so that the question of religious truth is the question of my own relation to the truth rather than any question of "objective truth" of that to which I am so related. At least on the level of religiousness A (in the *Concluding Unscientific Postscript*) the question is entirely one of the quality and intensity of passion in the relationship, "subjective" rather than "objective" validity, even to the point of the contention that the supreme subjective truth is compatible only with the greatest objective uncertainty.

Schleiermacher also made a significant contribution to this "turn." For Schleiermacher, theological assertions are to be understood as grounded in and drawn from the present faith, the religious consciousness, of the historical Christian community. Theological utterances about the constitution of the world and about the divine attributes and modes of action are to be developed as implications of the religious self-consciousness of the feeling of absolute dependence. Cardinal Newman's "illative sense" with its active judging and concluding out of which certitude arises illustrates this quite well. And all this irreducibly involves the believer's being in the truth.

A third stage in this dialectic is now becoming obvious in the post-Heideggerian thought of some Protestant theologians (for example, Bultmann, Gogarten, Ebeling) in the movement to the subjective view of the religious subject. Here *subjective* is intended to denote a way of viewing, a method, in which the subjecthood of the interpreter is involved necessarily. It refers to the insistence (the hermeneutical principle) that the realities of human experience (existentials) cannot be adequately explained apart from the investment of the interpreter's own self, the raising of questions about his own existence. A theologically sufficient interpretation of the faith can be given only by a method in which the question of the interpreter's own being is involved. And this involves qualifications deriving from particular existentialist analyses of the structures of human existence. Theology in this sense can really be said to be a true theological anthropology.

Rahner stands directly in this path of dialectical development. For he approaches the problem of God with data from theological anthropology as well as with the more usual principles of the magisterium and scripture. In studying the structure of teaching on God the question of the relationship between the natural and the supernatural

order, it is not enough to argue that dogma must obtain its
solutions from pure theological (and so not metaphysical
and epistemological) sources. Rahner cautions, however,
that it would be just as untheological if one were to act as
if he could develop theology as a systematic reflexion on
the Word of revelation without either scripture or metaphysics. The teaching about God can only concern itself
with propositions involving God's historical witness of
himself in His saving deed and word. But this experience
and its expression by man necessarily involve His metaphysical existence. So the more clearly man reflects on this
matter in order to become fully open for divine testimony,
the more purely he can restate the problem of God. It
must include the basic structures lacing the saving history
of God's action in the world. Rahner thinks that these
contents are usually distinguished insufficiently. God's
constancy, mercy, love, and so forth, that we experience
factually are not simply theological testimony of His necessary attributes and metaphysical essence. They are essentially more. God's constancy, love, and mercy which
He shows us He could deny us without thereby ceasing to
be true, merciful, and loving in the metaphysical sense.

Rahner finds that such an approach gives a better insight into the true heart of the Lutheran *theologia crucis*
and its value for Catholic theology. God's action in our
behalf (even more than His "attributes") cannot be unified in a single concept. His action can only be expressed
asymptotically in the converging statement that they must
all be one in God. For us the *mystery* remains without a
material synthesis. As we saw in the last chapter, their
effectiveness has a history in which a simple metaphysical
equilibrium regarding our behavior need not obtain.
Rather, we really must praise God's mercy more than we
must fear His justice, because God has let His grace
stream over us, and not His anger. The usual approach to
understanding God and the supernatural tends to conceal
this structure, since it is presented in seemingly unrelated

tractates. Rahner believes that if the teaching on God's providence and freedom in distributing grace, of the historicity of salvation, did not stand in an empty formality, we would have a theological counterweight to the secularized concept of the history of being represented, for example, in Heidegger's *Seinsgeschichte*.[1]

B. Trinity as Economy

Since our knowledge of God is analogous, we can never hope to penetrate the mystery that is the divine life. We can learn something through revelation of this inner life of God. But we must learn this in terms of God's relatedness to us. Father, Son, and Spirit each illuminate according to the scriptural testimony a true difference, a double mediation within the divine self-communication. But this double mediation (Word and Spirit) is not a created sort of thing at all so that God would not be shared really as He is in Himself. If following the witness of faith the "economical" participation in the divine life really is Trinitarian, if Sabellianism is really false, then the real mediation within the economy must be a real mediation of that inner divine life most proper to God. The "trinity" of the relationship of God to us in the order of the grace of Christ consequently is already the reality of God in Himself: three personal. So the economic Trinity is the immanent Trinity.

Rahner feels that the less a teaching on the Trinity is ashamed to stress this *economy,* the more it can truly say about the *immanent* Trinity and so arrive at a better and more existential understanding of the faith. For we know that revelation and salvation history display God's opening of self and man's transcendental nature as summoned by God in such a way that man is only present to himself when he finds God and that man could not find the true God if he only considered God in a relation "to us." Hence it is proper for man to speak first about God and not about salvation. This, however, does not exclude emphasizing that the real source of our knowledge of God is Christ the Redeemer.[2]

We have seen earlier how for Rahner reflexion on the question about being brings new insight into the characteristics of finite existents, so that man is led inevitably to some knowledge of absolute being as the condition of the possibility of the existence of finite beings. Such knowledge of finite being, since it is built upon God, is never complete. Transcendental philosophy can lead no further than to a knowledge of the existence of Absolute Being as such, which *as such* must possess an infinite wealth of spiritual-personal life since it is arrived at analogously. The question about God can then turn into a question addressed to God: whether He does not wish to reveal Himself to man. Man, tending to his dynamism, must be ready for any word God might wish to address to him. So Rahner, once he has built his fundamental theoretical approach anthropologically, then takes up the problem of God from the viewpoint of revelation.

The world is ordered as a whole to a supernatural end, the Triune God. We have seen how the whole development of the world—and we will examine this explicitly in the next chapter—is included under a theological *a priori*. Rahner says that we know the one God as beginning and end of the world, that we can know God with intrinsic certainty, therefore, "by the light of natural reason" from the objective world. But this means that knowledge of God is possible for *human nature*. The possibility of knowing God belongs to the constitution of man independently of revelation and the summons which elevates him in grace to participation in the life of the Trinity. This possibility still exists, even after an individual has lost the further possibility of participating in God's personal life. And only if it is in his nature that man have something to do with God can he freely experience God's self-disclosure as actually promulgated in revelation. So Rahner argues that precisely in order for revelation to be grace, man must have something to do with God from a locus, a place which is not already grace. It is important to note that this formulation does not say anything about the existing condition of man. Rather, it involves human nature as such.

This fact is important if we are to understand both the widespread failure of men to find God and when He is found, the multiple possibilities of error. Given man's real fallen state where sin ultimately is the will not to allow God to be God, so that every non-Christian religion will in fact be a polytheism in so far as it must be theologically qualified as sin, religion is bound to interpret God's infinity, for example, as an infinity of separate powers and forces active in the world. Still, for Catholics an additional danger exists, especially in the understanding of grace, of becoming factually *monotheistic* in the wrong sense, and so they do not really appreciate the Trinity and grace as a real *consortium divinae naturae* (share in the divine nature) following upon the Trinity. Even when Catholics say that grace was "earned" by Christ, they sometimes think of it as grace *Dei-hominis* (God-man) and not as grace of the *Verbum incarnatum,* the Logos. So we must see the doctrine on grace as a necessary corrective to a possible misinterpretation of the mystery of the Trinity.

Revelation has a real history. It is always a free event. It is not just because man is himself an act of God's freedom that God's Word and action are free. What happens in saving history is not the consequence of some unchanging ideal law, but is the free and ever new event of God's action. This has taken place in historicity. And this means that God has not established one and the same thing once and for all. God's central act is the single internal unity of the Incarnation, cross, and resurrection in which God has definitively communicated Himself to the world. But this is only revealed in the actions of Christ.

Rahner argues on the basis of the system of scholasticism that once the teaching on the Trinity has been presupposed, no real question remains (that is, once the linguistic usage of the New Testament has been taken to conform to that of theology). The New Testament makes the doctrine on the Trinity clear. Rahner's contribution here is a linguistic analysis of the concept ὁ θεός quite similar to the work of theological and philosophical analysts following the methods of Wittgenstein, G. E. Moore, and Russell. Rahner argues that the concept θεός ("God") in the New Testament signifies (significat) the person to whom the divine nature is proper. So "God" can stand for (supponitur) each of the three divine persons or for all three persons together. For example, when the Logos is called "Son of God," the word "God" stands for the Father. Or in the statement "God creates the world," the word "God" stands (in Latin theology) for the divine persons all three taken together in so far as they are one God in the unity of operation and so one source of the world in this operation "ad extra." Rahner argues further that in the New Testament ὁ θεός signifies properly the first person of the Trinity and does not merely stand for him. This applies wherever a different meaning is not clear from the context. So when in the New Testament we are called children of God, the question becomes whether we are children of the three divine persons or whether we are to understand that we are children of the Father. Rahner's argument makes it clear that we are to understand that we are children of the Father.

This matter leads to the theological problem of whether we are related specifically in grace to each of the three divine persons. The usual interpretation in Western theology of our "filiation" with respect to God tends to lead more into a moralistic attenuation of this relationship than would be the case if from the start we saw our relationship stressing a living awareness of the fact that the Father in the Trinitarian sense is our Father. Rahner holds that if "in prayer to God" we become more aware that we are calling upon the Father of Christ, the Trinitarian structure of our supernatural dimension will become more vital and will consequently sharpen our consciousness of Christ's mediation with regard to the Father.

Western theology (as opposed to Byzantine and Greek

orthodox) has tended to start discussing the problem of God from the unity of the divine nature as the condition for the doctrine of the Trinity, while the Greek theologians in the East have stuck more closely to the biblical usage. They begin with the three persons of a single divine nature: with the Father, the source from which the Son and through the Son the Spirit proceed, so that the unity and integrity of the divine nature follow conceptually upon the fact that the Father communicates His whole nature. Applying the analogy of faith, Rahner argues that we obtain a better insight into God's communication of Himself to us in grace if we start from such an approach.

This question gets at the heart of the problem of the real connection between the Trinity as economic and the Trinity as immanent, the entitative Trinity and the Trinity of revelation. If man really does have a special relationship to each of the three divine persons (because grace cannot be reduced to the concept of an effect of God's efficiency, an effect worked by the three divine persons in common), the opposition between the entitative Trinity and the Trinity of revelation is resolved at its very root: God both exists as Trinitarian and man is related to God as Father, Word, and Spirit.[3]

As noted earlier, Rahner complains that in spite of all the formulas and Trinitarian mysticism which has filled the history of the church, Christians tend to remain false monotheists when it comes to an actual belief in the Trinity. When we speak of the Incarnation we tend to think of the fact that God became man but not that it was the Logos who became man. Rahner says that this is a consequence of the nearly universal assumption in theology that any one of the divine persons could have become man in the Incarnation, so that the Incarnation of the Verbum would reveal nothing at all to us of the inner-Trinitarian uniqueness of precisely this person.

Rahner admits the validity of a theology of the Trinity built on the psychological doctrine of St. Augustine which culminates in a teaching paralleling the basic acts of spirit: knowing and loving. But he adds that in scripture the divine knowledge in the economy of salvation is given in terms of a revelation of divine love, in terms of a *personal* communication. Where our attention is focused on purely psychological speculation we tend to fall into the difficulties which too much speculation always produce: we start from an inner-worldly philosophical concept of knowledge and love, develop from this a concept of the *word* and of the attracting power of *love,* and finally end by applying this last concept to the Trinity. Then we admit that our application falters because we remain stuck in "essential" concepts of knowledge and love.

According to the Logos theology of the Fathers of the church and from the viewpoint that the economic Trinity *is* the immanent Trinity (and vice versa), a much deeper insight can be gained. The theology of the Trinity (and Christology) needs, Rahner thinks, a rather fuller development. And this is all the more important since the hypostasis of the Logos is precisely that whereby the Word is differentiated from Father and Spirit, and not just that wherein the three persons in one and the same general "Person-being" come together. If this hypostasis is that of the humanity of Jesus, it necessarily takes on a hypostatic function regarding what is essentially *other* (the one expression of God's Word as such). Only when seen in this light, Rahner thinks, can the unity of the doctrine on the Trinity and the Incarnation be made clear.[4]

Rahner is thus enabled to view God's unity as being in the same position regarding the Trinity as is His immutability in regard to mutability. In each case, the tendency of our intellect might lead us to a one-sided conclusion if we were not continually checked by faith.[5] The expression about God's immutability, for example, is a dialectical statement, like that about His unity. Both statements do not become really precise for us unless we think at once about other propositions (though it is not possible for us to think of one as preordained to the other). The doctrine of the Incarnation reveals to us that God's immutability is not precisely and of itself what distinguishes God, but rather that in His immutability God can truly become something. And this is the high point of perfection. Rahner's thought in this direction has only begun. It is to be hoped that he will continue to develop this line of speculation and that other theologians, following his lead, will take up the challenging outline he has drawn. This direction leads theology out of the impasse which modern criticism of traditional doctrines seems to have put the "orthodox" theologian.[6]

C. Different Modes of Relatedness of Graced Man to the Trinity

Rahner holds that the three communications of God are self-communications in the same threefold relative manner in which He subsists. The Father gives Himself to us as Father. Because He is essentially present to Himself, He expresses Himself and so communicates with the Son as His own personal self-opening, and thereby and in so far as Father and Son (receiving from Father) affirm the self in love which comes to self (as accepted loving, Spirit), God communicates Himself in a three-personal manner. God is related to us in these modes of the Trinity. This threefold (free and unexacted) relation to us is not just an image of the immanent Trinity but *is* this very communication. For what is shared is the triune personal God, so that this communication, when it freely happens, can only come in the divine manner of the immanent communications of the divine nature of Father, Son, and Spirit— because any other would not communicate what is here communicated: the divine persons, since these cannot be separated from their own manner of communication.[7]

The Trinitarian relationship of God to us in the order of Christ's grace is already the reality of God as it exists, *three personal.* Such a statement could be heretical (Sabellianism or Modalism) if the statement of the "modality" of the relation of God to the supernaturally elevated creature were to overlook the radical *self*-opening character of this "modality" (in uncreated grace and in the hypostatic union) and so not let God be what God is. When God is understood as so untouched by this relation that it implies no difference in God, we approach a proper understanding.[8]

D. Three Persons in God as Immanently Constituting the Absoluteness of the Supernatural

We have seen how the inner life of God is approached by Rahner. We have observed how the relationship of immanent and economic Trinity involve each other in our attempt at understanding this mystery. Rahner is here arguing that the only way we can learn the meaningfulness of God-language is to learn its usage. Some modern theologians object to such an approach, but their objection overlooks the real note of mystery in what is involved. Man is really to share in God's self-communication. He has an obediential potency for this sharing. But if the supernatural existential that is his really is supernatural, it must mean openness to the reality of God as such. This reality can only be the real life of the Trinity as communicated in a triune manner. Hence we must come to see the Trinity as immanently constitutive of what we mean when we speak of the absoluteness of the supernatural. We can gain some limited insight into what this formulation implies only by considering the radical importance of the hypostatic union and by considering what it is we really mean when we talk about supernatural life. This means that we have to think about grace in its very essence. The separateness of the usual tractates on grace and God make this unusually difficult. Rahner's approach may make it easier. And given the brief look we have taken at his Christology and his doctrine on the Trinity, we may be able better to appreciate his specific development of the teaching on divine grace.

II. PARTICIPATION IN THE TRINITARIAN LIFE OF GOD

There are mysterious similarities between God's Trinitarian life and our own supernaturalized life. These similarities reproduce within each of us what occurs in the life of humanity as it progresses toward its supernatural destiny. Rahner likes to say that there are three essential mysteries in Christianity: the Trinity, the Incarnation, and grace. All three are mysteriously related. But they remain forever mysteries and we cannot hope to attain a clear grasp of them or to form an adequate concept about them. But what we have already seen provides a good introduction to the mystery of grace. For Rahner argues that of all that man has learned by experience about God in saving history, the really decisive thing is that out of His grace God has called us in His Son to the most intimate company with Him. This, he says, we can summarize with St. John: ὁ θεὸς ἀγαπὴ ἐσ‑ιν (God is good) (1 John 4, 16).

Man continually trips over signs which urge him to be snatched up *per invisibilia ad invisibilium amorem* (through invisible things to the love of invisible things). God sanctifies and redeems His work by opening and lending man the needed dynamism to elevate himself into the mysterious darkness that is his own light.[9] This dynamism, which we earlier considered under its metaphysical form, is called supernatural believing love or *grace*. Grace becomes the source of a dynamics, a new principle of operation, so that when we possess it we are most truly sons of the Father and brothers of Christ and temples of the Holy Spirit. The three divine persons dwell inseparably and yet we are really sons of the Father and not of the Trinity. It is important to stress this if we are to appreciate Rahner's thinking on divine grace.

To situate the discussion we start from Rahner's formal principle of the self-understanding of the *one* man who is the partner of God. His partnership implies that he is

ordered inevitably to God and the explanation of himself is
that the inevitability of this relation to God can be what
saves him. Because man *exists* as partner on God's side
and not just by means of man's own actions, man really *is*
himself. This relationship means the historicity of man in
which he experiences that degree of intimacy required for
approaching God. And it is this degree of intimacy that we
call "grace." But man's *summons* to partnership implies
that man does not of himself assume the partnership. Both
man and his summons are established by God. So man as
he exists is constituted by means of a real unity between
creation and grace. Here, then, we come to see the complete meaning of Rahner's supernatural existential dimension of man. A real supernatural transcendence exists for
every man who has reached the use of reason.

The Christian experience of faith is an absolute fulfillment of the formal divine plan of saving history. In being
summoned as a creature, man recognizes himself as actually sharing in the divine life promised him in revelation.
Rahner usually approaches this matter from the viewpoint
of his metaphysics.[10] We have seen that being and self-
presence grow in direct proportion, so there can be no
created reality in which the higher is not more present to
itself than the lower and consequently less mysterious.

But paradoxically, the real mystery can exist where it is
a question of man's relationship to God and God's relationship to the created intellect. The plurality of divine
mysteries cannot be grounded by means of the plurality of
created reality.[11] And in this question of grace we have a
relation found nowhere else between knowing as a subjective act and what is known. The transcendental moment
(of being ordered to the Absolute in the spiritual acts of
knowing and loving) and the unthematic, non-objective
knowledge of the Absolute implied in this moment effect a
unique mutual dependence between reflexive knowledge of
God and direct (implicitly transcendent and objectively
direct) knowledge of God. So reflexion on the uniqueness
of man's transcendental orientation to God reveals the

mystery that God really is—in so far as this mystery can be expressed at all.[12]

A. Supernatural Sanctification

The starting point for the theology of grace, then, must be a *theological* statement of anthropology, out of which the differentiation of nature and grace and the concept of grace can grow as principles for coming to an understanding of grace. It is usual in Protestant theology to speak of grace as the free and unmerited activity of God for the benefit of the sinner which overcomes his bondage to sin and restores him to the life for which he was originally destined. Now an important tradition within Catholicism has insisted that grace is not exhausted in its function of overcoming sin. God is gracious to man as man. So man is brought into a relationship with God which is not an inherent possibility of man himself but is only made possible by God's self-communication.

Rahner begins by saying that the believing Christian must see himself as the one summoned by God to that most perfect relationship of the inner life of God. The determining point is that God does not give man just any saving love and presence (in the sense that might apply to a relation between creator and "innocent" creature), but summons man as partner, destined for eternal life face to face with God. The self-communication of God is both in itself and as given essentially free, personal, unexacted grace. It is a free gift to man. But man is included in God's saving will because all humanity is offered this divine self-communication. Furthermore, it is free because God's self-disclosure is a personal sharing love that is unexacted. Man experiences it in a dialogue which presupposes the one spoken to and so cannot be identical with the kind of existence implied in simply being a creature. In order not to dilute God's self-communication through man's acceptance and turn it into a finite event, this acceptance itself must be carried by God in the same manner as the gift itself. Rahner's hermeneutics, then, asking about the conditions for the possibility, give him the needed principles for developing a doctrine on grace which are fully in accord with traditional teaching.

To develop the question, Rahner continues to apply his method. He asks what conditions are needed for making such a communication possible. He says that a constitution for man is presupposed which includes two aspects. First, his nature so precedes the divine self-communication that man's self-performance is not itself already transcendental, although really ordered to a communication of God by means of his obediential potency and his supernatural existential. From the very nature of obediential potency it is clear that the positive orientation to God cannot be identified with the obediential potency as such, which is simply identical with nature as personal and spiritual. Its reality is the tremendous reality of spiritual nature; it builds on nature (*gratia supponit naturam*) but is quite different from it. Man's orientation is entitatively supernatural. This fact is important if grace is to be truly free and if man's refusal is to mean his personal failure. Second, Rahner presupposes that man would go on living even if man should close himself off to God's summons.

Grace is the perfection of man in every sense. God as Lord of nature can demand that man subordinate himself to the divine will, to a supernatural destiny, and open himself to grace. Man's obediential potency for grace exists, then, only in the most negative sense. For Rahner stresses that man's orientation to God is what makes him be what he experiences himself to be, so that he cannot deny himself without sin. What he is is affirmed (even if only in an *a priori* manner as an implicit transcendental) in his every human act.

Paradoxically, recent theological investigation has come to realize that the concept of the *supernatural* developed very slowly in theology. So today theologians realize that grace, viewed in relation to the whole of history, is a grace which effects the acceptance of what it offers. It is both the possibility and the realization of the possibility, both the capacity and the performance, both God's word and man's answer. Such a recognition has led also to a realization that grace has a wholly public character. For if theology is to agree with scripture, theology must say again what it usually forgets to say: that God has promised this grace to history as a whole. And God's self-communication effects its acceptance. If we gain some insight into all this, we begin to get at the meaning of *supernatural* existence. The grace of God's self-communication is supernatural. It is unexacted but offered *every* creature, even before the sin of man. It is not owed to man as an element of what it means to be a man, not a constituent of human nature as such, not given "of itself"—so that even if man had not sinned originally it would still be unexacted. It is wholly *super*natural.

Rahner observes how man forever finds himself existing in the double condition of being a creature and a sinner. Both situations condition and explain one another. The weakness of the creature is not itself sin, but sin is seen only in terms of this weakness. Man's sinfulness forces him to interpret himself as the absolutely limited creature for whom the gift of God is always grace. Rahner says that if we reflect on this also and on the history of the teaching on the supernatural, it is not at all surprising that the Council of Trent's in teaching about justifying grace, though "intending" the *supernatural,* did not conceive it under the schema of man's elevation but under the schema of giving grace to what has been lost. This fact has had a profound effect on the development of the supernatural.

1. NATURAL DESIRE FOR GOD

However differently grace may be understood within the different theological traditions, it must be considered at three points. (1) At its origin, grace is God's favor toward men, a free decision of love in their behalf. (2) Grace is also the communication of this divine decision, whether the emphasis falls upon historical events (as is the case with Rahner and much of modern theology), or upon words whose content is heard in revelation and thus becomes the saving power of God (as in classical Protestantism), or upon a special influence by means of which God acts inwardly upon men. The original divine life is effectively communicated to man, whatever the means may be. (3) Considered at its term, grace is viewed as the foundation of a new relationship of man with God, and, however differently man's life under grace may be understood, in all cases it is viewed as the intended aim of the divine decision and its communication to man. As we have seen, the root of the question is the crucial point that grace opens up a possibility that does not lie within the scope of man's natural powers and is not implied in his being as man.

In the Middle Ages a theme of a natural desire for the vision of God was an important topic. This theme has been revived in recent years as a means of showing that life under grace is not something secondary and adventitious. The doctrine is usually felt to be most persuasive when the desire is interpreted as a preconscious "desire of nature," a *desiderium naturale,* and more insistent than man's conscious life. Henri de Lubac views this desire for God as an orientation of man's being through which God grasps him and calls him to the full union of the beatific vision. But this natural desire has also been discussed in terms of Maréchalian-Rahnerian Thomism, wherein God as the source of all finite intelligibility and goodness is the motive, the dynamism of the human spirit. So a natural desire for God must be the secret foundation of all acts of knowing and willing. The existential appeal of this doctrine lies in calling attention to man's transcendence and his dissatisfaction with limited reality. But the problem with such a simple explanation is that grace comes to be viewed as an aid, a help to the attainment of something already desired in the depths of the self, the means by which man's capacities are fully realized instead of the free and gracious self-communication of God which calls for a corresponding decision on man's part. The human response comes to be seen as motivated more by what man is than by what God does, more by man's natural desire than by God's grace. In a sense, the doctrine of natural desire represents a kind of triumph of Platonism in early Christianity.

It should be clear, then, that unless Rahner is read carefully, he could be accused of positing a doctrine of natural desire in his supernatural existential. But such is not the case at all. Again and again he stresses the necessity of letting God be God, the unexactedness of grace, and the fact that even man's acceptance is carried by God's gift of himself. Rahner's solution to the problem of nature and grace (which we will examine more fully in the next chapter) clarifies his position even more. Briefly, he points out that the three characteristic doctrines under which the discussion on actual and habitual grace are unfolded and in the end made over-explicit are (1) that man has only an obediential potency for grace, (2) that man's desire for the vision of God is only a "velleity" or a conditional desire, and (3) that man could have been left without injustice in a "state of pure nature" without the offer of grace.[13] Now Rahner's main point is that he shows how grace can be an existential of man without being an existential of his nature. Nature is that theological remainder concept which with the aid of Christology is coming to be discerned more and more clearly. Man is the *other* of God. And this contribution moves the theology of grace a good step forward. Life under grace is twice removed from any "natural desire"; it is contingent upon the free action of God and upon man's free response as carried by grace. Rahner makes good use of his historical-anthropological categories and avoids naturalistic ones.

2. GRATIA INCREATA: PARTICIPATION IN GOD

Rahner thinks that in the doctrine on grace we still have a lot to learn from Thomas Aquinas. We can learn that medieval theology thought much more deeply about "uncreated grace" than has post-Tridentine theology, which has concentrated on the "indwelling of the Spirit" more or less exclusively in terms of *created* grace. For in its anti-Protestant zeal Tridentine theology was all too ready to call created grace simply *grace*. Rahner feels that pre-Trent theology made it easier to see that *the* grace of justification is wholly supernatural, is God's self communication of Himself. And this is *uncreated* grace. Naturally, if one thinks of grace as "something"—a quality handed over to the autonomous control of man—one will conceive of this uncreated grace wrongly. Derivative concepts such as "inhering," "accidental," and so forth, can depend on the question of the real difference between created and uncreated grace if properly understood. But the concept of uncreated grace implies that man himself is truly re-created (*umgeschaffen*) by God's self-communication, and in this sense supernatural grace is "created" and "accidental"—that is, not given of itself to man's *nature*. Uncreated grace, then, must not be regarded as a simple consequence of the creation of some "infused" grace which constitutes the state of grace as a physical accident. Instead, it is the very essence of grace, and this, Rahner maintains, explains how grace can be a strict mystery, since a purely created entity could never be a strict and absolute mystery. God communicates Himself to man, and this is the mystery of uncreated grace which means our participation in God. On the basis of this interpretation Rahner points out how the bridge to the mystery of the Incarnation and the mystery of the Trinity is easier to find.[14]

Created grace can be viewed as what is efficiently produced by God both as condition and consequence of uncreated grace in terms of a quasi-formal casuality. Such a view sees created grace as a kind of "material disposition" for the "form" of uncreated grace. This view approaches what Rahner himself holds. Another similar view, that of de la Taille, explains created grace as a moment of this uncreated grace (*actuation crée par l'acte incrée*). Both of these views diverge from the official Tridentine view which considers uncreated grace more or less as a simple consequence of created grace, so that the "indwelling" is given by created grace as such. Rahner will admit that there is a supernatural causality of God— especially regarding what we call the indwelling in the souls of the just—which implies an essentially new action of God superior to nature which transforms but does not suspend its laws and which does not imply a merely sporadic divine intervention but pertains to the normal structure of spiritual reality.

Grace, however, is the self-communication of God to man. Here God's work is really Himself. So it cannot be conceived as separable from God's favor and man's reply. An adequate concept of sanctifying grace must include uncreated grace so that created and uncreated grace condition one another. In stressing the essence of grace as uncreated Rahner appeals to traditional church doctrine (D 2290), which he says makes clear that uncreated grace as the primary and total gift of God to man has to be considered the carrying grace which alone explains its real supernaturality. We must always remember that God does not become less through the fact that we become more. And for Rahner's metaphysics of knowledge there is no special difficulty in seeing that transcendence to the Absolute, the supernatural, is not clearly distinguished from the transcendence of spirit as such—although both ways of transcendence are given consciously, the latter having the former as a necessary condition.[15] Thus a more precise understanding of uncreated grace results in a clearer concept of the fact that the Catholic theology of grace as sharing in the divine nature can escape the usual explanation of grace as an existing created condition, an "ontic physical accident." [16] Where spirit is experienced in the real order, it is supernaturally elevated spirit.

3. CREATED HABITUAL GRACE

The division of grace into "actual" and "habitual" is the result of a different approach to the problem of distinguishing grace. It stems from a particular historical situation. Building on the anti-Pelagian teaching about the necessity of created grace,[17] theologians came to view grace as help for an act and so "actual" grace. It is always offered as a *help*. Medieval reflexion on this grace as supernatural came to an understanding of what is called "habitual" grace, the grace of justification. So habitual grace came to be thought of as the *state* of actual grace possessed over a period of time. Eventually, the two came to be considered the same. Rahner thinks this fact demonstrates that up to now there has been no real agreement on whether "actual" grace is needed in addition to "habitual" grace for a saving action or whether habitual grace alone is enough. That the concept of supernatural help for every saving act may not from the very start be identified with the concept of actual grace (as is usual today) Rahner thinks is made clear on the basis of his approach.[18] In so far as doctrine of faith goes, the distinction simply says that "habitual" grace is the proferred supernatural self-communication of God (after baptism) and which if freely accepted by the adult is given freely. "Actual" grace is this same grace in so far as it actually carries the act of its acceptance (existentially ordered and always newly realizable) and therein actualizes itself. Rahner thinks that this distinction is truly helpful if we care to understand how it is possible to grow in grace.

4. LIFE OF THE HUMAN SPIRIT AND GRACE

An entitatively elevated act which on the level of awareness remains a natural act cannot be called an inner inspiration without being nonsense. Rahner believes that the fact that the Molinist school wanted to preserve this phrase and find a meaning for it illustrates the strength of the conviction within the tradition that a supernatural act performed by means of grace is different consciously and existentially and not simply entitatively from any natural act. There are impulses of grace which precede the acceptance of justification. If we think of God's invitation and summons of grace for the man compelled to make an existential decision not as an intermittent grace, only "actual" in the sense that is temporary, and if we see that man's freedom is not at all thereby curtailed, we can also see that supernatural transcendence exists in any man who has reached the age of reason. He can still be a sinner; but in so far as he has the possibility of performing good actions, he is open to transcendence to the God of supernatural life. The life of the human spirit is lived under a supernatural existential.

5. OUR AWARENESS OF GRACE

The man of today thinks "existentially." He strives to experience the reality of grace as much as possible. He wants to view supernatural grace as the entelechy and power of his existence. And in accord with other tendencies of our times, man wants to see grace not just as the presupposition and content of individual salvation but actually at work in himself.[19] Rahner asks if we can experience grace in this life.[20] That the mystics have experienced grace we admit all too readily. But this is an unusual occurrence. Rahner says that we should start an inquiry after our awareness of grace with the experience of the spiritual as such. He admits the difficulty of defining what we mean by *spiritual,* but he points out how we all think and study and decide and love. This leads us to some insight into what spirit is. But the problem is not simple. Just as transcendence is involved in every human act, so the supernatural is implicit in every supernatural act. Rahner says, then, that every time we perform a morally good act we experience the supernatural, every time we silently bear unjust criticism, every time we try to love God when we feel no natural desire to do so. In such and many other actions we experience eternity, the reality that the spiritual is more than just a slice of the temporal world. In such experience we factually co-experience the supernatural. It is there unthematically but can be experienced to the degree that we abandon ourselves to the working of grace.

In addition, Rahner thinks that there are charismatic moments when we can experience grace even more directly. He cites how St. Ignatius says when one is seeking to know God's will in the election, apart from and prior to "rational" consideration in the light of faith, there are "times of election" when one learns the divine will by God's direct motion, so that logical and moral reflexion is only a substitute should the divine motion fail or not be clearly recognized. Such a divine impulse analogous to the Ignatian election must be at work in the church. God speaks truth to us inasmuch as He acts. The concept of the revealing action of God demonstrates that in the real order even revelation as the communication of truth is only accomplished when by the communication of grace God gives us the ability to listen to His word which is at the same time the reality which He communicates.[21]

We shall have more to say about our awareness of grace at the end of the chapter, but to anticipate briefly, since this point is important for understanding what follows on the theological virtues, we note how spirit is transcendence. Spirit grasps in its striving for the Absolute its object. We can consider this drive, this dynamic striving as light or darkness; we can experience its wordless givenness because of its non-objectivity as divine darkness or explain it as the *lumen intellectus,* the light that sheds luminosity on everything else, since only in the drive toward it can any individual object be presented. This is that original and carrying ground, the ultimate condition of the transcendental possibility of categorial illumination which makes understanding possible. Analogously, the spirit that is supernatural makes everything else possible supernaturally, making it possible for man to know *truth* and to act upon this knowledge.[22]

On the basis of this experience of grace in our lives Rahner approaches the problem of the theological virtues. It follows as a consequence of his method that the virtues must be moments on the one supernatural life that is God's self-communication.

6. NECESSITY, NATURE, AND FORMAL OBJECT OF "ACTUAL" GRACE

Before going on to consider the theological virtues, we can summarize some of what we have seen in terms of the scholastic notion of the formal object of grace. From a more precise understanding of uncreated grace we see that grace is not just pardon for the sinner but is real participation in the divine nature. And this both shows us how necessary grace is and tells us something about its nature, that of supernatural divine life. Grace is God Himself. Since theology has to conceive the real as "real and existing" and has to express what is most sublime in abstract terms, it is possible to speak of the object of grace and distinguish it as actual and as habitual.

The teaching of St. Thomas on the object of the entitatively supernatural elevated act, an object which (as formal) cannot be attained by any human act, needs to be rethought and made viable again. For in this teaching, "object" does not mean what is "objectively given, distinguishable from something else by reflection while seen together with other things." A formal object is neither an object of knowledge nor just a bringing together of what is common to many individual objects by abstraction. For Rahner it is the *a priori* mental horizon of which we are aware in being conscious of ourselves, the context for all our knowing and ability to recognize *a posteriori* individual objects. Rahner says that if we take the scholastic teaching on the formal object as the *lumen* by which and in which all other subjects are seen, then we cannot object to the teaching of a supernatural formal object on the ground that it cannot be experienced. In Rahner's metaphysics of knowledge we have no difficulty in seeing that transcendence to the Absolute is not clearly able to be distinguished upon reflexion from supernatural transcendence to the Triune God, even though both kinds of transcendence (involving the formal object of natural spirit and the formal object of supernaturally elevated spirit) are conscious.

On this basis we can come to see how various inspirations and enlightments we received from God can be called supernatural actual graces.

B. *The Theological Virtues in Our Awareness of Grace*

There are three theological virtues, faith, hope, and love. Usually, they are treated separately. But there is no true pluralism in the virtues. They do develop historically, however, so we can distinguish them from a number of viewpoints. No virtue is given completely. It becomes and develops and only gradually comes to itself—which is to be precisely love, *caritas*. This point is important in Rahner's thought.

Can one virtue be possessed without possessing the others? This is only possible in so far as we understand that it is performed as a moment on the movement toward the complete acceptance of the entire personal nature of man and so is only completely possessed when integrated into the whole acceptance in love. So every virtue can be viewed as a moment on man's direction toward *caritas,* and only in this way is it possible to speak of separate virtues. But there has to be a beginning of this directed movement, a recognition of this goal, as it were. This is a logical process which we call the virtue of faith. Faith is the faith of personal decision.

1. LOGIC AND THE SUPERNATURAL: FAITH

There must be grounds upon which man can base his free decision. These must be the data of experience found in the actual question performed by every man, the existential question: Why am I? The modern problematic of the theological virtues has to consider several factors. First, the theological virtues are in their unity the transcendental foundation of man's relation to God wherein God is given in Himself. God gives Himself in an act which effects His being accepted. And this states what we mean by the theological virtues. For they only make specific in different terms what is meant by *uncreated* grace as the ultimate foundation for the grace-laden self-communication of God in its relation to created grace. Secondly, if the virtues are to be understood in their unity and difference, they may not be thought of so much as powers for different things. Together they form the one power of man's total relationship to God's self-communication and differ among themselves in so far as they express phases of this one self-communication of God. Man in history has to accept grace in the face of a pluralistic material world. The usual teaching on the virtues tends to note how that love integrates the virtues elevating faith and hope into itself as its own moments. And in this sense Rahner's approach is not new.

Thirdly, because of the dynamic unity of the virtues we

can ask whether the one performance of Christian existence cannot have epochally different significations named after one of these three virtues. In history we see some basis for thinking this way. Paul considered justification in terms of the virtue of faith. Today we understand the world as dynamically moving into a future which seems to see the love of God as being essentially mediated by means of the love of our neighbor, so that perhaps the epochal word for the coming age might be the future opening, hoping *caritas*.[23]

In the existential acceptance of himself man has a history. He continually bumps into dimensions of his own personal nature and the personal reality of others. Man can come to himself in respect to one existential dimension and not in respect to others. This same fact is true of the realization of the virtues. Man can have one and not another. But any virtue is only fully possessed when it is integrated into the whole acceptance of one's own nature in love. All other virtues are the crystallization of love in the enduring plurality of the many dimensions of human existence, so that love, different and yet always remaining itself, truly appears in them and still is not their sum. So the virtues can be realized in diversity without their having to lose anything of their own perfection and fullness. Rahner says we are called to love in Christ Jesus. Regarding the realization of the virtues in the mediation of the multiple dimensions of human existence, which in their plurality compel and allow different forms of human existence, every man has his own unique "calling" and "vocation." In this area we see the integration of what man does and his leading a spiritual life. If we understand this properly, we see how there is no difference so far as the supernatural goes between the vocation to the one state or another. The upshot is that Rahner says that it is not asking too much for man out of the experience of his own existence to experience real Christianity as the truth of his life. And the logic of this argument is the supernatural virtue of faith.

2. ETHICS AND THE SUPERNATURAL: HOPE AND LOVE

Courage to follow the light means the act of hope, of desire for greater illumination. The virtue of hope is to be on the way to the goal. And so the Christian virtue of hope means one has no fear that he will not reach the goal. If Christianity means faith, hope, and love, and if these three virtues are not three separate, externally ordered realities, each having a different source and nature, so that love or *caritas* is the concept for the fulfillment of the one whole act of virtue, then *caritas* should be considered the *epochal* term for this phase of Christianity. In this phase man is beginning to take seriously the fact that the love of neighbor really is the love of God.

Tradition has held fast to the teaching that love of neighbor is a moment of the theological virtue of *caritas* whereby we love God in virtue of the Spirit for His own sake. Hence love of neighbor is only a precondition and touchstone of this love of God. It is an act within the total believing and hoping abandonment of man to God which alone justifies, since it is carried by grace and really makes man one with God.

If the difference between natural and supernatural transcendental horizons is presupposed, Rahner says, it is easy to say that not every act of love of neighbor is also a formal act of love of God, in so far as love of neighbor intends an act in which the neighbor is approached and loved as a thematic object of conceptual presentation. But when one expressly turns in prayer, in hope and love to God, we have an act of the love of God and not of neighbor.[24] Measured in terms of the object, such an act of love is much more valuable than an act of love of one's neighbor. But where the whole transcendental depth of interhuman love—which can be *caritas*—is realized, such a love is necessarily love of God, has as its reflexive motive God (though in quite different degrees of awareness). This follows from Rahner's metaphysics of knowledge as a necessary consequence. When one's neighbor must be loved truly, as *formal object* and motive (loved for himself), no matter how one may want to explain the unity of the two aspects, real love of God is necessarily given. This still leaves the question open whether interhuman love may have as its own radicality something besides *caritas*. For Rahner, however, a true understanding will show that because of the inevitable transcendental horizon, for which God's saving grace is always present, such love is always (at least unthematically) ordered to God.

The thesis is presupposed that whenever man is fully engaged in a positive moral act, it is placed factually in the order of salvation and so is a supernatural act, performed in faith, hope, and love, in *caritas*. In the second place, love of neighbor is not an action like any other good act. It is the foundation and explanation of the really moral as such. For in man's confrontation with the world he has to integrate part of it to himself. But in the case of interhuman encounter, the world of humanity is basically one, the true solution to the anthropological problem of the one in the many and vice versa. The true environment of man is his personal human world. This world is what comes to itself in men. The thing-world is only a necessary moment of this world. We have already seen how for Rahner the plurality of objects must be given *a priori* in order that man can become present to himself by using them in knowledge and freedom. The thing-world is only a moment of the person-world as a possible object of man. This can be seen in the fact that *being* and the *good* are identical: the morally objective good is truly given in *personal* being. A good that is not a person or ordered to the person cannot be called a real value. In short, the world is the mediation of self, wherein the personal-world is what is most important. A known, personal other, a *you,* is the proper mediation of the subject's becoming present to self. The case of freedom makes this even clearer. Free self-disposal as morally proper is precisely loving intercommunication with a human *other,* a loved one.

Because knowing (since it already is an internal operation) is only successful in an act of freedom, must "elevate" itself in freedom in order to be itself, the knowing act achieves its wholly human meaning when in freedom it is integrated in loving intercommunication with a personal other. The act of personal love of one another is therefore man's all-inclusive, basic determining activity. And if this is so, it is an essential, inner moment of the completion of transcendental consciousness. And this *a priori* basic determination is really experienced in man's encounter with other men. That basic act wherein man really becomes present to himself and really disposes of himself freely is a communication (involving love or hate) with a living person. In this relation man experiences *a priori* his relatedness to a personal other. Everything else becomes but a moment in this relatedness as either condition or consequence. And in the present order of salvation history this basic act is elevated supernaturally by God's self-communication in uncreated grace and the powers of faith, hope, and love, wherein the *caritas,* theological love, necessarily integrates faith and hope into itself. So the true human act, love of another, of neighbor, when it is genuinely given, is *caritas,* the goal of man's life.

Rahner's transcendental reduction of man's spiritual life to love of neighbor as *caritas* does not limit itself to the tangible every day, but gives this act a character of mystery, even when we do not consider the specifically theological. For to say that the one self-understanding of man as the collection of his knowing and self-determination for eternity takes place in the act of loving communication with another (so that everything else is but a moment in or precondition of this communication) is to say that in the act of love of neighbor is collected man's entire mystery and performance, to say that all anthropological propositions must be read as statements about this love. This is not just an isolated event in man's life but is the whole, and in this he meets the crisis of his nature. Love of another person is in reality the performance of total transcendental consciousness. Rahner thinks that if we understand this it will be easier to see how in the present salvific order such love can only happen as *caritas*. For *caritas* means nothing else than the absolute radicality of the love of another in so far as it is opened to the immediacy of God's self-communication in grace. Thus we see how Rahner interprets the proposition that the absolute, unlimited transcendentality of man's spirit is obediential potency for grace. This obediential potency is realized transcendentally in love of another person, and if it is properly understood it gives insight into the importance of the hypostatic union personally and into what a real "encounter" with Christ implies.

Rahner is arguing that love of neighbor is the only categorial act wherein man reaches the categorially given wholeness of reality, wherein man performs himself completely, and so already really experiences grace.[25] Other thematic religious acts remain derivative of this love-grace experience.

An intellectual being perfects himself through love. In Rahner's system this means the self-transcendence of knowledge in so far as it elevates itself into another in the sense that the subject implies more than knowledge. A supernatural love includes God and other spiritual creatures in their unity in the Kingdom. This has a theological and an ecclesiological character in as much as it is founded on Christ and His church and works toward the destiny of universal redemption. Love as *super*natural frees man and his world from self-centeredness, and so it has an eschatological-transcendental character, open to the present but hidden life of God. It can be called transcendent to the extent that this love is ordered to God as the supernatural goal of the self and so surpasses the world. It is eschatological to the extent that this love (though ever present in the world by the merits of Christ) is in the world because the eschatological event of Christ exists in it for all time. All human existence that is related to what has meaning in the world is capable of being transformed by divine love. But of its nature this symbolic character of the world tends to hide rather than to display this truth.

The universality of the offer of grace in salvation history, an offer to man to share in the three-personal life of God, is what Rahner intends, then, when he speaks so often of God's supralapsarian economy of grace.

APPENDIX TO CHAPTER FOUR

1. See *Lexikon für Theologie und Kirche*, vol. 4, "Gotteslehre," cols. 1122, 1123; and Claude Welch, "God, Faith and the Theological Object," *Harvard Theological Review*, 59 (July 1966), pp. 213–226.

2. *Lexikon für Theologie und Kirche*, vol. 4, col. 1121.

3. This point has more than just polemical significance. If it is not taken seriously, Rahner's positions on Christology and the doctrine of grace lose much of their force and contemporary importance. Failure to appreciate this point helps explain some of the inability to accept Rahner's positions on these two doctrines.

4. See *Lexikon für Theologie und Kirche*, vol. 5, cols. 953–961.

5. Dom Illtyd Trethowan may represent those theological thinkers who object to this point. He writes, "This seems to me, to put it mildly, dangerous ground. It is tantamount to saying that the doctrine of the Three Persons involves a contradiction. Certainly it does nothing to show that Rahner's formula for the Incarnation does not involve a contradiction." "A Changing God," *Downside Review*, 84 (July 1966), p. 254. Rahner is not attempting a sort of "double-think" but a logical clarification from within his metaphysics of what is and must remain a mystery. If one thinks of the Trinitarian speculation of the Victorine school much of what Rahner is attempting receives a clearer situation and historical development.

6. This issue will become more and more important as theologians begin to take seriously some of the objections of the "death of God" theologians. For the scholastic importance of some of these modern objections see John Lachs, "Two Concepts of God," *Harvard Theological Review*, 59 (July 1966), pp. 227–240.

7. See *Schriften*, vol. IV, p. 125.

8. *Ibid.,* p. 127.

9. *Schriften,* vol. III, p. 48.

10. See *Schriften,* vol. IV, pp. 59 ff.

11. *Ibid.,* p. 66.

12. Hence we must stress not just the fact of a possible knowledge of God but also must pay closer attention to what kind of knowledge this is. Only in this way will the uniqueness of what is known be clarified. Rahner believes that the question might be asked whether the fundamental delineation of our relationship to God (beyond theoretical acceptance in knowledge) would have to be presented, since this relation is not developed as a whole.

13. For a brief résumé of this question see Henri de Lavelette, "Bulletin de Théologie dogmatique," *Recherches de Sciences Religeuses,* 54 (January–March, 1966), pp. 140 ff. De Lavelette clarifies the exact relationship between the theory of de Lubac's *Le Surnaturel* and Rahner's position, pointing out that too much emphasis has been given the importance of the "natural desire" controversy in the formation of Rahner's thought. See especially Ulrich Kuehn, *Natur und Gnade: Untersuchungen zur deutschen katholischen Theologie der Gegenwart,* Berlin, 1961.

14. Usually one considers the relationship between the Incarnation and the order of grace as simply factual. Rahner feels that God has willed that the order of grace factually depend on the *Verbum incarnatum.* One presupposes silently that this could have been different. But Rahner asks if this presupposition is correct. The order of grace and the Incarnation rest on the free grace of God. But does it follow that these two objects of God's free grace, in which He shares Himself in both cases to the *other* are really *two* different actions of His freedom? Who could argue against the assumption that the very possibility of creation rests on the possibility of the Incarnation, even though the reality of creation (as nature) does not necessarily include the factual realization of God's incarnate self-expression. If one assumes this, then grace receives a much more radical Christological character; the Logos becomes not just the factual mediator of grace but is also the one who in becoming part of the world establishes the world as a precondition of His becoming man, as the condition needed for His nature and environment.

15. On the basis of such a consideration the Thomistic position is wholly defensible. It is recommended as a metaphysical-theological translation of the conviction expressed repeatedly in scripture. For if we take scripture seriously, Rahner says, and do not suppose that it does not say this because it could not, then we have to say that scripture states that the sharing of the spirit (the divine *pneuma*) is not just an entitative "elevation" beyond awareness but remaining existentially the same, but that it is "life," "anointing," "light," and so on. *Pneuma* is more than *nous*. Rahner thinks it would be beneficial to confront the scholastic controversy with this teaching of scripture. We might then free ourselves from the opinion that in a religious question there may be more to learn from scripture if the matter has been debated in school theology. The point is that if various questions could easily be resolved, obvious answers would exist for their resolution. See *Schriften*, vol. IV, p. 226.

16. See Michael Schmaus, *Katholische Dogmatik*, vol. III, 2, "Die Göttliche Gnade," München, 1965; E. Schillebeeckx, *Theologische Peilingen, deel I: Openbarung en theologie*, Bruxelles, 1965.

17. In the form from the time of Augustine: grace as the inspiration of justifying love.

18. If in the Thomistic (as opposed to Molina) teaching it is presupposed that the grace given the act itself elevates man's powers, then it is possible to say from the point of view of faith that there is no difference between actual and supernaturally elevating grace and habitual grace—only in so far as it is certain that there are saving acts by means of which the unjustified individual prepares himself for the necessary grace of justification. Whether this necessary grace is the same as or different from God's self-communication and whether in the adult "habitual" grace is the same as or different from this divine self-communication there is neither an official explanation nor a consensus in the teaching of theologians. For Rahner's most complete exposition on this and related questions see his *De Gratia Christi*, Summa Praelectionum in Usum Privatum Auditorum Ordinata, Innsbruck, 1959–60. Rahner's positions in this work are put forward in the light of the history of church teaching on grace.

19. See *Schriften*, vol. IV, p. 219.

20. *Schriften,* vol. III, p. 105.
21. *Schriften,* vol. IV, p. 54. As we observe continually the tightness of Rahner's system we see how significant in Rahner's *rationes theologicae* are his hermeneutics.
22. *Schriften,* vol. IV, p. 59.
23. See *Lexikon für Theologie und Kirche,* vol. 10, col. 80.
24. See *Schriften,* vol. VI, pp. 284 ff.
25. *Ibid.,* p. 294.

For most of the material covered in this chapter the following articles by Rahner are basic: "Theos in the New Testament," *Theological Investigations,* vol. I, pp. 79–148; "Ueber die Erfahrung der Gnade," *Schriften,* vol. III, pp. 105–110; "Bemerkungen zum dogmatischen Traktat 'De Trinitate,'" *Schriften,* vol. IV, pp. 103–136; "Vom Geheimnis des Lebens," *Schriften,* vol. VI, pp. 171–184; "Zur scholastischen Begrifflichkeit der ungeschaffenen Gnade," *Zeitschrift für katholische Theologie,* 63 (1939), pp. 137–156 (*Theological Investigations,* vol. I, pp. 319–346). For his doctrine on grace the codex of his Innsbruck lectures is invaluable and contains much bibliographical information. Also helpful are Charles Baumgartner, *La Grâce du Christ,* Paris, 1963; Henri Rondet, *Essais sur la théologie de la Grâce,* Paris, 1964; Bernhard Stoeckle, *Gratia Supponit Naturam, Geschichte und Analyse eines theologischen Axioms,* Rome, 1962. See also Karl Rahner, Hans Meier, Ulrich Mann, Michael Schmaus, *Religionsfreiheit,* Munich, 1966.

CHAPTER FIVE

THEOLOGICAL ANTHROPOLOGY: CREATION

The previous chapters considered questions of method and process, principal concerns in theological argument. They took up the problem of mystery in Christian life as seen in the absolute mysteries of the Trinity, the Incarnation, and grace. In looking at these questions we have observed Rahner's method at work, but we have not yet really considered his metaphysics of becoming. With this chapter we move, then, into an examination of this problem as we see how Rahner examines the problem of creation. As always Rahner takes a specifically anthropological starting point, asking the general question about the relationship between Creator and creature. Rahner sees man as openness to a possible revelation, as transcendental consciousness. But just how does this *openness* fit into the over-all relation of every creature to God?

We have seen that man is the creature who listens and that God speaks in His self-communication. But because what God speaks—revelation—has a determinate character, philosophy can lead man but a little way on his road to destiny. Revelation has a tendency to mold human questions rather than be molded by them. So metaphysics can only demonstrate that man is obediential potency for a possible revelation. And once philosophy is confronted by revelation it can be stripped of its ungrounded aspirations to do more. Still, philosophy has its uses. It reminds man that he is so embedded in and ordered to sensible reality that his dim awareness of an inescapable thirst for infinity can spill over into a self-defeating appetite for the finite.

PLAN OF CHAPTER

This chapter builds on the previous ones by clarifying the relation between matter and spirit, between man and the world. It asks about man in his origin and so takes up the problem of biological evolution. In this, Rahner's views closely resemble those of Teilhard de Chardin, but they are theologically and philosophically subtler and more sophisticated. For Karl Rahner attempts to interpret the modern evolutionary world outlook in terms of a biblical, realistic eschatology. After considering this problem of the relationship of matter and spirit, we will proceed to a refinement of this question, the problem of nature and grace, completing some points initiated in the last chapter. Finally, some of the interconnections between these two problem areas are illustrated by discussing the hard-core problem of man's corporeality and what it implies. The chapter ties these questions together again by repeating Rahner's understanding of *mystery*.

A theological-anthropological understanding of man's essence which includes knowledge about the possibilities of his nature has to rely on a twofold method corresponding to material covered in the previous chapters, on a transcendental method, and on a careful reflexion on the historical experience man has of himself.[1] The very first question, then, that any theological anthropology has to consider is the relation of creation to the Creator.

I. RELATION OF GOD TO THE WORLD

Karl Rahner's thought is anthropocentric—or better, as we have seen, Christocentric. But prior to considering man

as such and his relation to God, we must examine the
more general problem of the relationship of spirit and
matter. For man is spirit in the world. Rahner first looks at
the concept of the *world*. And the problem or theme of
this first section deals with the self-discovery of matter in
spirit by means of self-transcendence. Where matter comes
to a definite breakthrough, man's nature is seen as the
midpoint of a total understanding of the world.

A. Creation and Becoming

That everything that is, heaven and earth, is created by
God is a matter of faith. This is only to say that all
diversity springs from a single source. (Again the basic
paradigm of multiplicity in unity!) For only an infinite and
all-powerful cause could create totally diverse things. But
this manifold diversity displays an internal similarity and
community. Rahner says that creation may not be thought
of simply as disparate or composed of contradictory elements. The manifold and variegated world is one in origin,
perfection, and determination. It is really one world. So it
would be a huge mistake to think of matter and spirit as
wholly disparate realities. It would be error to imagine
man as a kind of orphan spirit forced to wander about lost
in the world. "It is a matter of course for both Christian
philosophy and theology that matter and spirit have more
in common (if one may put it in this way) than different." [2]
And what is common manifests itself most clearly in the
very unity of man himself. Matter and spirit are moments
of the one individual man. They can only be thought as
separate from the point of view of man's performance—
where they are understood as related to one another. Accordingly, we have the teaching that the perfection of
limited spirit—man—may only be thought of as taking
place within the perfection of the cosmos.

For Rahner the term *cosmos* is wholly relevant. In an
evolutionary setting it concerns the origin and develop-

ment of the universe as a whole. This would be opposed to a modern cosmogony (which treats of local systems such as the formation of observable planets and galaxies). Hence Rahner's concern with the world is more theoretical. Though he speaks to sciences whose concern is with cosmogony (which the biological sciences exemplify) and so are practical, Rahner does not hesitate to theorize. That is his function as a theologian. And in his theorizing the problem of extrapolation from known systems is definitely a construct. Yet no *scientific* assumptions are entangled. His argument, as usual, springs from his own method.

The current view of the world is stamped with a predisposition to unity and evolutionary theory. This current view gazes at matter, life, and spirit in terms of a single history of unfolding. Such a view need not be false provided it remains discrete and in touch with reality and does not try to level off essential differences within the unity of the whole.

A theory of evolution includes an essential self-transcendence, since otherwise nothing could become really *new*. If we presuppose essential self-transcendence under a divine dynamics, we can state summarily that natural life by transcending itself in the process of cosmic history unfolds into spiritual life. The history of nature and of spirit has a unity—the unifying principle of life. This life finds its supreme coronation in God's self-communication (as we saw in the last chapter). This is Rahner's theory in thumbnail form. How does he explain it?

Rahner first disposes of the problem of scientific method. All sciences have the same relation to theology that philosophy has to theology, since all sciences deal ultimately with the same thing. Further, Rahner argues that science is a moment of man's total knowledge and so is ultimately self-knowledge of his radical orientation to ineffable mystery. This knowledge encompasses a great deal of information about matter. It determines ever more

precise functional relationships among the appearances of
nature. But because science works apart from man in a
deep methodological abstraction, it can learn a great deal
about matter and yet cannot know matter, even though a
knowledge of the functional and temporal relationships of
isolated objects does lead inductively to man. The field of
a scientific discipline, its totality as such, cannot be determined using the same methods as those used to determine
the parts. Only man can express what matter is. Matter
cannot express what man is. If everything were matter, the
process would be self-defeating. For matter can express
nothing about spirit. And it is only man, not spirit, who
can say what matter is (and thus what might smack of
Platonism is neatly side-stepped by Rahner). Out of
man's experience of himself, he can say that spirit constitutes the one man in so far as he comes to himself by
means of an absolute being-given-over to self. This happens through the fact that he is ordered to the Absolute.
Man's return to himself and his relation to the totality of
possible reality (and to its ground) condition one another
(as we observed in the first chapter).

Man must return to self by means of the "phantasm."
So in understanding himself man *sees* his relation to the
world. He returns to himself (*reditio completa*) by means
of his encounter with individual, *material* things. Man
experiences himself as matter and his immediate world as
matter. Hence this matter is the condition of the possibility
of every objective *other*—the world and man himself, the
condition of what man experiences immediately as space
and time. This is the condition of that otherness which
estranges man from himself in order to bring him back to
himself. Matter is the condition, then, of that immediate
intercommunication with other persons in space and time
and in history which enables him to achieve completion.
Thus matter is the very ground of the givenness of the
other as material for freedom.

In Rahner's discussion of matter and spirit we see a

clear instance of the pendulum-like motion of the transcendental method at work. The movement proceeds from
reductive to deductive moments and back again within the
basic paradigm of the one and the many. Time and matter
in a sense constitute man's prehistory, and as the source of
his reflective freedom time and matter have to be understood as ordered to the very history of human spirit.
Hence matter and spirit are *two* related principles, insepa-
rable, irreducible moments of *one* man. An inevitable
multiplicity of moments in *one* man can be expressed in
the same way as the *one* essential difference between matter and spirit. It is rather important to stress this, because
only in this way can our view remain open for *all* the
existential dimensions of the *one* man in all their possible
expansions. The difference between matter and spirit is not
one of opposition or disparateness. Both have a unity in
their history. Man's reflexions cannot run ahead of his
actual historical development.

Rahner concludes that determining just what matter is
poses great difficulties. Spirit is already determined in the
very question about it and is thereby already experienced.
For spirit lets itself be developed from the question about
it in a transcendental deduction. Only an existential ontology, however, can decide what matter might be, because it
already recognizes spirit; and out of the metaphysical experience of spirit such an ontology can express what matter
as such must be: *that which is closed to the experience of
transcendence to the Absolute.* In a theistic philosophy
matter is conceivable only as a moment of spirit. So in a
sense matter is "frozen spirit." [3] Of itself there can be no
leap of matter into the Noosphere of Teilhard de Chardin.
The liberating of matter is performed by spirit, especially
where spirit so penetrates matter that spirit differentiates
itself from matter and holds it as a moment of its own
development, its own coming to self in man. So matter is
the bringing of self to appearance of personal spirit in the
dimension of the finite. Matter really does tend to evolve
toward spirit. How is this the case?

B. Becoming in General

Rahner argues that if there is a real *becoming* (that this is so is not only a fact of experience but also a basic axiom of theology, because otherwise freedom and responsibility for self-performance would make no sense), then becoming cannot be simply becoming *other.* Rather, it must be a becoming *more,* a development of the more "real," a performed attainment of a greater fullness of being.[4] This means becoming involves self transcendence. Becoming is a genuine surpassing of self, a self performed transcendence from the lower to the higher. And a real becoming as transcendence of self demands Absolute Being as the cause and primordial ground of the self-performance of the becoming. The Absolute must be the cause in such a way that the self-performance has this primordial ground as an inner moment of its act and so is really a surpassing of self and not just a passive being overtaken. Still, the process cannot involve the becoming of Absolute Being, because as inner moment of the self-performance the Absolute remains free and untouched. If this is rightly understood, Rahner claims that the limited existent can actually effect more than it is, but only in virtue of the power of the Absolute. The limited being is powered to a real self-transcendence and yet is so completely different from the Absolute that the Absolute remains undisturbed.

To save the concept of becoming, then, Rahner says that we must emphasize *self*-transcendence. And this must include the leap to an essentially new and higher grade of being. The nature of the existent which can transcend itself must not be seen as a limit on what it can become but as a *real symbol,* indicating how something "more" must and does become from a limited potency. This possibility is not always realized, for natures do not always evolve. Still, the nature remains as a sign of what it is yet to become.[5] The nature of an existent further signifies that the beginning of the performance, the essence of the thing moving itself, always remains a law limiting what can *become* immediately. The starting point, even when once surpassed, can still be a sign or real symbol of that toward which the whole process strives and of how far it can progress immediately. Once we presuppose this, we have implied in an ontologically valid concept of becoming as genuine self-transcendence the fundamental possibility of essential transcendence.[6]

Given the unity of matter and spirit and the legitimacy of a self-transcendence in the essential order, the evolution of matter toward spirit is a philosophically and theologically valid theory. And the supreme degree of all productive becoming is human spirituality. Matter strives toward this spirituality as to its ultimate essential and formative principles. For man is the goal of all productive becoming. History, as the one history of matter, life, and man, always evolves, always becomes "more."

Since the higher order always includes the lower, the lower of itself is a prelude to self-transcendence. And as the lower gradually approaches those limits in its history at which real self-transcendence occurs the disposition becomes more immediate. Just what these limits are can only be recognized after they are surpassed. Yet they are never exactly specified.[7]

Rahner says that this fact only becomes truly clear if we consider that spirit, as self-consciousness and freedom, arrives on the stage of the experiential world at a moment temporally much later—at least it seems to arrive much later—than the material world and the consequences of its evolution. Human spirit makes a very late entrance and at a narrow doorway in cosmic history. Hence the question arises not only whether the history of nature and spirit really do form a unity (if and to the extent that both are presupposed as given), but also whether they constitute one history, that is, whether spirit may be seen as the result (product) of natural history when it reaches a definite point, or whether this would violate the Christian notion of the difference between matter and spirit and so, for example, destroy God as creator of the human soul.

Before giving his answer to this problem, Rahner recalls that all reality, in its becoming and being, has its ground in God's creation and conservation. Still, it might seem at first glance that a negative answer would still have to be given, since on the one hand spirit is not simply an immanent product of evolution. Spirit must spring from a creative initiative of God. However, Rahner believes that we need not be in a hurry to give a wholly negative answer. For according to St. Thomas Aquinas, God as Creator is the transcendental ground of everything, but is not thereby a categorial and spatio-temporal cause of any definite individual. God acts through "secondary causes."

C. The Becoming of the Human Soul

Rahner asks whether we should consider the creation of the human soul as an exception to the normal relationship between first and second causes. As a *terminus* the relation of God as Creator to the soul is quite different from what it is in the case of sub-human material beings. So a satisfactory answer requires that the concept of divine causality (as the active and conserving support of all reality) be so developed that precisely this causality appear as the ground of possibility of limited being, of active self-transcendence, and so that this apply in particular to the creation of the spiritual soul.[8]

Creation of the soul can be thought of as effected by a second cause only if God and His power are considered a moment of the causality of the limited cause and not simply as support of the secondary, received causality. The traditional doctrine of the *praemotio physica*[9] is not enough. This is too static and too objectivized and so falls into categorial causality. Hence a *praemotio physica* by means of the limited createdness and its difference from act cannot be considered a meaningful ground for increase in being. Instead, Rahner suggests two principles for a solution. First, a genuine ontological concept must be shown as valid by means of a transcendental deduction.[10] Secondly, the ontologically first and basic determination given man is that he is a knowing being.

What being, what causality is first experienced by the knowing subject himself and in his performance of self-possession? The performance may not be separated intentionally from the real performance of the being of an existent. Rather, what is realized and experienced—the intellectual event is the ontic, true event—is one act. And that this takes place by means of the physical simply indicates that it is a deficient mode of being. So if a concept of a real becoming is to be attained, it must be in the case of the causality of knowledge.

We have already seen how for Rahner man is a limited intellectual being; that is, he is present to himself by means of the fact that he is present to a particular existent which he encounters *a posteriori* and by the fact that he has a spontaneous drive to the Absolute. The goal of this transcendence may be considered not just an object of knowledge. Rather, it is the horizon, the condition of the possibility of objective knowledge, of the return to self and of freedom. For Rahner this goal has to be given for any intellectual act to be possible at all. And the goal of transcendence is so interior to the performance that it only has "interiorness" to the extent that it stands above the performance and is "untouched" by the performance. The goal is what moves. It is not just a "finish line" but the real causal ground of the whole act. All other efficient causality can only be seen as a deficient mode of this causality.

Self-transcendence, then, takes place through the fact that Absolute Being is the cause and ground of the self-performance in such a way that it has in itself this basic ground as an inner moment on its performance and so is really a genuine surpassing of self and not just a question of being passively overtaken. And just as in the knowledge act the Absolute is unaffected, so is this the case with self-transcendent essential becoming.

Now as far as the creation of the human soul is concerned, Rahner observes that if we examine a medieval
doctrine (which is enjoying an increasing popularity) that
the spiritual soul enters at a comparatively late stage of
embryonic development and not at the moment of conception, that between fructifying the ovum and the presence of a human organism several stages of non-human
life are visited, then an ontogenesis of the human phylo-
genesis is not impossible. A biological organism not yet
human drives toward the condition in which it will have
the requisite biological substrate for the origin of a spiritual soul. Hence the causality of the parents in conceiving
belongs to that kind of created efficient causality in which
the cause with its nature-placed limits essentially surpasses
itself by virtue of the power of divine causality. Such a
doctrine on the origin of the human fetus has several
practical applications, not the least being a realistic solution for those who fret over miscarriages.

D. Spirit in the World

Man is the transcendence of living matter. And the history
of cosmos and of spirit form a graded unity in which
natural history has evolved toward human history, and
human history moves in the direction of completing the
history of spiritual being. So natural history finds its destiny in the free history of spirit. To the extent that human
history bounds natural history as history of living matter, it
is always supported in its freedom by structures of the
material world. And to the extent that the history of the
cosmos *is* the history of free spirit, it is the history of man.
The world finds itself in man, and man's place in the
cosmos becomes clear. The world finds itself many times,
and each time in a unique fashion; for it finds itself in
each individual man. Yet it seems that in this way the
world never completely finds itself and that it never has or
will. Yet this finding of itself by the world must have

occurred, even though we in our limited natural experience cannot know this. But as Christians we call this fact the immortality of the soul. This means that we need to see clearly how such a perfection of man, his immortality properly understood, is the complete finding of itself of the cosmos. So immortality has nothing to do with the picture of a separated, distant, free-floating soul independent of the world and its matter. The self-transcendence of the cosmos in man is only possible when the cosmos receives not merely the createdness of its being but the immediate self-communication of the ground of its being. And this comes with grace and glory. God did not just create the *other* but gives Himself to the *other*. And the nature of created being as a real symbol points to what it is to become eschatologically. Hence we gain insight from the point of view of the cosmic evolution into the significance of the Incarnation.

Rahner concludes his observations on the relation of Creator to creation by noting that if the history of cosmos is basically the history of spirit and of spirit's desire to come to itself and its ground, then the immediacy to the ground given in God's self-communication to the creature and through the creature to the cosmos is the only rational purpose of evolution. This, of course, implies that the cosmos *can* achieve this goal and is moved toward it by the Absolute. We as individuals experience only the physically conditioned extreme beginnings of this movement toward Infinity. Still, we live under a formal anticipation of it, and this is what makes us different from animals.

The spiritual freedom of the world is the history of the self-consciousness of the cosmos, a history of the intercommunication of spiritual persons. For the coming-to-itself of creation in persons is necessarily a coming-to-other in which in diverse ways the whole becomes present-to-itself. Otherwise, this coming to itself would divide the cosmos instead of uniting it. God's self-communication involves the ultimate sharing in freedom and intercommunication of many cosmic creatures. This can only take place through free acceptance of God's gift of Himself by the creature throughout common history. For this an event is required which happens at a definite point in historical space and time. And it is here that the theology of the redemption and Christology begins. And this should give yet another insight into Rahner's position on Christ as the center and crown of creation. For the supreme point of God's self-communication to the world is the hypostatic union in Jesus Christ.

Rahner's hermeneutics yield yet a further dimension for man. As listener to a possible revelation, as obediential potency for grace, man is now observed to be that point where time and eternity meet. Man's immortality becomes a truly existential dimension. These dimensions build in Rahner's anthropology on the foundation of that doctrine of being which is the basis of that realism which, even in its somewhat debased forms, the church has always embraced as its own. The question of man's being involves the real symbol of man's openness to mystery, where mystery is now seen to be the mystery of an intelligibility that would take possession of itself. Summarily, God's revelation presupposes man as listener. As a transcendental, limited, historical, spirit-in-the-world (and in virtue of the structure of being as open and illuminated, in virtue of the world and of history) man is the place where time and eternity meet, the place of revelation, the very place ultimately of God's word as word of God in grace. This determination of man hinges on the place of the one who reveals, Jesus Christ. Christ's relation to the world and the cosmos is that of Logos, the ground, head, and goal of all creation.

E. Theological Anthropology

Man's condition of standing before God presents several problems. An understanding of the impact of various definitions of self-concept and other psycho-sociological emphases in American theology tends to compound these problems. Rahner is going back away from such notions and is calling attention to a definition of man that echoes emphases of Newman and the Oxford Movement as well as the more modern personalist school. For Rahner asks how it is possible that man's concept of self seems betrayed, despite the fact that what man hears in an encounter and so *a posteriori* is heard under the mass of the *a priori*. This is Rahner's determining question for the condition of a real theological anthropology. It asks why an explanation of man which comes from outside historical contingency, in order not to come too late as man's basic determination, can be an answer at all (even though man cannot previously discover his nature as self-possession). And Rahner uses the transcendental method to arrive at a preliminary answer.

Rahner suggests several possible approaches. First, we have the fact that an adequate *a priori* self-concept includes the light of faith as a *supernatural existential*. This means that previous to justification by means of sacramental or extrasacramental sanctifying grace man already stands under the salvific will of God as a redeemed subject, absolutely obligated to a supernatural end. This "situation" ("objective justification" as opposed to its subjective acceptance in sanctity) which surrounds man's free act and influences it, consists not only in the intention of God but is a real ontological determination of man. This "supernatural existential" pervades man's "world," coming to his essence as "nature," and it is never absent from man's real world. This is why man can never be indifferent to his supernatural orientation—even in refusing grace! Man is always more than just a *nature* in the cosmos (in the theological sense of *nature*). So the light of faith as a supernatural existential does not encounter a self-concept alien to itself.

Secondly, man cannot dispose of his relations to the historical *a posteriori*. Theologically perfect luminosity and *a posteriori,* historical coming to self are not opposites. For prior to every reflexion, man has a transcendence as its condition. Heidegger speaks of this in terms of man's being unable to free himself entirely from the *facticity* of his already being thrown into the world, so that in the projection of existential possibilities he is guilty essentially and his creativity and freedom are limited. For the Christian, man is thrown into the world as guilty, it is true; but Christian man knows himself in spite of his createdness and sinfulness as the one historically addressed by God.

Because man's theology is his talk about God, and because man is ordered to God and only so properly present to himself, theology dare not neglect a single one of man's existential dimensions. Thus a theological anthropology would need to consider man's physical being with its extensions in the communion of sex and society. It would include a theology of the family. Indeed, most of the current theological tasks, Rahner thinks, are those of theological anthropology. But until recently the core problem of the relationship between Christology and theological anthropology was overlooked. Everybody claimed to know what a man is. Hence to say that Christ was a man did not present any special problems. Since Karl Barth and K. Heim the problem has to be faced more squarely. Rahner observes that Catholic theology needs to reflect more profoundly on the fact that many of its statements about man—for example, those of grace, the resurrection of the body—are only meaningful because of Christology.

II. PROBLEM OF NATURE AND GRACE

Obviously connected with the problem of creation and Creator is the more specific problem of nature and grace. It is a good introduction to many of the questions about man's existential dimensions. The fact that non-human being is wholly incapable of receiving revelation shows that it is not a false problem. Rather, the problem of nature and grace is one of the most important in Catholic theology.

A. Theological Meanings of Nature and Grace

On the basis of Heidegger's doctrine of existentials, Rahner suggests that man's situation as listener involves a "supernatural existential" which is a constant structure of his existence. In order to show how this can be a general structure applicable to all men at all times, Rahner attributes it to the effects of God's continuing action on man. It enters into man's very constitution and orientates him toward the faith. The notion of the "supernatural existential" is a miniature solution to the problem of nature and grace.

As preliminary definitions Rahner calls grace the *a priori* ability of connatural acceptance of the self-communication of God in the Word (and in the theological virtues) leading ultimately to the beautific vision. Grace is a biblical and dogmatic concept. Nature, on the other hand, is a theological term made legitimate because it is needed to understand completely the revealed doctrine on the gratuity of grace.

Rahner calls *nature* the abiding constitution of man presupposed by his ability as a listener, since the sinner is really able to close himself off from God's self-opening. The non-believer can lock his heart to God's offer of love. So nature is an obediential potency for the supernatural communication of God. This includes the supreme completion of man's nature in its assumption by the divine Logos. Considered as existence, nature as transcendence makes possible nature as existence; that is, human nature in and through its transcendence is made present to itself: it is *Existenz*, person. Nature is interior self-realization as existence. By means of his nature man must *become* what he *is*. This real, irrevocable *becoming* lies on the way of human freedom under the horizon of human nature itself.[11] If we see this, we grasp the importance Rahner attaches to the problem of *becoming* which we discussed earlier in the chapter.

To appreciate Rahner's solution to the problem, it is important to gain perspective. The distinction between nature and grace is not derived directly from scripture but is a byproduct of theological reflexion on the kerygma as a whole. It was developed by Augustine and the scholastics, who argued that man, even as originally created, enjoyed communion with God and was destined for a future perfection which could not be the result of his human capabilities alone, even those of a humanity free from original sin. For eternal life is always a free gift of God. St. Thomas put it this way: man under sin does not need grace "more" (magis) than he would apart from sin, for eternal life is always beyond the natural capabilities of a creature. He does need grace "for more" (*ad plura*) because of the added difficulty of sin.

Christ has overcome sin. But sometimes the Incarnation is viewed as having occurred only for the purpose of liberating man from sin, as we have seen in Chapter Three. Yet whenever grace is interpreted as Rahner does (and we saw this in the last chapter), Christologically, as always being the grace of Christ, it follows that the Incarnation would have occurred even apart from sin and is the completion of the spiritual history of man.

We leave further discussion of Rahner's treatment of grace and refer to the previous chapter. But to understand grace as a decision of God which is communicated to man and calls for man's response provides us with an important clue for understanding the distinction between nature and grace; namely, that grace opens up a possibility for man which is utterly beyond the scope of his natural powers. Grace, as we saw, is not implied in man's being as man.

B. Approaches Toward a Solution

According to the biblical view, the beginning is made with God's turning his face toward man in the covenant. Man's role is seen in scripture as one of response to the God of the covenant. The Protestant discussion of the problem tends to take this as the whole picture.[12] Rudolf Bultmann, for example, views the Christian life as "authentic existence" toward which man naturally tends but which cannot be actualized in sinful man until he is liberated by God's grace, coming in the form of the kerygma. In general, the Protestant tradition has stressed man's sinfulness. In emphasizing the fact that the function of grace is to restore man to his original possibilities, it has tended not to ignore entirely but to give inadequate theological attention to other aspects of the biblical message which suggest that grace is the free decision of God to enter into communication with man in history.

Within the Catholic tradition are two conflicting approaches to the problem, so discordant that the possibilities of mediation are limited. A decision has to be made between two perspectives on human nature. The first conceives of man in accordance with St. Augustine's saying at the beginning of the *Confessions,* "Thou hast made us for thyself, O Lord, and our hearts are restless until they rest in thee."

And during the period of high scholasticism when this question was first being elaborated, it was turned into the theme of the natural desire for the vision of God, a topic which we covered in the last chapter. There we saw that this theme has been revived in recent years, and noted its philosophical connection with the work of Maréchal at Louvain. In this view a desire for God is the condition of the possibility of all knowing and willing. The human spirit is considered a dynamic openness for the whole of being, that is, a potentiality which is nevertheless devoid of content and so strives toward being as that object whose possession by means of acts of intellect and will brings fulfillment. Since "being in general" is only a formal concept without reality, Maréchal argued, it cannot be the motive goal of the dynamism of the spirit. God, however, as *ipsum esse subsistens,* is the source of all finite intelligibility and goodness, so a natural desire for God must be the secret foundation of all acts of knowing and willing. For Rahner this drive in man is more insistent than man's conscious life, even though its conscious expression may have different degrees of explicitness.

A natural desire for God does not include its own exigency. This fact is important, because what it is to be a spiritual creature would make sense even without the gift of grace. Man, however, as limited spirit is essentially paradox and mystery; because he is spirit, he is capable of the infinite and really only finds rest in the vision of God; because he is limited, he cannot of himself arrive at immediate knowledge of the infinite and could not be summoned by God. So the natural desire or tendency of an intellectual creature for being is "elevated" by grace and transformed into an *a priori* active orientation to the Absolute, to God. Grace, then, founds in man a supernatural intentionality, an elevation of his spiritual faculties toward the supernatural formal object. It can do this because of man's supernatural existential dimension. Thus life under grace becomes the true beginning of man's end.

The data upon which this doctrine is founded are widespread. For it is undeniable that man's thoughts and desires reach out insatiably beyond the range of his own capacities of actualization. And this aspect of transcendence is the expression of a secret desire for the knowledge of God face to face.

Opposed to this doctrine of a properly interpreted natural desire is another approach in Catholic theology dominant since the Council of Trent. This latter teaching emphasizes the freedom of grace as a kind of superstructure beyond man's conscious spiritual and moral life. Naturally, the neo-scholastics acknowledged grace as an object of

178 THE ACHIEVEMENT OF KARL RAHNER

faith and saw that it was the life of God. But they tended
to argue that nothing at all can be known about this life.
The simplest kind of experiences as well as the teaching of
Trent [13] would seem to endorse this view. Only nature and
its acts are experienced. Nature is what we know of ourselves apart from revelation. "In short, the relationship
between nature and grace is thought of as two layers laid
very carefully one on top of the other so that they inter-
penetrate as little as possible." [14] Accordingly, nature's
orientation toward grace is thought of as negatively as
possible. Man's nature is considered in his fallen state
"sicut spoliatus a nudo"—as the man who has lost his
clothes differs from the man who never had any. Lack of
grace is seen as deprivation, because God so decreed (that
man have grace) and Adam lost it. It is not as if the lack
itself were any different in the two instances.

Revelation tells us that sinful man is called in Christ to
participate in divine life through faith, hope, and love (the
theological virtues) and ultimately is summoned to glory
in the vision of God. So redemption means not just freedom from sin but also the "divinization" of man. The
implications this has regarding the option of the two theories seem clear. And it makes a great deal of difference
which theory one adopts. Rahner's solution seems to provide a unique possibility. From what we saw in the last
chapter we can already predict the lines which his solution
will take.

C. Rahner's Contributions Toward a Solution

The distinction between nature and grace brings no dualism along with it, neither in the intention of God nor in the
existence of man. God, the source of nature and of grace,
has ordered the creation of the world and of man to
Christ, in whom and through whom humanity is summoned to participation in the very life of God. The unity
of the divine plan of salvation history orders reality hier-

archically, orders nature to grace and creation to redemption. Man in his nature is himself *imago Dei, capax Dei,* that is, openness for grace and the free self-communication of God. Man's nature as transcendental consciousness is really openness for the supernatural, for grace.

Although some indications of Rahner's solution have been adumbrated in the last chapter and in situating the problem, we have not really focused on his specific answer as such. Briefly, Rahner argues that God creates a creature whom He can love. He creates man in such a way that man can and must accept grace for what it is: the marvelous and wholly unexacted gift of love. Man must be able to receive this love which is God Himself. But man must have a congeniality for it. He must be able to receive God's love as one who has room and understanding and desire for it. So man is really created from the start as capacity for God. And this is man's most central and determining existential dimension. The real man as partner of God must be able to receive love as a free gift. Because of man's desire, his orientation, his existential for supernatural grace only allows grace to be free when it is itself unexacted and at the moment when fulfilled by grace it becomes aware of itself as supernatural—that is, appears as unexacted. Man is unable to see himself as simply another part of God's free creation. Rather, since man exists, he is to accept God's love as a gift and an unexpected mystery. If man were nothing but this existential, this desire, if man were simply a *nature* (and here we have the theological concept of *nature* clearly drawn for the first time), that is, if man were in no way able to be dissociated from what he is otherwise and from what he could understand himself to be, then he would as a free agent continue to act contrary to this nature in spite of God's love. But he could not accept this love as given freely. He could not really become a partner of God. If man were only this existential and were this his "nature," then it would be unconditioned in its essence, that is, once given, the love that is God would be given necessarily by God.

So man who receives love will recognize his existential dimension for this love as something unowed him. And this recognition is what allows him to distinguish and delimit what he always is (his indissoluble "quiddity") into what this unexacted receptive dimension is, his supernatural existential, and what is left over as a remainder, his "nature."

When man reflects on himself, he experiences himself in his every judgment about himself as an object and so sees himself in his transcendence to the infinite as what he is of necessity, a unity which cannot be broken down into separable parts. He exists as a whole or not at all. Man grasps his metaphysical essence, his spirit, in transcendence and freedom. Out of a transcendental analysis of what goes on in every human act, man must come to view other things as "essential" to him—his being in the world, his corporeality his membership in a community, his sexuality, his need to love his neighbor, and so on. Real human nature, therefore, is a nature in a supernatural order. Man can never escape his supernatural existential dimension. Nature "superperformed" (which does not mean "justified"!) by the offer of supernatural grace is man's existing condition. And once man recognizes by means of revelation that this supernatural order of grace exists for him, he is forced to notice that much of what he experiences within himself is due in fact to the operation of what he knows from revelation to be unmerited grace. Man experiences both grace and nature together. "For we experience our nature where we experience grace; grace is only experienced where by nature there is spirit. And vice versa, in fact; as things are when spirit is experienced, it is as a supernaturally elevated spirit." Perhaps some of what was rather abstractly considered in the last chapter on Rahner's understanding of grace and our awareness of it is now somewhat more understandable. We see that his hermeneutics continue to refine and develop a few insights by continual application of the transcendental method.

D. Resurrection of the Body

Perhaps by looking at one or two applications of some of Rahner's principles discussed here on the relation of Creator to creature, of matter to spirit, and of nature to grace, we can gain help in focusing our attention. Rahner's consideration of the resurrection of the body might be a good illustration, since it ties these questions together. The resurrection of the body involves the questions of life, of matter and spirit, of nature and grace.

The resurrection of the body is identified with *eternal life*. What is theologically exciting about the concept of life is that in the history of revelation life itself has a history. It proceeds from the vivid experience of human life and death as principle and stands at eternal life as term. One of the key words of revelation is eternal life. This is not to say that "life" is the only key word for man's perfection and for theological anthropology.[15] (It must always be viewed in connection with other revealed truths and theologoumena which make up our understanding of man.)

Matter as "dead" is the asymptotic zero point for life. What is simply matter is apparently open indifferently to all of material being, because it is a pure function. But out of the concept of life, spirit and person can be drawn as a radical surpassing of life itself. Man's world develops from his material environment, but he becomes a person out of his interior world, out of his assimilation of the material environment by means of nourishment and cultural and technical adaptation. Man makes progress by integrating his cultural environment. And out of his limited openness for the *other* represented by *his* world, man becomes infinite, transcendent to being as such. It is a movement, a progression, toward the perfection of matter in life and spirit. This is another facet of what was earlier discussed in terms of man's immortality.

We saw, then, how for Rahner theological anthropology

emphasizes this fact. Theological anthropology, Rahner thinks, should also reflect on man's state when this goal has been definitively achieved. As a listener man is destined for eternal happiness as spirit-in-matter, as spirit in the world. While asking the right questions, Rahner questions what we can say about this ultimate situation of man. He asks what is it that we mean by the "resurrection of the body." By *body* he understands the whole man in his proper corporeal reality. *Resurrection* means the termination and perfection of the whole man before God.[16]

Man is a many dimensioned being. He encompasses matter and spirit, action and passion, nature and grace. It is not surprising, then, that the process of man's completion is not a simple and uncomplicated progression. It is not surprising that the "moment" of perfection is not the same for each of man's many dimensions.

Spiritual union with God may be thought of as something growing in inverse proportion to belonging to matter. The soul's separation from the body as such, however, does not really mean greater nearness to God. Remoteness from the world and nearness to God are not convertible notions, however much we may be accustomed to think in this way. The world is many things striving to become one. The deceased remain united to the fate of this world in its eschatological striving. But biological and spiritual life share the common unity of the one human life. At the start of this chapter we noted how for Rahner the world as a whole has a beginning and a public history. It moves toward a point which is not the end of its existence but simply the completion of its incomplete and self-developing history. As man learns more and more about the physical world and its evolutionary character (especially in this age of physical and space science), he becomes more and more aware of the possibilities for change in the world. Rahner states, "If we allow the 'becoming,' time and history, to be really temporal and do not in the end turn them into a false eternity, then we may (very carefully) say: it is not against the nature of the world that this open, self-propagating history has a beginning and an end." [17] And personal spirit penetrates the whole reality of the world with significance. Personal spirit as human is material, mundane, incarnate. So the end of the world must share in the perfection of this spirit. The world remains forever the connatural surrounding of achieved spirit which finds its destiny in communion with God. The spirit performs its own history and that of the world as well. The end of the world is the total performance of saving history, which first became wholly operative and victorious in Jesus Christ and His resurrection. The history of each individual who has worked out his own personal completion finds its goal and ultimate expression along with the consummation of the world in the resurrection of the individual. The resurrection of the body, then, pulls together the many various interrelationships among matter, spirit, and grace into the final and definitive perfection of human spirit.

III. MYSTERY

We will conclude this chapter with a study of some of Rahner's thoughts on the source of man's dynamism and his spontaneous goal, the source of the power in creation. *Mystery* is the essential property of the "object" toward which the intellect is primordially situated and which forces a knower to elevate himself into an acceptance of this mystery as such. Man must accept mystery in love and in so doing attain his own perfection. By the very nature of man's spirit *mystery* cannot be the previous limiting concept which the theology manuals usually make it out to be. We can see how sharing a mystery, when spoken by God, can only happen in grace. Mystery demands as its own transcendental condition, the condition of its possibility, that it be heard by a subject divinized in grace.

Rahner observes that if being and presence to self progress in the same measure, then in created actuality the higher the being the more self-present it is and so less a mystery. Mystery, then, can only exist where it is a question of a relation involving God and the created intellect. Concepts about God, however necessary they may be, always live off the unthematic, non-objective experience of transcendence as such. Whether human knowledge recognizes the fact and reflects on it or not, a knower always presupposes the primordial difference between the Absolute as the goal of transcendence and the existent, in order to be able to differentiate even one existent from another.

Rahner applies his transcendental method again to arrive at an outline of what a mystery is. He begins with man, as usual, in his natural and supernatural transcendence. Briefly, if the goal of this transcendence is that which while it opens itself, gives its essence to itself, and if transcendence is the condition of the possibility of all understanding and conceptualizing, and if the goal of this transcendence is mystery, then this holy mystery is the only possible explanation for the entire process. All other understanding must be grounded in this transcendence. And by "absolute mystery" we mean what we want to understand by the concept "God," that absolute mystery which we think implicitly at least as the presupposition and ground of our encounter with everything that is not ourself, whether we will it or not. God remains the ground and inclusive unity of our experience of both spirit and the material world in their oneness.

This deduction has a number of applications. Here let it suffice to indicate a theological purpose. Rahner notes how the real argument against Christianity is the terrible experience of everyday living, that darkness which lurks behind all the disciplined arguments of the scientists and the sciences. But it is just this terrible everyday experience that is really the chief argument for Christianity. For what else does Christianity preach than that mystery remains eternally mystery? This mystery is that infinite, that ineffable mystery we call God, who gives Himself in self-communication to the human spirit right in the very heart of this terrible experience of limited emptiness. This very nearness of absolute mystery transpires not only by means of what we call grace, but also in an historically experiential form which we call the God-man who revealed the Trinitarian personality of the one God, Jesus Christ. These three mysteries of Christianity (grace, the Incarnation, and the Trinity) are experienced whenever man feels himself grounded on that abyss of unshakable mystery. Man experiences this mystery in the depths of his consciousness and in the crystallization of his own personal history (both of which are constitutive of his personal existence), and man accepts this mystery, in what we call the act of faith, as the only possible solution to life's problems.

A proper conclusion to the discussion of mystery can only be indicated. It cannot be stated explicitly. Two unique words and realities converge, man as the infinite question and the infinite mystery as unlimited, absolute response—and because the mystery still remains, we have that orientation of man and God. So the God-man is the unique and definitive answer. After Christ there can be no new mystery, no new revelation. We gain further insight here, then, into Rahner's understanding of how revelation is complete in Christ and how theological anthropology is ultimately Christology.

We can summarize some of these thoughts by noting that theological anthropology sees that man by spiritually recognizing himself and by identifying himself freely can and ought to open out in the direction of immediate, personal communion with the Infinite which is made possible by the self-communication of the Infinite. Man's self-fulfillment, the gaining and preserving of his pre-established dignity, constitutes itself the final and definitive dignity of man. This can never be lost. The fact that it could be lost and the consequences of this loss for individual men make up the matter of the next chapter. Man's personal nature includes his definition as spirit. This means that he is freedom; he is individual; he is dependent on a community; he is a person in the world. Man is a corporeal-material living being, a spiritual, personal, religious, God- and Christ-centered being. He is God-centered by nature and grace and he is Christ-centered because his being has an ontic and spiritual-personal capacity for communicating with Christ. While these many existential dimensions must be distinguished upon analysis, they cannot be separated in reality. The lowest dimension is determined by the highest and the highest by the lowest. Man's supernatural existential penetrates his most physical self. The implications of this in terms of man's so-called "physical" acts, his sexuality for example, need to be developed. It is in bringing out the true theological importance of such points that Rahner is most exciting. He remains theoretical in his hermeneutics, sometimes angonizingly so. Yet his deductions point to important practical conclusions which he leaves, for the most part, for others to draw.

APPENDIX TO CHAPTER FIVE

1. Rahner himself makes this observation. See *Theological Investigations,* vol. II, p. 237.

2. See *Schriften,* vol. IV, p. 188.

3. *Schriften,* vol. VI, p. 203.

4. The question how something can be more *real* than something else often provides a point for modern philosophical analysts to attack transcendental philosophy. But implicit in their attack is the self-defeating pronouncement that everything that is is matter. Rahner cautions that the "more" must not be thought of as something added on. Rather, it must be seen as evolving out of what was previously there and constituting its own internal growth in being. This means not just simply becoming something else, as a horse that dies becomes a mountain of cadaverous flesh.

5. This is the case "Thomistically" because different essences are not disparate quantities but different limitations on being. The lower is not opposed to the higher but is simply a more limited degree of being. The problem of becoming as essential self-transcendence by virtue of the divine power involves the question of a more precise ordering of the "stages" of progressive becoming. What and how something can be followed by something else in a series can only be discovered *a posteriori* and is a most difficult scientific question. See Paul Overhage and Karl Rahner, *Das Problem der Hominisation,* Freiburg, 1961, esp. pp. 43–89.

6. Rahner indicates how this ordered system might be considered according to St. Thomas. The form of every being is essentially its "idea." Whatever reality we properly identify as unconscious is considered metaphysically that being which only has its own idea, is caught up wholly in itself alone and so is unconscious. Hence it can be considered as a step toward consciousness and becomes more and more complex in terms of organization so that it finally is able to achieve self-

consciousness, even though this self-consciousness includes a real transcendence of matter when considered in the light of its previous unconscious condition.

7. An analogous example may help make this clear. A hundred years ago people thought they knew the limits of man's ability to manipulate the universe. Now we are only beginning to see darkly just what may be done in this regard. Specifying the possible limits of such manipulation becomes more problematic every day.

8. According to this understanding, the active becoming of limited being must appear as active self-transcendence in which the existent overcomes itself by itself precisely as an act of God. This applies to the asymptotic nearing of a being higher (than itself) by means of its self-performance.

9. In general, this theory holds that grace is to be placed in some quality or motion, which help is a physical, not a vital entity (because it comes not from a potency but from God), is not intentional but flows from itself. This motion puts the potency in first act and is called *"praemotio physica."* This is the general Thomist explanation, but some theologians such as Billot and Boyer have rejected it. This is not the place to go into the whole Molinist controversy, but let it suffice to note that Rahner's doctrine on grace keeps this old controversy alive. For bibliography and his observations consult his Innsbruck codex, *De Gratia Christi,* esp. pp. 129–186.

10. That is, its validity is to be shown through the fact that it is demonstrated to be implicitly affirmed where it is questioned or even drawn into doubt.

11. See *Lexikon für Theologie und Kirche,* vol. 7, col. 807.

12. For example, Karl Barth stresses this viewpoint. See Hans Urs von Balthasar, "Deux Notes sur Karl Barth," *Recherches de Sciences Religieuses,* 35 (1948), pp. 92–111. See also Hans Küng, *Justification: The Doctrine of Karl Barth with a Catholic Reflection,* New York, 1964.

13. For example, see Denzinger, nos. 802, 805, 825, 826.

14. *Nature and Grace,* p. 117.

15. Rahner develops this point in *Schriften,* vol. VI, pp. 174 f.

16. It is only because Christ Himself arrived at that furthest point of human existence which we call being dead that a

resurrection exists. That is why man is saved through and through, and is capable of God's beatitude with his whole undivided being. The heart of the earth has accepted and received the Son of God, and it is from a womb so consecrated that the saved creature rises up. See *Theological Investigations*, vol. I, p. 219.

17. *Theological Investigations*, vol. II, p. 212.

Extremely helpful in gaining understanding of Rahner's doctrine on nature and grace are the works by Kuehn and Stoeckle listed in the appendix to Chapter Four. The bibliography found at the back of *Nature and Grace* among the footnotes beginning on p. 143 is also very useful. A good general article on the problem is Eugene A. TeSelle, Jr., "The Problem of Nature and Grace," *Journal of Religion*, 45 (July 1965), pp. 238–250.

CHAPTER SIX

THEOLOGICAL ANTHROPOLOGY: REDEMPTION

Man has a history wherein he moves toward destiny, but he is threatened. The ability to refuse God's communication of Himself belongs to man as a spiritual, personal existent. And external and internal threats to man's disposal of himself mutually condition one another. Theologically, the fact of being threatened externally is a consequence of man's perversion from within. At the same time, the danger from without is a situation in which man's internal defection from his nature achieves itself in concupiscence, so that for man, prior to the revelation of God's judgment, both guilt and fate become entangled. Heidegger speaks of man as being both fate-laden and guilt-laden. And one of the results of man's fate-laden condition, of being continually threatened, is that he inevitably discovers himself poised between a state of guilt and redemption. The present chapter is about this fate-laden condition of man. Rahner discusses this condition in terms of the experience of fate, indicating the relatedness and the difference between fate and faith. There is always a fate-laden condition for the Christian in so far as his free act always occurs in terms of an *other*, over which he has no control.[1]

PLAN OF CHAPTER

The chief concern of this chapter is the possibility of rejecting revelation as this is developed in Rahner's theological anthropology. We will consider man first as "person" and "nature" somewhat more fully than in previous chapters. Then we take up man as "sinner." This implies considering the relationship between sin and freedom, the problem of original sin, and the concept of concupiscence. Since the problem of sin and of the struggle with sin must be seen in a social context, we are led into a brief discussion of the implications of this context for the sacrament of penance. Finally, we discuss specifically the question of the relation between the orders of creation and redemption. Since God has spoken His word of redemption, any discussion of man as sinner is necessarily incomplete without a discussion of man as redeemed.

In virtue of his orientation to the world, man is forever threatened. His opportunities encompass historical threats. As a corporeal being he is open to seizure by other creatures prior to any decision of his own. Material forces and other persons are able to exert an influence over his freedom. Although a final damnation can only come as a result of man's own free decision, these external influences can facilitate it; and no existential of the human person is hidden from such influence.

I. POSSIBILITY OF REJECTING REVELATION

Karl Rahner begins by affirming that we know that man's total responsibility consists in disposing of himself in freedom. But man can fail in this by wilfully going against himself in any one of his existential dimensions. For such offenses touch the very core of man. "The use of freedom necessarily confronts man with the choice of either degrading his dignity or of preserving it by means of God's grace and converting it into achieved dignity." [2]

A. Man as Person and as Nature

The unified picture of man as transcendental consciousness and of revelation and saving history given us in the New Testament permits us to understand dogmas about man both in their unity and in their articulations. Indeed, dogmas may be so understood that other teachings about man's *nature,* made available to man's understanding of self, can be seen as real statements of faith. We have touched on the question of man's "createdness." Suffice it to repeat and stress the fact that man as a whole, the *entire* man, is created. Independent of anthropological and evolutionary concerns, man is created and has no way of governing his origin. Man is the creature who necessarily recognizes this in terms of his fate-laden subjectivity, even though he does this unthematically (or even in the way an "atheist" expresses himself through hostility). So this knowledge also belongs to the constitution of the person. Man is essentially a person.

1. MAN AS PERSON

Man is a person in spirit-body unity. His soul is the *forma corporis,* and so this unity is existentially *a priori* to the real and experienced plurality of moments on this unity. So Rahner begins a transcendental reductive analysis of man in order to understand him as "personal." Man as person means that he is spirit, constituted by an immortal soul capable of knowing the Absolute Truth and of exercising freedom in orienting himself to mystery (the absolute mystery which we call "God"). Wherever spirit and person are given we have a transcendence to the infinite.

We have a knowledge of the individual both from without and from within only to the extent that the intellectually knowing subject opens himself to the infinite. In so far as this spirit experiences himself *in* time as a process of perfecting self and recognizes this process as performed in freedom and as absolutely decisive, and in so far as it involves an experience of responsibility, it necessarily excludes the possibility of a flight into nothingness. Because man is such a spirit, he recognizes himself as a person who is immortal.

But man is a *body*-person. The performance of personal spirit always involves *passion,* a passive and active suffering that are inseparably united, that is, always taking place in terms of an encounter with the one *appearance,* the sign or real symbol of what man must become in making objective his personal act of freedom. This uncovers the original act of subjective freedom and also throws a veil over it, because this makes the original nature of man's free act incapable of absolute determination. In both phases man's corporeality appears as person and as nature. In his corporeality man performs as receiving person, ordered to another in an I-You relation. So it is found in the most varied forms, chief among which is the relation of man and woman, in the performance of a real historicity. Just what Rahner intends by this will become clearer, but we should recall the importance of "love of neighbor" in achieving the self which we saw in Chapter Four.

In so far as man's *nature* always finds in the performance of his freedom this nature as the previously given space and limit of his free, active self, he understands and actually experiences himself as oriented to God by means of a real relation. This means that the transcendental structure of his nature is affirmed implicitly in every free act of knowing and willing in which he disposes of his "nature" by means of grace as a "person."

2. MAN AND FREEDOM

To clarify this point we can see that man's double character—as person and nature (which does not imply a real dualism)—can only be understood by a more careful consideration of freedom. Rahner spends a great deal of time trying to clarify his concept of freedom. We have seen some of this effort already. Let us now try to refine this concept in terms of man's disposal of himself as a *person*. For freedom is the clue to man's responsibility. If man were not free, he could not be guilty of rejecting revelation. Chapter One defined freedom as the *transcendence of the particular by means of the spirit.* Just as the ontological structure of any being determines its activity, so man's essential freedom implies that he is bound to be and become the person he is by the exercise of his freedom. Freedom is the basic condition of personal being, but since it is basic, it is hard to describe. Freedom is the possibility of personal disposition in such a way that this cannot be broken down into something different from itself in terms of which it could be deduced. Rahner argues that freedom cannot be resolved in such a way that in any case it would be and be so because its prerequisites happened to be such and such and not others.

Let us consider what freedom does *not* mean, though it can give us insight into what it should mean. I can give you, for example, the fullest possible advice about what to do, but I must omit one piece of counsel, since I cannot in the same breath advise you how to take the advice I give. So there is no paradox in saying that while normally I am not surprised to find myself doing or thinking what I do, yet when I try to anticipate what I shall do or think, then the outcome is likely to falsify my expectation. As Gilbert Ryle puts it, "My process of pre-envisaging may divert the course of my ensuing behavior in a direction and degree of which my prognosis cannot take account." [3] In other words, the one thing man cannot prepare himself for is the next thought that he is going to think, since the future is always elusive. But any performance can be a concern of a higher-order performance, to use the terminology of linguistic analysis. If we take this notion and apply it to the question of the transcendence of spirit, we can see what freedom really means for Rahner.

The causality of man's free act should be understood as his free openness to more than what is simply realized by his decision. In terms of our analogy of futurity, there is always more that I can anticipate in my behavior. Freedom is only possible as the transition from the open choice of an infinite number of possibilities to the limitation of a finite realization in which and passing through which man's destiny is either gained or lost personally. Hence freedom hinges on man's transcendental openness and orientation to the Absolute. Freedom is the self-performance of the person using the finite material of his world laid open to him before the Absolute. Therefore, freedom is *the* central datum of theological anthropology.

Rahner's analysis involves use of the reductive moment of the transcendental method. For without prejudice to man's spontaneity, Rahner is arguing that freedom is preceded by conditions wholly different from its act. The condition for this is a law of both ontological and ethical orders. It involves man's ability to say yes or no to a summons. Just as anyone can be given advice but cannot be advised how to take the advice, so man's freedom is his ability to say yes or no. Man's freedom is not absolutely creative. Preliminary conditions make possible its exercise which are themselves limited and so limit the possibilities of freedom. They are not in every case the same, they can be changed. Herein consists, by the way, the ontological and ethical basis for a legitimate limitation on human freedom. Equality of rights can only mean that everyone shall have his rights protected, rights which coincide with the rights of others only in certain definite areas but not at every point. The tendency toward attainment of a material equality of rights for everyone would only mean the oppression of everyone, since it would have to be based on interfering with the different scope for freedom objectively ordained for every individual.

Freedom does not involve a totalitarian equality. Rather, it is the manner of the appropriation and realization of the person and of his absolute dignity before God and the community of other persons in his use of the finite materials of his world. On the other hand, freedom, Rahner thinks, should not be conceived of as just a formal capacity which receives its importance from the result realized at the end of life. For the person and freedom are both absolute values. It is a real transcendence of the particular, the spring of man's dynamism, existing for its own sake, and its frustration would mean an attack on the dignity of the person.

Rahner says that a philosophy of the person and of freedom could demonstrate that there belongs to the nature of personal self-performance in an historical decision of freedom a daring leap into the *open,* a trusting thrust into the future. This involves a definite kind of not knowing. Freedom always demands an indefiniteness as its space, an accepted basis of emptiness as the dark ground of itself, as the very condition of its possibility. This implies that there exists a form of not-knowing which is the condition of the performance of freedom, and this is more perfect than the knowledge which if given in the performance of freedom would take away freedom. In this sense, freedom is more of a higher-order performance than knowledge. We can think back to the problem of Christ's immediate vision of God and recall how in this vision a certain kind of not-knowing was requisite for Christ to grow in self-consciousness. Paradoxically, in this question of freedom most linguistic analysts come closer to Rahner than many theologians of the tradition.

If freedom in itself (freedom of exercise) belongs to personal dignity, and if it depends for its exercise on the conditions given externally and internally, then the concession of these possibilities for the exercise of freedom is demanded by the dignity of the person. For freedom is the hidden capacity to effect oneself, to project oneself once and for all into finality. An important consequence is that any attempt to legislate away moral evil or to make it impossible by means of coercion is not only utopian but must degenerate into a morally wrong attempt to eradicate the scope of freedom itself.

Rahner explains further how the moral law is not such a limitation on freedom. The moral law presupposes freedom and orders it to its own destiny, the true achievement of the person. Freedom of personal decision is a higher-order performance, a higher value than any material security of physical existence.[4] However, there can be a just limitation on the exercise of freedom. It might seem that man must needs have free and autonomous access to salvation. But in this case his salvation would be ultimately himself and this is wholly false. God can never be just another word for the splendor of human self-disposal any more than He can substitute for the sublimity of human knowledge and transcendence. We see once again how Rahner's thought converges; for he explains freedom ultimately in terms of grace. If God is to be God, that alone which makes freedom truly free, He must act by refusing Himself and by declaring Himself, by both remaining distant and by drawing near. God is the freedom of man's freedom by the grace of His self-communication, without which man's free will could only choose slavery. God's self-communication, His grace, is the *terminus ad quem* of freedom. So man's freedom is preserved from the dilemma of being either a freedom given over to the question of choosing from among finite particulars or of starving to death because of its own emptiness. It is a true transcendence of the particular ordered to the freedom of freedom that is grace. Hence it involves an element of mystery, so we cannot expect a crystal-clear explanation.

To look ahead for a moment, however, Christ and His salvation is not simply one of two possibilities offered man's choice. It is the very act of God which in overtaking man springs his dynamism, breaks open his possible false choice. In Christ, God gives not just the possibility of salvation which must be worked by man, but the actual salvation—no matter how, as precisely given by God, it includes the proper free decision of individual men.[5]

3. MAN AS NATURE

Morality is the free personal acceptance of one's own previously given *nature,* the admission of self in trust into all one's given existential dimensions, primarily in turning in love to another. It involves the acceptance of nature as belonging to the mystery of love. This acceptance of nature has its own history. It is not (as is the case with the angels) given all at once. It becomes in time. This means, however, that something already *is* at a definite point of time and yet still has to come to its own perfection. And in this it is important not to underestimate the element of temporality in man's existential dimensions.[6]

The matter of man's use of freedom has been discussed by Rahner in several connections. One of the most frequently misunderstood is related to man as nature and involves his concept of "situation ethics," or as he prefers, "existential ethics." This concept includes the attempt of some theologians to develop in moral theology alongside the *essential* moment an *existential* moment of moral obligation. Existential ethics attempts to bring out the real aspect of moral obligation in a clearer light. Moral action means that an individual has to realize himself in that manner in which he finds his obligation presented. To the extent that the act is not determined by more general norms, it becomes a question of existential ethics. Rahner holds that the individuality of the person and his own value falls, as does all being, under God's obligatory saving will. So a positive individual act, in so far as it is more than just an *instance* of the universal, belongs to the moral order. Real obligation is not just an application of a general law (though it can be this also), but is more than just a special instance or case. Instead, an individual act corresponds with an individual summons and demands just as individual an answer. Here we cannot know the positive uniqueness of the content of moral obligation. A good deal of unthematic knowledge is involved. Hence existential ethics should be understood as a complementary concept of universal or general ethics. It is neither what traditionally goes under the name of "special ethics" nor "situation ethics." Given Rahner's understanding of freedom and of man's nature, it is possible to better understand his call for an "existential ethics."

B. Man as Sinner

Rahner thinks that a community of situation is applicable to the freedom of all men. This community of situation is the basic reason why by divine decree the offer made man in the liberating freedom of freedom (sanctifying grace) depends on an acceptance by the first man. And this offer was refused. So man is a slave to "sin." In as much as this offer of freedom given the first man no longer exists in that way, as at first, man no longer finds himself on a plane where his exercise of freedom remains free simply because of God's offer of self-communication.

The systematic connection of the human existentials of person, nature, and freedom needs to be seen against the background of their denial, against the darkness of sin, the actual misuse of freedom and the person. Rahner has made a number of important contributions to the doctrine of original sin. He has clarified the problem of transmission by his explanation of *monogenism*. Since this question is important for the unity of humanity, and since its denial is central to a number of modern theories on original sin, it is well to see how Rahner approaches monogenism in somewhat full detail.

1. MONOGENISM

a. Relation to Unity of Creation

Christ has become one of us, not merely having the same nature in the abstract. Christ belongs to the one human race which is not just the sum total of all human beings but an actual unity in the will of God. "However difficult it may be to find categories to define it, this unity is manifested in the monogenetic descent of all men from the one Adam, is raised to a supernatural destiny, and unfolds in original sin and the one history of the human race in salvation and perdition." [7] That unity is confirmed, increased, and made definitive in the Incarnation of the Logos. Hence Rahner thinks it reasonable to follow this principle in discussing the problem of monogenism.

b. Monogenism

The doctrine of monogenism states that all men spring from a single biological pair, the biblical Adam and Eve. It is opposed to a polygenism which holds that man springs from several Adams. Rahner develops a lengthy demonstration to prove that monogenism is the official teaching of the church. And after showing this possibility of proving monogenism from scripture and tradition, he gives a unique metaphysical demonstration.

Prior to the encyclical *Humani Generis* it was customary to offer a simple proof of monogenism which if applied to anthropological transformism would lead to its condemnation. *Humani Generis* seems to forbid a positive defense of polygenism even as a scientific hypothesis! But a precise theological qualification is not given. And the only such qualification obtainable from the encyclical itself is that monogenism is "theologically certain." Rahner states that there is no question that *Genesis* 2, 3 sets an individual man before us and that before this Adam there was no man who could cultivate the earth. Now, does the fact that the Adam of *Genesis* is portrayed by the inspired author as an individual mean that he *was eo ipso* an individual? Given the state of exegesis today, a simple affirmation that monogenism is unmistakably meant is no longer possible. Rahner argues negatively that pure exegetical methods, however, will provide no conflict with the unity of the human race.[8] The inspired author sees himself faced by an ethnological and cultural plurality and he reduces it to a more primitive unity. Rahner argues that the unity of man is prior to this plurality and that the inspired author intended to act as a guarantor of monogenism.[9]

Generation Rahner understands as the only genesis of the human individual within a species. Hence wherever "polygenistic" phenomena are found we are in the presence of the genesis of a metaphysically new species. It is impossible that the same thing have two categorially different causes. The first man is established by the Absolute. If the Absolute, without being obliged to achieve itself in an institution of the conditioned, actually does institute the conditioned, and if this conditioned can produce effects proper to its nature, then the Absolute is not able to reproduce that which it creates as cause distinct from itself. The Unconditioned can do what the conditioned can do. But it cannot will to repeat without the performance of the conditioned what the conditioned is capable of performing once it is so established. Otherwise it would be to will and not to will the same thing at once, a metaphysical impossibility. However, Rahner observes that a moderate theory of anthropological evolution maintained simultaneously with monogenism does not lead to compromise. For both theories arise in the same way from a single principle, the transcendence of divine causality influencing the course of the world in the most discrete and economical way. "What the world can do by itself, it must do in the

highest possible way; and that includes both the preparation of the biological substratum which was to 'become
man' and the spreading abroad of the one stock." [10]

Monogenism actually states a fact which establishes the
unity of all men at different levels of one human reality. It
also expresses a task and is a condition of the possibility of
the unity (and catholicity) of the church. Monogenism is
also important because man's intellectuality allows the
possibility of a common history despite the divinely willed
plurality of people, cultures, and civilizations. It most
importantly provides a foundation for the unity of salvation history which is God's universal salvific will regarding
all men.

2. THEOLOGY OF CORPOREALITY

Before we take up the question of original sin and of sin in
general, some further remarks on man as "nature" are
needed. Since Christ, theology is always theological anthropology; so corporeality and sexuality can be seen in
their meaning within salvation history in terms of their
symbolism. The body, as we saw, is the symbol of the soul.
The symbolism of man's corporeality may be illustrated as
a theological principle by noting how Rahner treats sexual
differences, which, by the way, represent the typical European viewpoint which still suffers from a way of looking at
woman as a sort of incomplete man.

When it comes to salvation, Rahner says neither man
nor woman has any particular advantage. But each exists
even before God as heterosexual. Man exists as a whole
and as one. God created man, however, as man and
woman. The sexual aspect of the human being is not just a
defined sector of human existence, so that it becomes a
religious matter only in terms of the moral law. Rather,
one's sex rules the very being of the whole man in all
existential dimensions. One is everywhere man or woman.
And because revelation summons the whole man to per-

fection, it cannot be other than as man or as woman.

Rahner singles out for particular attention the call of St. Paul (1 Corinthians 16, 3) to be a man as meaning an exercise of male qualities in the life of the church. But for Rahner, what these qualities are is a difficult question. Because sexual differences penetrate all dimensions of human life, a specific question about man is as problematic as one about human being. Rahner says that one would have to begin with the question why the gospel always called God "Father" and not "Mother." Then one would have to ask why the eternal Logos became man and not woman. Further, Rahner wants to stress the masculine concept of ecclesiastical history and the fact that only men are ordained priests.

Rahner lists several specifically masculine qualities of human nature. As opposed to woman, man is turned toward the external. He is concerned more with accomplishment and less with feelings. He is concerned more with fact and less with persons. He is more analytic and less intuitive, acting in terms of principle, and he feels more honored to be called just than loving. Man finds it easier to differentiate between thing and person (which in the ultimate analysis is not an advantage). He finds it easier to be alone. While he is a prophet, woman is a mystic. Man lives more with his head than with his heart and likes his life to be in agreement with his theories, so he builds his outlook around his actions, while woman can more easily bear contradiction between theory and practice, as long as the theory is intellectual.

Rahner says that woman is usually taken on the average to be more pious than man. The female sex actually constitutes a statistically larger sample of churchgoers. One even expects a woman to be more "religious" than a man. And the situation is such that in Europe (and to some extent in America) a holy man is considered to be somewhat effeminate. Rahner asks where such a situation comes from and why contemporary religious life is ordered more to woman than to man. He says the reasons are many, but cites two significant ones. First, the history of religions shows that religion historically was as much a concern of man as of woman, and Christianity itself has nothing specifically feminine about it. So the answer must lie in the fact that historical Christianity has assumed characteristics more in accordance with feminine piety, so that it is easier for woman to be "religious." This means that a real imperative exists for the church to make some changes.

The church needs to consider becoming more masculine. The man of today does not rejoice over long sermons the way men did before newspapers and television.

Secondly, men feel that perhaps too much is asked of them, because most of them feel they do not have the chance and grace to become "professional" saints. A real man tends to feel out of place among "model" Christians. Rahner notes, "We do not want to praise men's absence from Sunday Mass . . . and set this up as a model; but perhaps one could still say that this involves a more genuine Christian mentality when there is still earnestness in the feeling that one does not have to place himself before the alternative of either going to holy Mass every Sunday or giving up his Christianity altogether." [11] Rahner thinks that it is possible to get the impression, at least in Europe, that Christianity is seen as a fixed sum of accomplishments which one performs wholly or not at all. Communism, on the other hand, has not only party members but also its "Friends of the Soviet Union." Christianity should not imitate this but might take a leaf from their book. For even Jesus did not tell His apostles everything at once. He drew them slowly into His teaching and left a great deal to the Holy Spirit.

Religion, to anticipate the last chapter for a moment, has a double element, the categorial and the transcendental. This means that God may never be identified with *religion,* the formula may not be confused with the fact, the accomplishment with the goal, the sacrament with grace, the church with the Kingdom, no matter how intertwined elements of one or other may be found. One can be in the church and still far from God. Man has more understanding for the transcendental element than has woman. He does not think automatically that a longer prayer must be better than a shorter one. But today man is in danger of being made irreligious by religiosity. In this area there is much room for reform in the life-style of Catholicism.

Women would probably find a number of points objectionable in Rahner's treatment of sexual differences, but his position is really quite favorable and mild regarding woman when compared with the views of the typical European clergyman.

3. SIN AND FREEDOM

Man performs himself in freedom. But a bad free decision is a failure properly to dispose of himself, not only because he misses his proper object, the essential good willed by God, but also because he lets the inner nature of real freedom escape him. For a morally bad realization of freedom, though still free, is a false realization of its purpose, since God created freedom not as the possibility of subjectively performing good or evil, but as the possibility of the creative positing of the good as such. Consequently, freedom mistakes itself in committing sin, the ultimate negation of itself. This negative moment we call guilt.

Heidegger's concept of guilt says that man is not merely laden with guilt; he is guilty. The state of being "laden with guilt" originates in the circle of celebrations and cares, but guilt itself has no specific origin whatever, since it pertains to the very being of man. Rahner counters by emphasizing the fact that given the nature of freedom and responsibility, guilt, considered theologically and essentially, is man's decision against God, his no to the summons to participate in God's self-communication. So it is a rejection of man in himself, a rejection of the horizon under which he performs all his moral acts. In this sense, then, guilt is theological and metaphysical suicide, without the subject's really being able to see into his nothingness. Though the possibility of committing this suicide is always contained in man's existential dimensions, it is in no way constitutive of his being. This is important, because at this decisive point we find a chasm between Rahner's subjectivism of the person and that represented even by Heideggerian existentialism.

Rahner asks us to observe that sin does not happen in the simple transcendental interior of a noumenal subject but in actual deeds of the flesh which are apparent and palpable. Yet because a totally definitive judgment can oppose man's *nature*, theological guilt can be admitted into man's disposal of himself. But because of the various levels of man's dimensions, this can be admitted in various existential degrees. It can even come under the guise of good. We see this in many instances. A good intention, for example, may often lead us to use a bad means; or we often perform good acts with bad feelings. In short, it is impossible to discuss freedom and responsibility apart from their various relationships, to transcendence and to genuine subjectivity. This means that we must see guilt in terms of man's nature as an existential dimension. And this fact is usually discussed under the phrase "original sin."

4. ORIGINAL SIN

The doctrine of original sin is a basic thesis of theological anthropology. Only on the basis of this doctrine can man's renewal by means of his redemption in Christ be understood. Original sin should be described as a violation of and a challenge to something stamped permanently in man's structure. Original sin is internal to man because it sets up a conflict within an intrinsic orientation to the beatific vision. In a sense, it is the source of man's being threatened from within.[12] From the beginning man was seen as a partner of God. God was to share out of absolute "otherness" His divine nature with man, and because of this supernatural elevation, man was free. So Rahner views original sin in terms of man's prehistory which has the character of situation, that of the beginning of history. We can only know this through an aetiology of statements in scripture. Adam as essentially the first of many men could represent man and be *the* man simply. And the sinful decision of Adam is ratified (Romans 5, 12) with regard to accepting or rejecting the offer of grace, so that Adam's decision is definitive for all men in such a way that his rejection is included in God's more powerful acceptance, in God's decree for the Incarnation and salvation of mankind.[13]

Essentially, original sin is the absence of that supernatural elevation planned originally for man. This "situation of incompleteness" really divides man from God. However, as such it is not real, personal sin and can only be called sin analogously. It belongs to man as *nature,* even though real man is "wounded" by this original sin and consequently is deficient in his natural powers.

This means that the beginning of mankind has been partially determined by guilt. On the one hand, it was a free act of the first parent (historical because *constitutive* of our space of experience and not "historical" in the sense of fact *within* this space), and on the other hand it so determines man's existential situation that he lacks supernatural grace and in this sense remains interiorly a sinner. This situation understood by original sin remains in existence essentially even after individual justification has transformed it fundamentally. For man's condition of being-unto-death, his historicity, his guilt and concupiscence, indeed everything that makes it difficult to posit a personal moral decision, remain. And in so far as this sin is situated at the beginning of mankind, we know that man's space of existence is to remain determined up to the final, eschatological elimination of guilt. Rahner notes how without this teaching being understood historically, the multi-dimensioned history of penance in the church, including its roots in the Old and New Testaments, cannot be understood.[14]

To summarize the problem of sin briefly, for Rahner the unity of the history of spirit and matter of the one cosmos of corporeal and spiritual reality must not be so considered that this unity implies an exclusion of sin and guilt, as though guilt could not find a place within such a unified structure of the world. The real evolution of the world is toward spirit, toward transcendence and freedom. But where freedom exists before the reality of the world as a whole in a transcendence to the Absolute, guilt can make a grand entrance. For real freedom must include the possibility of rejecting God. Since the Incarnation is the high point of creation, we must see that to the extent sin exists in the world it must be included in the beginning as a moment of God's saving will of forgiveness. God's will to save is salvific because of Christ and not because of man's sinfulness. Guilt is allowed to transpire because as limited it must be comprehended in God's offer of Himself to a world in need of redemption. Hence we are to understand Rahner's statement that we are saved through Jesus Christ from our sins in the sense that Christ's action does not move God's will to forgive but that God's will to forgive effects Christ's action.

Another way of looking at original sin is to realize that a plural world of numinous powers receives its meaning and justification from the God of Christianity. The effort it may cost us to hold onto this world is the price of conquering original sin. We are forever prey to the dilemma: God or world. A polytheistic, slavish adoration of inner-worldly powers is but the reverse side of the same dilemma, the numinosity of the world without God, the Godlessness of the world. But Rahner observes how today our real danger lies in worshipping God and still letting the world be without God.

Recent theological attention to the problem of original

sin may highlight Rahner's contributions.[15] Schoonenberg says the doctrine of original sin is at a standstill and is in urgent need of integrating other elements including (1) a deeper view of the sin of the world considered actively and passively; (2) the realization that when the scriptures speak of Adam and his sin as the source of sinfulness for all, they do not exclude but rather include other sinful causes; (3) the fact that monogenism has been upheld in classic theology as a necessary presupposition for safeguarding the dogma of original sin as understood in the past. Schoonenberg wants a new concept developed which would leave the door open for polygenism. "There is no difference between original sin and the sin of the world" considered actively and passively. The rejection of Christ consummates the history of the sins of humanity, a history initiated in the sin of the first human beings. This definitive sin begets a totally sinful and graceless situation, at least for all men born after Christ's death. It is not generation itself which is instrumental in the transmission of original sin, but the sinful state is caused by the historically graceless situation in which our parents live. Rahner would affirm much of what Schoonenberg wants done, and much of Rahner's doctrine already goes beyond this, especially regarding a "sin of the world" considered actively and passively. But Rahner would reject out of hand a possible polygenism, not because it is essential for preserving the classic doctrine on original sin, but because it involves the unity of mankind with Christ as head.

5. CONCUPISCENCE

Some of Rahner's thought on sin and freedom can be compressed into his discussion of the problem of concupiscence. *Concupiscentia* in the narrower sense, he argues, is the act of the appetite in regard to a determinate value in so far as this happens spontaneously within consciousness on the basis of man's natural dynamism. It forms part of the necessary precondition for man's personal decision. For the act of desire responding to an object on the basis of natural dynamism is a prerequisite for free choice. So with the same metaphysical necessity with which a limited freedom must be given its object if it is to become active at all, there precedes the free operation an act of the appetitive power which is none other than man's dynamic spontaneity. So a freedom from *concupiscentia* in the theological sense cannot be a freedom from every kind of spontaneity prior to free decision.

The usual description of *concupiscentia* in the narrowest sense, and this is what Rahner means by concupiscence, is man's spontaneous desire precisely in so far as it precedes free decision and resists it. A free act is one which sets man explicitly or implicitly before the Absolute and in which man comes to a decision regarding the Absolute. This is true to the extent that God is comprehended at least implicitly in every morally free decision of self-disposal. Because man can only be free regarding finite values in virtue of his dynamic orientation to the infinite, every free decision is a disposal of man before God. The principles of transcendental hermeneutics, then, lead Rahner to his redefinition of concupiscence.[16]

Man's tendency to dispose of himself freely never wholly succeeds. There always remains the tension between man as *person* and man as *nature*. The person never wholly absorbs his nature. Nature, as we saw earlier, includes everything that must be given previous to self-disposal as object and condition of this possibility. Person means man in so far as he freely disposes of himself.[17] Man's spontaneous act of desire belongs to nature, as one of the necessary presuppositions for a free act. The end toward which free decision is ordered is that everything which is in man (as nature) should be a symbol, the expression of what man as a person wishes to be. So a free decision must comprehend and infuse the spontaneous drive to become not just natural but personal. But because this drive is prior to any personal act, the person never wholly becomes what he truly is. Hence it follows that the analytical dualism of nature and person, which Rahner calls concupiscence, is something within man at work for both good and evil. It is just as important that it works for good. For instance, a man wants to be brave, but he still goes on trembling in the face of an enemy's gun, although he would like to be so brave that he does not tremble. Or a student feels that he should write his mother a letter, even if he does not get around to it. Both good and bad decisions encounter the resistance of nature. "Concupiscence in the theological sense shows itself, for instance, just as much when a man blushes in the act of lying as when the 'flesh' refuses to follow the willingness of the spirit for good."

Man cannot determine exhaustively the whole extent of his real being. His free act *does* dispose of himself, in so far as it is a free act of the man's personal center. Yet his being is not wholly engaged. In the course of temporal self-determination a person suffers the resistance of nature and never wholly succeeds in making man wholly personal. Something remains which is impervious to existential decision. On the other hand, it is integrity that makes possible an exhaustive realization of that tendency associated with every free decision, the tendency of the person to dispose of himself totally before God. An individual's spiritual-personal free decision does not involve merely implementing a universal law in an individual instance. It is rather a realization of a personal, supernatural individuality in obedience to a personal summons from God. And this is no less individual and unique because it often announces itself through the drabness of everyday occurrences or by force of external circumstances.

In the usual non-existential teaching about sin a distinction is often made between *peccatum personale* and *peccatum naturae*. Yet in this very terminology we find existential ideas about the person at work. Reflexion on this distinction allows the thought to become clear that where there is a single person, there is a single freedom in rela-

tion to which any other reality can only be its manifestation or expression. Yet this is precisely not the case with
Jesus. And so this is what makes us different from him
who is like us in all things except sin.

C. Sin and the Struggle with Sin

The entire being and action of the church constitute a
rejection of sin. Man as sinner is also a social being.
Whatever man does affects his fellow man, and sin is no
exception. Sin has a real social character.

1. SOCIAL CONTEXT AND NATURE OF SIN

Rahner brings out the social context of sin in discussing
the relation of the sinner to the community of the people
of God. He gives the words of Matthew about "binding
and loosing" an interpretation which refers them to the
sacrament of penance. He argues that the passage concerns how the people of God are to deal with the sinner. If
a member of the elect sin grievously, in the sense of
personal sin, it cannot be a matter of indifference to the
church. For the church of its nature is to proclaim the
victorious grace of God, and to be indifferent to the sinner
would be to betray this function of the church. The church
has to react, because the holiness of the church is to be a
symbol of God's grace. So the church "binds" the sinner,
that is, draws away from him by some kind of exclusion
(*not* excommunication). And this means that the sinner is
no longer seen by God as a member of the people of God
and therefore cannot share in God's self-communication.
But if the church "looses" the sinner, that is, raises its ban
by a recognition of the sinner's reconciliation with the
church, "to that extent we may say that this has a sacramentally symbolic value, the sinner is 'loosed' also in
heaven. God effectively regards him in the full sense a

member of the community which the Son has collected on earth." In this sense, God forgives him his sins. Reconciliation by means of the church is therefore reconciliation with the church. Hence Rahner's emphasis on the social context of sin is developed within the framework of his examination of the sacrament of penance.

2. PENANCE

The acts of the penitent in confessing to the church are constitutive of the sacramental sign. This means that sinner and the church together constitute the real symbol in which both the acts of the sinner as a member of the church and the reconciling action of God become manifest. What happens here in penance is an actualization of the essence of the church and so really is a sacrament, a necessary moment of the self-realization of the church.

The best approach to the many problems surrounding penance starts, Rahner thinks, with the fact that the institution of penance has undergone enormous changes. This is so true that if it were not a fact, most dogmatic theologians would consider penance impossible because it would seem to contradict the essence of a sacrament. St. Joseph did not fashion the first confessional. Centuries passed before confession of non-grievous sins took place. The saintly bishop Gallens typified the attitude of the church for centuries when he preached that one should *do* penance but not go to confession until one was on one's death bed. Even Councils warned against confession for a young dying man because he might recover his health and an entire lifetime of penance would be too hard. And for centuries one could receive the sacrament of penance only once in a lifetime.

Between the eleventh and the thirteenth centuries theologians taught that the sacrament of penance did not destroy guilt before God but had only secondary effects. Thomas Aquinas taught that the penitent came to confession already justified by sorrow. Beginning with the most difficult of penances, the accent in the sacrament moved toward internal sorrow, then to the shame of confession, and finally was placed on the priestly absolution. Nearly thirteen centuries went by before the church distinguished between perfect and imperfect contrition. Before the time of Aquinas, theologians taught that the decree of the Fourth Lateran Council obliging one to yearly confession included those who had no serious sin on their souls. Thomas and later theologians saw theologically deeper and affirmed the opposite. Rahner says that this practice today has caused this explanation to disappear so that even pious souls unconscious of any grave sins approach Eastertide with fear and dread. The sacrament has undergone many other changes also. Rahner argues that all these prove just one thing: that it is alive. What lives changes, even though its essential ordination remains the same. And anyone who has any knowledge of history knows how absurd the notion is that because something once was the case it could be that way again.

Rahner asks whether it is possible to predict future changes in penance. He says that we have neither the power nor the right to change anything in existing theory and practice. But within the framework of the present teaching exists a large area for change. Just as Irish and Saxon monks in the fifth and sixth centuries initiated a new era of vitality in the sacrament, so today we can do something about the matter of habitualness in the sacrament.

Rahner suggests that future teaching and practice will tend to make penance both fuller theologically and personally. He says there is today a legalistic, magical tendency in current practice. Many elements based on casuistry display this. In the past, mothers who died in childbed would often be relegated to a particular section of a cemetry. The *Roman Catechism* orders three days of continence for married people before receiving communion. The idea obtains that the more Masses one has said the better one's chances of getting something. Examples could be multiplied. But in the sacrament of penance many such superstitions remain. For example, a penitent is anxious over whether he had "bad" thoughts three or four times. A list is repeated in confession after confession because it "sounds good." A bedridden parishioner confesses missing Sunday Mass because it makes him "feel better." These and other tendencies display the residue of an aura of magic and superstition. Such formal ritualism tends, Rahner thinks, to develop a situation in which penance is reduced to priestly absolution from sins together with the necessary predisposition in so far as this is absolutely essential, and so penance comes to be valued as a mechanical process (often involving the false appeal of *opus operatum*). And in these results lurks a primitive, legalistic, magical instinct which is wholly opposed to the true nature of the sacrament.[18] As far as frequency of confession goes, this is a matter of individual decision. But it needs to be emphasized that one good confession is certainly better than three "habitual" ones. The criterion must be genuine progress in spiritual life, and where progress is absent, frequent confession is no better than none.

Rahner says that we should free ourselves from the prejudice that God established the sacraments so that we would have it subjectively easier. Such an opinion stems from the fact that modern theology (as opposed to the theology of the Middle Ages) gives a one-sided emphasis to the fact that in confession attrition is enough for justification but is not enough outside of confession. Rahner does not oppose this thesis, but says it does not justify the resultant prejudice. Whoever has attrition has no difficulty having contrition; the only difficulty with contrition is attrition, that is, obtaining real distance from sin.

In the second place, penance needs to be experienced more fully theologically. It is not simply absolution in the name of God. It is a mystery of Christ. The same judgment is passed over the sinner that was passed over the world on the cross. It is the judgment of the future transpiring now.

It is dialogue between God and man. It is liturgy in which total responsibility for the church is involved. All these factors need emphasis so that penance become more itself and not be simply an act of juridical absolution.

In the third place, the actual confession of sins is a part of the sacramental sign ordered to the absolving words of the priest. Confession is matter of the sacrament and must be handled as such. It must be understood that there is no question of being judged by the priest. So there must be stress on the fact that personal guilt must be conscious guilt. Then in the matter of giving a penance, Rahner thinks that it would be naïve optimism to think that the average educated Catholic believes existentially in purgatory. If we did not think of the onus of punishment quite so juridically this situation might be different. If we should say that the *reatus poenae* is really myself, my guilt-laden egoism which implies that a vast spiritual development must be undergone before that state of purification in which the total integration of my personality can take place, the real meaning of the doctrine of purgatory would become once again viable. Instead, the average Catholic thinks that if he lives a reasonably good Christian life, juridically on the safe side, he may have a couple of years of purgatory but everything will be all right then. And even enough indulgences could take care of this. In reality, this life is but the beginning of our turn from evil in integrating ourselves and our culture, in developing ourselves as the persons we are to become. In the light of this problem the concept of doing penance needs to be made meaningful once more.

Rahner observes that we are a long way from banishing everywhere the thought that confession is a necessary preparation for communion, that the eucharist is somehow a reward for penance. There needs to be a functional ordering of the practice of confessing venial sins. The more genuine a spiritual life is, the more it evolves from the depths of one's being. A knowledge of one's being as sinner is not in itself contingent upon frequent confession. Augustine could pray his *miserere* on his death bed without ever having been to confession. Every confession in its turning to the historically palpable protest against all disguised rationalism is an admission that it is the act of God alone that destroys our sins. Every confession confesses that man can find in this way a forgiving God. That such an attitude is important in the formation of a sound spiritual life should be clear. As far as venial sin goes, do we really know that apparently venial sins, those which do not disturb the basic attitude of man to God, are really venial? Naturally, when measured against objective norms they are venial, that is, such things as small unfriendly acts against the neighbor, a distraction in prayer, an act of impatience. But we tend to overlook how these little things may fit into the total structure of moral behavior and so condition the ultimate attitude of our religious situation. Man does not commit individual acts one after another strung out on the thread of time. Man lives out of a basic attitude either turning him toward or away from God. Might not the fact that man is always committing venial sins mean that he is in a much deeper and more radical sense a sinner? This does not mean exclusion from the people of God. But properly understood, such an appreciation that we are sinners can give new meaning to our lives. In the light of such considerations Rahner thinks that the distinction between mortal and venial sins needs to be rethought, no matter how objectively correct it may be, because in reflecting on human existence such a distinction cannot be adequately made. Where "mortal" sin is involved, where it is given genuinely and subjectively, there is realized a control by the subject over his salvation. And in so far as the real theological nature of freedom is realized (even when such an act is definitive only on the basis of the whole of life and a "fundamental option"), we have a lengthy temporal process. In the case of "venial" sin, freedom is had in the sense of an active choice between two possibilities. But it is so given that a real control over the self regarding one's destiny does not happen. Factually, we must continually recall that we are on the side of sinners who hope in God's mercy. On the other hand, we are justified. And this justification is not a static possession. It is continually threatened by the world, the flesh, and the devil, externally and internally. The condition of grace is always open to man's freedom, which in turn can only receive grace in and through the free grace of God without any merit on our part.

II. REDEMPTION

Any consideration of theological anthropology including man's fate-laden situation of sin is incomplete without considering at the same time that it is a discussion of redeemed man. Christ is the historically real presence of God's eschatologically victorious mercy. The Incarnation, Rahner repeats continually, is not just the constitution of a subject who if eventually he is willing or is given the task by God can intercede for sinful mankind. If this were the case, nothing would have been determined by the Incarnation in regard to redemption. We must consider the "physical" view of redemption found in the Greek Fathers of the church and continually ask ourselves why the hypostatic union continued even after the crucifixion, why Christ died the death of sinful man, the very manifestation of guilt. In the Incarnation God accepted the world once and for all in His mercy. And the Logos redeemed by actually identifying Himself with the sinner. Consequently, the whole of mankind in principle is already accepted for salvation in the member and head of mankind who is irrevocably united with God in the unity of person. From the moment of assumption of human nature by the Logos the redemption of sinners cannot be halted.

A. Creation and Redemption

In the Incarnation God Himself becomes a creature in the supreme creative act of God. So created reality from this point of view most closely belongs to redeemed reality as the self-communication of God in the Incarnation. And created reality is the condition of the possibility of itself as a transcendental condition. Redemption in the Incarnation gives the world in all its dimensions a supernatural meaning. Something more needs to be said about this openness of created reality for grace as a conclusion to this chapter's discussion of theological anthropology. We must stress again following Rahner's method that given the nature of redeemed reality and the real order of God's self-communication, each created natural reality, and primarily man, is so ordered that it can only maintain its natural determination as completed through effort toward integration into the supernatural order of grace. And out of this results the Christian's concern for the world. The Christian cannot make a god of his world—though this is a continual threat and danger. Nor can he abandon the world. Rahner uses this fact to explain the distinction between the various states of life in the world and the religious life. Neither condition can be indifferent to the order of creation or of redemption. The religious may not think he is handed over to the order of redemption and has no obligations to the order of creation. Nor may the layman so seek the world as though he had already found God if he remains true to it. Either case would imply that the order of creation would be identified simply with the order of redemption (and so sin, for example, would be problematic). A division in the tasks of religious and layman follows upon the fact that the task of the church is divided and articulated in its functions. The Spirit can infuse each partial function without prejudice to the uniqueness of the whole.

The church does not order every phase of life. The church cannot decide one's vocation, one's summons from God in a sense. It cannot say whether a man should become a doctor or a television producer. For this is an individual matter. Yet such a decision can mean individual salvation or damnation and imply a great deal of good or evil for the world. This expresses in germ what the world's salvation implies. There is no such thing as existing in a chemically pure "world." The true Christian attitude is not just an honest, factual approach. Rather, this honest approach is the condition for a genuine Christian attitude. The two moments make up the one reality. The Christian cannot exist without being an honest man of the world, but just being that does not guarantee being a Christian. Both must complement one another.

For the order of redemption includes the order of creation as an essential inner moment. Creation must be so conceived that each thing is meaningful for everything and everything meaningful for each. Christianity knows no creations, just creation. The interdependence of everything, from highest to lowest and back again, is essential, so that the lower order exist for the sake of the higher and all for the sake of the highest, the mystery of God. So the closer man comes to God, the more he really becomes man. The more the life of God lives in man, the more independent that man becomes. Creation is not like the morning fog that vanishes when the sun grows warm, so that the more man might know the Absolute the holier he would become. We may be tempted to think this way, but this is a result of original sin and is un-Christian in the extreme. We tend to overlook the fact that conditioned being is the condition of unconditioned love, so that it has a value which makes it more than just a forerunner announcing something to come. We must learn to value creation anthropologically.

APPENDIX TO CHAPTER SIX

1. See *Lexikon für Theologie und Kirche,* vol. 10, col. 888.

2. See *Theological Investigations,* vol. II, p. 242.

3. Gilbert Ryle, *The Concept of Mind,* New York, 1949, p. 192. Ryle is a good example of contemporary philosophers of the linguistic analysis school who, believing they are forced to reject the concept of the supernatural as involving a false dualism, nevertheless admit the evidence discovered upon analysis and attempt to explain it either in terms of higher order predication or think of "mind" as a sort of spiritual matter no different really from other matter. Various physical theories can be involved. What is significant is that their reasoning processes quite often resemble those of transcendental philosophers, often without either side being quite aware of the fact.

4. *Theological Investigations,* vol. II, p. 249.

5. See *Schriften,* vol. V, p. 146.

6. Here the mystery of the temporal moment in the history of a temporal being receives emphasis. In order to be able to be a moment in history, it must itself be "something," must have a "nature" in the widest sense. Precisely this moment may not exist for itself but must point away from itself in transcendence, coming to itself when it enters into the greater whole of the mystery. This is the mystery of the dialectic of individual historical moments which is one in the mystery of the dialectic of the whole.

7. See *The Church and the Sacraments,* p. 12.

8. "We can and must go on to add positively: what Genesis says is positively open to a revealed doctrine concerning monogenism arrived at elsewhere and by other means and guaranteed by the magisterium; and in this sense it is now possible to say that monogenism belongs to the contents of Gen. 2." *Theological Investigations,* vol. I, pp. 247, 248.

9. Rahner explains that in any case the narrative of a single

ancestor is a declaration about the original, divinely willed unity of mankind and its history. For this follows from all that has been said in the narrative. Rahner says that similar arguments can be given for *Wisdom* 10, 1 and *Acts* 17, 24–26. Rahner's scriptural argument takes the following form: scripture knows of a common situation of salvation and damnation only in so far as men are of one stock. Only an original member of a community could establish a situation of damnation for the whole membership, though a later member could redeem. The historical origin of the situation of damnation at the beginning can only come from one individual. So monogenism in scripture is not something attested marginally by this or that brief text, but is closely identified with the scriptural conception of salvation history.

10. See *Theological Investigations,* vol. I, p. 296.

11. *Sendung und Gnade,* p. 298.

12. The capital catastrophe of hell, for example, lies in the fact that the damned has lost the God of the beatific vision and yet by an energy and dynamism planted in his very being is forever being urged toward this God.

13. *Romans* 5, 12 is an important text in Rahner's doctrine of penance. He uses it in his development of both the doctrine of original and of personal sin. See Rahner's *De Paenitentia,* Innsbruck, 1960 (mimeographed fourth edition), vol. II, for his most complete exposition on the question. The first volume is an invaluable historical-dogmatic investigation of the development of the doctrine of penance and contains valuable bibliographical material.

14. For further explanation consult J. B. Metz, "Konkupiszenz," *Handbuch theologischer Grundbegriffe,* vol. I, Munich, 1962, pp. 843–851; Bernhard Stoeckle, "Erbsündliche Begierlichkeit," *Münchner Theologische Zeitschrift,* 13 (1963), pp. 225–242; K. Rahner, "Gerecht und Sünder Zugleich," R. Kösters, "Luthers These 'Gerecht und Sünder Zugleich,'" *Catholica,* 18 (1964), pp. 48–77; 193–217. Most important for concupiscence is Rahner's "Some Implications of the Scholastic Concept of Uncreated Grace," and "The Theological Concept of Concupiscentia" in *Theological Investigations,* vol. I, pp. 319 ff.

15. Paul Schoonenberg, S.J., *Original Sin,* tr. by J. Donceel S.J., Notre Dame, 1965, esp. pp. 150–177.

16. Rahner's argumentation follows his transcendental deduction of the conditions of knowing and willing wherein the subject brings to completion *a reditio completa in seipsum,* and Rahner stresses this here because the subject otherwise would only suffer a free decision passively and not really place it.

17. The dualism of person and nature is rooted in man's limitedness (as essence and existence, matter and form). In reality, the whole of nature given prior to the exercise of freedom offers resistance to the person's free and total disposition of himself, so that the boundary between person and nature stands vertically, as it were, to the horizontal line which divides spirituality and sensibility in man: for example, the condition which makes a *passio* possible in both senses of the word.

18. For Rahner's explanation of *opus operatum* consult the next chapter. What is important here is that Rahner stresses that the sacrament does not work automatically or magically. Its effectiveness (*in actu secundo*) is measured and limited by the disposition of the penitent. And this means that where such disposition does not grow by means of frequent reception, no practical meaning can attach to it, even when viewed from the point of a moral theological minimalism and is not received sacrilegiously. On the other hand, Rahner notes, the fact that there does not seem to be any growth is no reason for stopping reception of the sacrament (this phraseology is bad because it hides the involvement of the penitent) and that would not accomplish anything.

In addition to the two-volume Innsbruck codex, helpful for obtaining greater insight into the material discussed in this chapter, are Rahner-Metz, *Handbuch der Pastoraltheologie,* vol. II, Freiburg, 1966, and the article "Busssakrament" in *Lexikon für Theologie und Kirche,* vol. 2, cols. 826–836. See also "Unbefangenheit und Anspruch," *Stimmen der Zeit,* 178 (August 1966), p. 97. For freedom see Rahner's article, "Theologie der Freiheit," *Schriften,* vol. VI, pp. 215–237.

CHAPTER SEVEN

THE CHURCH OF CHRIST

The church is not an institution humanly established to satisfy a demand for religion. Men did not found the church in the same way they set up educational, political, and economic institutions. God willed salvation history and a moment of it became the church. God's design for the Incarnation includes within itself the founding of the church. In the second place, the church is an eschatological structure; it is the church of the last days, the final and irrevocable plan of man's salvation. So God does not merely appropriate the church to Himself like other works of which He is the transcendent cause. This chapter takes a closer look at the question of the church as seen in Rahner's ecclesiology.

PLAN OF CHAPTER

We first discuss the church in its basic structure as the total sacrament of Christ. This is followed by a consideration of the presence of the truth of Christ in scripture and tradition. We are then taken up with a discussion of Rahner's theory on the articulation of the mystery of the church as total sacrament and the realization of this in individual sacraments, with particular attention given to the eucharist. The chapter concludes with Rahner's eschatology and extremely influential theology of death.

224

I. BASIC STRUCTURE OF THE CHURCH AS THE TOTAL SACRAMENT OF CHRIST

God does not appropriate the church as He does His other works, and this for two reasons. First, the church proceeds from God's will (understood as determinate action and not "faculty") which is absolute. It is prior to man's action and yet includes his free action within itself. God wills all creation absolutely, but this does not necessarily include the creature's free activity but precedes it. However, when something comes into being which, though still a free act, is so predefined by God that He reveals his will and effects it in a miraculous way, we have what is a qualitatively preferential will of God. And we find this at special points within saving history. Further, this historical action of God attains its climax in Christ and the church. The objective realizations of divine action exclude the possibility of rejection in the case of Christ and the church. For they exist as the definitive presence of God's grace in the world. In short, God appropriates to Himself the founding of the church in a unique fashion, because it is the work of His formal predefinition which is within the context of saving history and has an eschatological character.

Rahner argues that the apostolic church, then, was subject to divine intervention in a qualitatively unique way. But the church should not be discussed in purely "actualist" terms, as though it were nothing more than the ever recurring event of faith in history. The church has in addition a divinely willed institutional character and as such is historically palpable throughout history. This implies that it began to exist at a given point and then continues in existence in such a way that the qualities found in the beginning continue as the determining qualities or properties of its lasting existence. What comes later rests on what came earlier.[1] This point in Rahner's ecclesiology will require some clarification.

The church is the lasting presence of Christ in the world. It is the continuation and extension of the primal sacramental word of grace which is Christ in the world effecting what is expressed by being expressed symbolically. Simply in being the enduring presence of Christ the church is the total, fundamental sacrament, the wellspring of all the other sacraments. From Christ the church has an intrinsically sacramental structure. The church is historically visible in space and time through its character as people of God and its juridical and social organization of this people. The lasting presence of Christ in this church is the real symbol of the fact that God identifies Himself with the world in Christ. And because the church is the lasting sign of this triumphant grace of God, this sign can never lose its meaning. As an historical entity, the church is the real symbol which always effects what it signifies.

In explaining this fundamental nature of the church, Rahner sketches a comparison. He points out that the existence of a political association having a common territory, civilization, and purpose constitutes a *state*. It is the common cultural life and historical unity of the people which are the basis of the state. And the state exists logically because the necessary preconditions already are given. A similar situation obtains regarding the church. Christ became a member of the human race. This race has a unity because of the monogenetic origin of all men. Since Christ is man, all mankind has been divinized and by means of grace participates in an immediate presence to God. So Christ's membership in the one human race means that mankind as a whole is called to supernatural life.[2]

The association of men summoned to redemption presupposes the consecration of the whole of mankind in the Incarnation and redemption. So as a social and juridical organization of the people of God the church is not at all some sort of "spiritual-welfare organization." Rather, it is the abiding presence of Christ and the life He brings, the historically real and eschatologically triumphant grace of

God. This favorite theme of Rahner means that the human race is already accepted in Christ for salvation. In emphasizing that Christ is the historical presence of God's mercy, Rahner intends that God's grace is established as present as a real part of the world and its history.

This grace of God is given in Christ and promised to the individual in so far as he belongs to the *people of God.* The promise and presence of this grace has a thoroughly public character. Just as the history of a state is not the sum total of individual private lives of the citizens, so is the same thing true of salvation history. Christ belongs, as we saw in Chapter Three, to public saving history. In such a dimension of belonging to the πόλις [3] of salvation, Christ is the primal sacramental word of God. The church is the historical extension of this primal sacramental word.

So Rahner understands the church as *the* continuing presence of God's salvific will in the world.[4] Since the church exists in this way, it is the total sacrament of Christ, having an intrinsically sacramental structure received from Christ. The church signifies a real incarnation of the truth of Christ in history. The formal teaching authority and the assistance of the Spirit promised the church make up the guarantee that its teaching belongs to the sign which signifies what the church really is. We shall have occasion shortly to examine Rahner's understanding of the presence of this truth of Christ in the church in scripture and tradition.

Seen as united to Christ, the church is the lasting promulgation of His presence. Seen in relation to individual sacraments, the church is the total or fundamental sacrament. Actual expression of the church takes place in historically conditioned ways manifesting themselves with greater or less intensity. This is particularly true of any community dependent on the higher-order personality—in this case the spiritual dimension of man. Any such community can only be recognized as an institution by means of derivative operations which of themselves do not express the reality of the church. Still, the church must function continually; for any institution or society which renounces its purpose ceases to exist.

II. PRESENCE OF CHRIST'S TRUTH

Just as the act of being born is qualitatively different from the act of carrying on life, so the beginning of the church is qualitatively different from its extension in time. This does not mean that whatever happens after this beginning involves the purely human. Yet the beginning period, the apostolic church, was the work of God in an eminent sense: *Deum habet auctorem.* As we saw in Chapter Two, the apostolic church is the permanent foundation and norm of all later development. On the day of Pentecost the church received its basic legal structure and was infused with the Holy Spirit. Yet it was not wholly complete. The church whose mission it was to conserve and interpret revelation did not exist as such; for there was public revelation after Pentecost. Revelation did end, however, with the death of the last apostle. But all the public revelation received its objective form in the period of the apostolic church.

A. Presence of Christ's Revelation: Tradition

If this church is the presence of Christ in the world, then salvation is offered to every man who enters into communion with this presence. But a relationship of communion may enjoy different degrees of intensity. Still, if any individual is to attain salvation, it can never be wholly absent. This means that a denial of the ecclesiastical character of grace would imply that grace has no relation to the Incarnation and to history. And this would be to say that a redemption exists apart from the grace of Christ. How is the individual to find this grace of Christ in the period following the Incarnation and redemption? Where is the truth of Christ preserved?

Christ's revealed truth made complete in the apostolic church is made incarnate for the rest of time in tradition and scripture. It is incarnate in tradition in the teaching of the church when it preaches Christ's precepts. This tradition is the effective presence of revelation. It could not be replaced without the church's losing its reality. All tradition involves an amalgam of human and divine tradition, and every moment on the evolution of dogma and the history of theology confirms this fact. Every actual tradition demands a criterion which can be called *traditio divina* and what can pass for *traditio humana.*

Tradition means handing down; something is passed on from generation to generation. Originally, Christianity is God's truth announced to man in public revelation. But this obviously is not what happens in dogmatic principles or in catechisms. It takes place in *events.* Tradition is not abstract truth grasped in a clear and distinct idea, but is primarily *the* event in which God in His grace acts upon us. The incarnation of truth which stems from the Incarnation of the Word has to filter down to us through a *parados,* a *traditio,* a handing down. The source wells up from the Last Supper (in conjunction with Christ's death and resurrection) and is continually re-presented in the eucharist. And this is the fundamental tradition wherein occurs the unique event of salvation. This implies there must exist a tradition of the *word* as a constitutive element of saving reality.

The whole of tradition then becomes the norm of any theological utterance, since any one moment of tradition cannot assume its total meaning except in relation to the whole. The diversity of tradition, too, Rahner says, is not understood properly until it is studied in the light of the whole tradition. The basic unity of theological thinking is not a specific moment of revelation, but rather another way of stating that no single material statement of faith can be allowed a normative function. Instead, each statement of faith is properly understood only in the context of all other statements. Originally, the question of handing on the actions of Christ was oral, but as such was also eschatological tradition. What was done in the apostolic church became nevertheless the abiding norm for all later times.

Rahner ties this point together by observing that a proper understanding of the role of scripture implies that the postulate of a materially rich tradition would be of no practical worth as an independent material source of faith.[5] But this is not to say that consciousness of the faith is always an authentic norm for interpreting scripture. Tradition is that living understanding of the church itself. And the teaching office is not a source of the content of faith (since it receives no new revelation), but it is the deposit of the faith which it must shelter and interpret. Where, then, is the faith of the apostolic church manifest today? It is preserved in scripture.

B. Scripture

Scripture is pure *traditio divina*. So it can function as at least one criterion for deciding within the general tradition about the necessary truths of faith. This does not exclude the fact that such a process of decision making takes a long time and is itself historical. Rahner feels that here, too, it is important to place this question in context. We recall that because the total revelation of God is given in Christ, saving history has already entered upon its final phase. In this sense, all revelation is closed and definitive. What happens after the time of Christ must take place in a confrontation with temporal extension and historical "material." It must display the character of an *anamnesis*, a conscious, existential reference to its origin (which already includes the end). The necessary condition for this is that the origin exist eschatologically. And it implies a conceptual expression of the faith of the apostolic church as a normative beginning. This is precisely what we have in scripture. So Rahner approaches even the matter of scripture and tradition from the viewpoint of the transcendental method, asking what conditions are needed for their very possibility.

1. AS THE WORD OF GOD: INSPIRATION

Scripture became the work of God through inspiration.[6] Since the apostolic church confessed itself as a true follower of the Old Testament and considered the history of the Old Testament its own prehistory, the Hebrew scriptures are a moment of the apostolic church. And this means that the Old Testament belongs to the norm of the later church also. Because it is an expression of the beginning of the faith of the early church, scripture participates in the historical and evolutionary character of the early church. This is already apparent in scripture. Once the origin has been established as the completion of the apostolic church, there can be no other beginnings. But it also belongs to this origin that it cannot be the end. Scripture is not the end of theology nor of the development of the faith.

Rahner applies his hermeneutics to the question of inspiration. By the fact that God creates the apostolic church with a formal predefinition, God wills scripture in such a way that He by His inspiration is the author. God creates the essential preconditions of the church. For example, the Old Testament is the authentic crystallization of these preconditions as history, and so God inspires the Old Testament also. No one but God can become an author by making someone else write. For only God can direct man's free activity in such a way that his freedom is not diminished but actually constituted and made most itself. Human authorship has an obediential potency for divine action, so that God can make it His own work and still not diminish the human act but rather perfect it. This thought is a good example of Rahner's use of the analogy of the faith. Just as the free and intellectual self-possession which constitutes man as "nature" has an obediential potency for achieving its ultimate perfection in the hypostatic union, so man's ability to be an author is capable of being assumed by God and perfected.

To solve the problem of explaining inspiration in this way, Rahner says that it is not enough to appeal to God's transcendent causality and His concursus with the operations of the world. True, there is a case in inspiration of a double cause of a single act (since two causes are operative though on different levels), but God's action as literary cause of scripture puts God on the level of categorial and not transcendental causality. This means that not only the thing caused but also the causal operation itself must fall within the dimension of created reality. God's transcendental causality of scripture would be insufficient to make Him a real author. His action in inspiration, therefore, must be understood in the same way that we are to understand the Incarnation. Both the inspiration of scripture and the Incarnation represent miraculous insertions of God into saving history, and both have (precisely as divine action and not just as effect) a definite place in space and time.[7] So we see that Rahner is able to reduce even the problem of the inspiration of scripture to theological anthropology as Christology.

As noted, the apostolic church in its initial stages had only an oral *paradosis*. But God made the bible a constitutive element of this apostolic church. Following the transcendental method, Rahner says that the essentially constitutive elements of the apostolic church must necessarily include everything that belongs to the church as such. So by the fact that God willed the church with a predefinition, He willed scripture as a necessary condition. And the bible belongs to these constitutive elements as the qualitatively unique work of God and permanent "canonical" origin of the later church. In as much as the early church crystallized its belief in writing, it thereby formed scripture. And God is the real author if He effectively sees to it that the human author conceives the judgment about what is to be written, decides to write that down, and then writes it—no matter how more exactly we consider the execution of this divine predefinition. Both God and the human author do not produce the same effect in the same respect. God wills to become an author because the kind of church He wills to establish demands this as a precondition. And God can effect this will only by causing man to write. God appears as author only during the formative period of the church, and once the church is established, His authorship is completed.

2. AS BOOK OF THE CHURCH

Since scripture is one of the constitutive elements of the normative apostolic church, it follows that scripture is *the* book of the church. It can only be recognized, therefore, by the church itself. God wills a community of salvation which makes itself objective in a book and in later times continually rediscovers itself in this book. In remembering that scripture is God's word to us, we should not overlook the fact that it is also the original representation of the belief of the early church. In and through this belief the early church realized itself. Thus the scriptures are in a sense a distilled form of the tradition of the early church. So the infallibility of the teaching office of the later church is by definition the unerring interpretation of this scripture, because it includes by definition a relationship to the tradition of the early church.

3. AS EVER NEW TRUTH:
RELATION BETWEEN SCRIPTURE AND TRADITION

The relation between scripture and tradition is another fundamental question. We have already seen part of Rahner's answer. For asking how an individual as well as the church knows about divine revelation we always ask fundamental questions. And when we ask where is the faith of the apostolic church and say it is manifest for us only in scripture, we ask implicitly about the tradition, the handing on of this manifestation of the faith of the early church. Scripture is the word of the living church carried by a living tradition. On the one hand, scripture is the tradition of the saving event of Christ as received in the church and made objective.[8] Rahner notes that oral tradition is not only preserved in scripture but also witnesses to the canon of scripture as such. But he goes on to ask whether oral tradition has other material contents which are not witnessed in scripture. He says that if we simply identify tradition with the teaching office, the formal authority of tradition cannot be removed in favor of scripture. For even scripture has to be witnessed to by authority.

In the second place, a Catholic interpretation sees that a true development of doctrine involves a real development of the faith. Church dogma and the immediate word of scripture, however, cannot be identical—even on the assumption that all church dogma rests on scripture. Thirdly, in so far as tradition witnesses to a canon of scripture, tradition (at least under this viewpoint) is for the Catholic a constitutive material source and norm of faith. Hence the question about the relation between scripture and tradition as far as recent history is concerned is whether in comparison with tradition scripture is materially insufficient, or whether one can affirm the sufficiency of scripture without violating the Catholic principle of tradition.

After asking the question in this way, Rahner says that we first have to admit that there is no clear tradition on which to build an answer. In other words, he says, "A clearly thought-out, generally accepted answer to this question cannot be found in the tradition of ecclesiastical theology, but there are different opinions and concepts

being represented right up to the present day." [9] Part of
the reason for this is that the question of the development
of dogma did not become a real problem for the church
prior to the end of the 19th century. And where this
problem was not recognized, we cannot expect to find
materials for solving the scripture versus tradition problem. There were theologians in the Middle Ages who
argued for the necessity of tradition independent of scripture, but these theologians had no idea what a tremendous
possibility for development even one truth of scripture was
to have. Rahner says further that an appeal to oral tradition to explain why this or that proposition of faith could
be an apostolic divine revelation does not lead more readily to a solution than when the other "side" tries to found
this or that contemporary teaching on scripture. We can
admit, however, that theologians have always argued for
the supreme importance of scripture within the entire belief of the church. Even the Council of Trent said nothing
more than that *both* scripture *and* tradition exist as norms
of ecclesiastical faith and in *this* respect (not in every
respect) are to be handled with equal reverence. Trent
said nothing about the relationship of scripture to tradition
or vice versa.[10] It left this question open. After the Council
of Trent, theologians tended to adopt an anti-Protestant
position, opting for the existence of truths independent of
inspiration and the canon of scripture. Rahner thinks that
we really should not expect an answer to this problem in
the near future. And in this respect Rahner is somewhat
conservative. He himself holds, however, that it is possible
to formulate a completely Catholic *sola scriptura* principle, provided by "Catholic" we understand the necessary
authoritative witness and interpretation of scripture by the
church and its teaching authority. He further remarks that
one should not explain a *sola scriptura* principle unhistori-
cally in the sense of a petrified prohibition on a living
development of the faith of the church.

In weighing this question it is important to remember
that no material theological source from the first three

centuries beyond the content of scripture exists. And this means that when we now confess that something is not found explicitly in scripture, we cannot demonstrate that this truth was believed explicitly in the first two or three centuries of church history. In other words, we must fall back in this case on a process of explication the more precise nature of which we explained in Chapter Two, and admit a progressive realization of truths found in scripture. Rahner adds by way of conclusion that an appeal to tradition does not facilitate the theologians' work of historical demonstration nor make it any easier than a properly interpreted *sola scriptura* principle. There is yet a further argument adumbrated by Rahner for the sufficiency of scripture. If we are to make sense of the statement that the scripture is the faith of the apostolic church made objective, scripture must be sufficient; for we cannot imagine the apostolic church lacking in the fullness of faith. If God really did work the miracle of inspiration, then scripture must be inspired to give witness to the faith of the apostolic church for all later generations. Rahner's argument builds on the *unity* of the object of faith, its inner consistency of manifold divinely revealed truths, which makes it at least improbable and ultimately unthinkable to assume two materially different sources of faith, one scripture and the other tradition. Both belong on the basis of their origin much closer together than the somewhat primitive and comfortable "two-channel theory" of traditional faith.

C. Articulation of the Mystery of the Church

The church viewed in its relation to the sacraments is the total sacrament. It is the presence of Christ's grace, and its sacramental structure is founded on the unity of grace and its historically manifest embodiment. Any event which transmits grace has a quasi-sacramental structure, sharing in the character of Christ as both human and divine. When the church in its public capacity as source of grace encounters an individual in its most proper function, we have a *sacrament* in the fullest sense of the word. The individual sacraments should be seen as such functions. Rahner's contributions to sacramental theology focus around a development of the theory that the church attains its highest actualization in the sacraments. For Christian saving reality is necessarily sacramental.

To the internal constitutive elements of the presence of a saving event the word belongs as a sign. The word belongs to the basic structure of sacramental reality, so that a "sacramental" function attaches to the word precisely when it first appears. If Christianity is not primarily sharing truths but sharing the reality of Christ, and if the originality of this Word belongs to the church as a necessary element, then the word is in its origin *sacramental,* the real symbol wherein God's saving will is made present for us.

1. RELATION OF WORD AND CHURCH

Rahner says that as soon as we inquire what God's word in the church is, how God really utters it, and what conditions are presupposed in speaker and hearer, we see an amazing parallelism with what is said regarding the sacraments in general. Word and sacrament are so similar that we have to ask about their foundation in order to gain a theological understanding of them. In addition, Rahner indicates how both word and sacrament constitute the church. More precisely, the power of preaching the word of God and the power of performing the sacraments are the basic powers of the church. Rahner's method permits him to say that these two powers cannot merely stand next to one another without an internal relatedness, since they must constitute the one church as the one total sacrament of Christ.

He says that we are used to speaking of the *word* as a formal part of the sacramental sign. If we really want to avoid being superficial, we cannot interpret this sacramental word like any other word. It must be spoken with God's authority because it is His word. It effects what it signifies and makes present what it proclaims. The word spoken by the church retains this character of God's word, since it is in the church as God's saving action and not just a forensic pronouncement of Christ's justice nor as a proclamation of God's future deeds. This word presupposes man's personal cooperation as an inner moment of the utterance. In so far as a gift of grace can be qualified as an "inspiration" or an "illumination," it is already by definition a *word*. If not, it would be an unthematic, transcendental intuition of God's grace-giving action. And if this alone were enough for salvation, man could always perform his salvation at the unreflexive pole of his nature, while the dimension of the categorial world would remain divorced from salvation history. Consequently, man would not be approached by God in every one of his existential dimensions. And secondly, man would know about his state of grace and already have the blessed vision, since to reflect adequately on one's own inner divinization is by definition *visio beatifica*. Thirdly, man's social dimension would be ignored by grace. All these factors imply that the proclaimed word, in so far as it is carried by the historical action of God, is an inner moment of the saving action of the community (the church as total sacrament) and so belongs to the necessary inner moments of God's saving history.

The external word explains the internal word, bringing the internal to reflex, categorial expression and so persuading man to adopt an attitude to the internal word. Thus man is led by grace into a communal dimension where the word is made present in society (and it is here that stress on Christian social awareness needs to be placed). The word makes possible the spread of grace into the historical world.

The inner word as the light of faith and divine connaturality infuses man with the power to listen to the word which comes from outside. Both moments mutually condition the normal performance of the personal opening of self to God. The good news heard in faith becomes not just an assent to propositions but a reception of that reality which the propositions relate. So the word effects what it signifies, making present the grace of God. But the effectiveness of this word has an essential variability. We can see this most clearly in the church. For everyone admits that not every word of the church binds in faith. This same quality is true of the word that makes present what it proclaims.[11] Rahner concludes that both word and sacramental gesture participate in the one character of the sacrament as a real symbol. So both have the character of the word. Every gesture has a word character. Indeed, some sacraments have only words; for example, in penance and matrimony the words alone constitute the sacramental sign.[12]

2. EFFECTIVENESS EX OPERE OPERATO

The effectiveness of the sacraments *ex opere operato* Rahner explains on the basis of this understanding of the word. He says that two points taken together make up the concept of *ex opere operatum:* "Word as the most complete actualisation of the church in its absolute engagement and word penetrating the determinate saving situation of man." [13] We know that the world is a redeemed world. And we know that Christ founded the sacraments because He founded the church. The sacraments are moments in the foundation. So *opus operatum* cannot be limited by the fact that a decree states in formal, juridical fashion that such a process exists and is effective without the cooperation of the one in whom the process evolves. *Opus operatum* does describe the effectiveness of the sacraments, but does not imply any magical connotation.

Rahner says that we must come to see *opus operatum* as the last step in the process of the actualization of the church, the true act of self-realization. We will then see how such an act participates in the very nature of the church when expressed as a sign of God's promise of Himself. This means we have a complete engagement of the personal individual in an act that is critical for his salvation; and God's word of mercy is so promised for such an act that the symbol effects what it signifies. In this process, though the dialogue is conditioned by the human partner, we have what must be called *opus operatum.* God's promise is infallible; only the human actor can spoil the dialogue. *Ex opere operatum,* then, means for Rahner the eschatologically unconditioned word of God to man made effective in the self-performance of the church as the total sacrament. Rahner stresses that where the effectiveness of the word is concerned, the engagement must be absolute when the salvation of the individual is intended.

If we ask what such basic self-performances of the church come into question, we see where individual sacraments have their place. Critical moments in the lifetime of the individual include matters of initiation and reconciliation, intercommunication and propagation, actualization of the church, and preparation for eternal life.

3. ARTICULATION OF THE MYSTERY OF THE CHURCH IN INDIVIDUAL SACRAMENTS

A community having an organized structure only becomes real for an outsider when he enters as a member. A society must enroll non-members. Initiation into the church is a sacramental act, the rite of entrance. Full admission involves baptism and confirmation. Baptism clearly establishes the individual's relation to Christ and the people of God; it symbolizes God's grace as grace of dying with Christ, a grace of the cross and of the downfall of the world. All of this is expressed in baptism as a descent into death with Christ. At the same time, the grace of Christ is the grace of the Incarnation, a grace of accepting the world for its transformation. This is the symbolized grace of confirmation, the sacrament of sending the Christian out into the world to transform it.

Man's social and sexual nature has a decisive meaning for the community, particularly as related to marriage. Marriage is critical for the church and so is an essential moment in the life of the ecclesiastical body. Marriage is a real sign of the love between Christ and church. Such a sign cannot be an empty symbol in the new covenant. So the church finds itself in this sign and achieves self-realization. For the presence (in the sign) of grace in the sacrament is simply the actualization of the church as total sacrament. And the church only attains its own supreme actualization when grace is realized in the individual.

God's self-communication and sacramental activity are not the same thing. The sacraments are only one of the possible kinds of God's saving action. In others such as prayer or whatever else an individual does privately to which God attaches His grace, the prayer, for example, can be intrinsically fragile, can be vitiated of itself. In the case of a sacrament, matrimony for example, the sign is a sign of God's eternal covenant with man, and as such can never lose its quality of being an expression of God's response to man. From the time of Christ, man cannot prevent this word from being addressed to him.

III. THE CENTRAL SACRAMENT OF THE CHURCH: THE EUCHARIST

The celebration of the eucharist is the absolutely central event of the church. Rahner likes to consider the sacraments from the point of view of individual realizations of the total sacrament that is the church. And from this viewpoint the eucharist is absolutely central. He notes, however, that even today the fact needs to be stressed that the Mass should not be viewed by the faithful merely as the production of Christ's real presence for the purpose of communion. The Mass is so much the sacrifice of the church that even a priest's private Mass is always the sacrifice of the church and as far as possible must always appear as such.

A. The Word and the Eucharist

The church realizes itself as a community of salvation in the sacrifice and meal of the eucharist. The eucharist is the perfect word of the church, not only making present the grace of Christ but also the very source of this grace. It is the event toward which the other words of the church point. Rahner reminds us that the human word is of longer duration than its physical vibrations and phonetic tone. A word of love, a promise, a threat (what J. L. Austin called "performatives"), for example, continue to exist long after acoustical expression vanishes. In this sense, the word of the eucharistic symbol remains, constituting the real presence under the symbol of bread and wine. The word of the altar sacrament, the presence of the Lord, is then carried by the faith of the people of God who hear this word and give it reality, that of the powerful lasting word. This is not a matter of the faith of the individual as individual.

The effective word of the eucharistic liturgy, Rahner says, is preaching the original kerygma of the death of Christ. And all other preaching in the church somehow participates in this. For where the word attains its supreme effectiveness as the incarnate and eschatological word of God and as the absolute self-expression of the church as a whole, there we have the eucharist.

Participation in the physical body of Christ by reception of the eucharist imparts the grace of Christ to us. For this partaking of the one bread is a real symbol of the renewed and personally ratified participation and incorporation in the body of Christ that is the church. Christ is present in the eucharist as a bond of unity, as a real foundation for the covenant between God and man. So because Christ really offers Himself as sacrifice for the church and of the church in a visible, tangible form, the church exists. For the church is most manifest in this its most intensive realization, the celebration of the eucharist. The words of the anamnesis make present what they signify. And all other words of the church are only a preparation for this event, an exposition and a defense of this presence in which the incarnate Word of God becomes physically present to our individual space and time. Each celebration of the eucharist involves the entire church. Only that individual who is prepared to hand himself over to the whole saving action of the church happening in the eucharist shares in the grace of this sacrament.

B. The Liturgy

Rahner argues that cult sacrifice and sacrament are *"in recto"* the dimension of the symbol. They are the sign of what is signified and not the thing itself. They do contain what they signify: Christ and covenant. But what they signify is presented not simply under the one sign. The eucharist is the unique sacrament. The other sacraments signify the same grace. Rahner warns that "in spite of all the romantic overemphasis which occurs here and there in the liturgical movement (which praises the Mass and indicates its central position in history), the Mass never was so absolutely the midpoint of all Christian existence that one would have to let everything begin with it and refer everything back to it." [14] No Christian ever argues for just one-way streets.

There is a real need, however, to encourage more personal participation in the liturgy. Of course, mere cultic performance in a liturgical participation through recitation, song, and so forth, is not enough to realize that inner condition required for the mystery of Christ in the Mass. This must be realized in man's heart. So all liturgical reform and education must be ordered to producing that faith, hope, and love of God in the depths of the person. Simply to order the external procedure is not enough. But Rahner admits that there is need for even greater effort within the liturgical reformation in order that it reach the most suitable form wherein the spirit of the Christianity of the heart is achieved in the most suitable fashion.

Rahner has some liturgical advice for his fellow clergy, but it is just as valuable for the laity as participants in the priesthood of Christ. Rahner says that at Mass we lend Christ hand and voice in order that He bring through us the sacrifice of the new covenant to the Father. We cannot be His liturgists in any other way than through the fact that we enter into the sacrificial attitude of Christ upon whom all the value of the liturgy depends. We must have an inner disposition of abandonment and readiness to suffer in order that we be not simply external participants. In receiving His body and blood sacramentally we proclaim the death of the Word.[15]

Liturgy has a special significance, because the church is the worshipping community. It is the one place where the explicit memory and hope of God's saving acts finds preservation and celebration. This is the only conceivable reason for its existence in the world. Liturgy is an essential moment of the visible expression of the church. To be sure, the forms of liturgical-sacramental life need to change continually in order to be more faithful sources of the faith. The liturgy must be clearly relevant to all aspects of life and wholly accessible to modern man.

IV. ESCHATOLOGY

The church is the presence of Christ's grace unto the end of time. Eschatology must be ordered necessarily within ecclesiology. Rahner argues that the existential theology of a possible revelation of God in history has been replaced by a theological eschatology. The theology of revelation has only a retrospective significance (an anamnesis) and no longer any prospective tendency. Expectation of the revelation of God in history has been superseded by expectation of that revelation of God which will end history. Rahner feels that a proper, unified approach to understanding eschatology as a whole still needs to be developed. Christian eschatology is not an anticipatory report of what is to happen eventually, a kind of false apocalyptic. Rather, it is a necessary preview for man's spiritual free decision. It is based on salvation history (as the aetiological ground of knowing) on which the final end of man helps illuminate his ultimate decision regarding the unknown. The Christian must accept his present as a moment in the realization of the possibility of his future salvation.

Regarding the contents of eschatological propositions Rahner says that we need to develop first the inner historical form of time from a real beginning to a real definitive end. Secondly, the character of each unique event within salvation history must be illuminated. Thirdly, the themes of death and time must be emphasized. Fourthly, it must also be emphasized that in the Incarnation the end has already come. And finally, the question of the natural convergence of man and cosmos needs to be rethought. Rahner's eschatology therefore involves his customary themes considered under the light of man's destiny.

Rahner says that particular attention should be given to the dialectic of statements of individual and universal *eschata* which deal with human nature and its completion. These must include all of man's existential dimensions and should not simply be compared one with another, although this is what usually happens in eschatology. Matters such as the beatification of the soul, the resurrection of the body, the last judgment are usually handled in isolation. Neither individual nor universal eschatology should be overlooked. For man is a union of body and soul and this fact may never be overlooked.

Rahner has addressed himself specifically to the problem of developing theological principles for the hermeneutics of eschatological statements. He recognizes the special problems of this area. Interpreting scripture, for example, about eschatological questions is quite different from the problems of ordinary hermeneutics. Rahner compares the state of affairs in eschatology with the problems found in philosophy before the rise of epistemology and the metaphysics of knowledge. The advent of theory of knowledge gave philosophy a subjective turn (on the continent). And Rahner feels that an epistemological consideration of the nature and extent of eschatological statements both in theology and in the area of knowledge in general will be beneficial. He says that the entire controversy over "demythologizing" shows that this is a real question. Rahner asks, then, what meaning can eschatological statements have.

The church is the believing community existing in the present as a response to God's summons. As the "primary archive of the consciousness of the church," scripture is the norm of theological activity. Its interpretation is subject to the teaching authority and *sensus fidelium* of the church. So a theologian's task is not just exegesis but involves expressing the traditional faith in a way comprehensible to his own generation. The critical point is reached when the dogmatic theologian asks the exegete to discover not an explicit but an implicit expression of a later dogma of the church in the New Testament.[16]

Rahner argues that there must exist in any understanding of the faith a real eschatology that intends a real future. Christian understanding of God comprehends the possibility of His revealing the future. Still, the question about an *a priori* space of eschatological statements, about a real horizon of understanding, should be asked. This horizon (and its accompanying hermeneutics) is established and limited by two statements which condition one another. (1) Scripture says that God has not revealed the last days of man, and (2) man's nature includes his historicity. An anamnesis and a prognosis belong to man's existential understanding of himself. Man's present is his *being*-pointed-to-the-future. And this is more than what Heidegger intends by man as being-unto-death. Knowledge of the future, in so far as it is yet to be achieved, is an inner moment of man's self-knowledge. (If we recall Rahner's doctrine on freedom, we see an obvious relationship here and gain yet further insight into the tightness of his theological anthropology.)

The content of eschatological knowledge is needed in order to understand the present existent. This self-knowledge is a moment on man's being as personal spirit. For Rahner, the future must exist as unseen and uncontrollable—because only so can it be the space of freedom—and as truly, really ex-sistent, ordered to the hidden future. Rahner says that this leads to a question about the source of these eschatological statements.

The climax of revelation highlights the fact that God revealed His three-personal communication of self in the grace of Christ. Any statement concerning the present condition of Christian existence includes this fact. Man knows his future because he knows both himself and his redemption in Christ through revelation. And what he knows of the *eschata* is not a further communication added on to theological anthropology and Christology, but simply a transposition into an expression about the state of man's destiny. The source of eschatological statements, therefore, is the experience of God's saving action which we have in Christ.

Since such statements comprehend all of man's existential dimensions, we can see how they refer to present Christian existence. "Biblical eschatology must always be read as a statement about the present as revealed which refers to the real future, but not as a statement about an anticipated future already made present. Speaking out of the present into the future is eschatology; speaking out of the future into the present is apocalyptic." [17]

Rahner distinguishes between the mode of an expression and its content. He does not intend to divorce thought from image, because no concept exists without some intuition, without its *conversio ad phantasma*. But when many statements are taken together, the relationship between expressed content and the manner of expression as a single statement can be confused. As a result, it is difficult to say whether one or another expression adequately states what is intended.

Rahner concludes that eschatology does not place salvation and perdition on the same level. The church, for example, can pronounce about the salvation of martyrs and saints because the grace of God is promised invincibly. But the church can say nothing about the damnation of anyone. In the second place, eschatological statements must recognize the same dualism considered by other statements of theological anthropology which speaks of the one man who is both individual and social, both personal spirit and corporeal nature. A proper interpretation of both aspects of the one man would lead to a clearer understanding of what is really meant by *purgatory,* a concept expressing an intermediate condition, a reality which Rahner says must be respected as legitimate.[18]

Rudolf Schnackenburg indicates the real problem most exegetes and biblical scholars would have with Rahner's eschatological principles. Schnackenburg writes,

We are thankful to Karl Rahner for his essay on the theological principles to be used in explaining theological sayings. . . . These principles are prudent and well balanced. The difficulty arises only with their application to the actual sayings of the New Testament.[19]

Unquestionably, it is difficult to move from the level of Rahner's principles to practical biblical exegesis. It is difficult to apply such general principles to specific New Testament pericopes. But one illustration given by Rahner may help clarify their value and real usefulness. He says the New Testament speaks of the parousia of Christ. And Rahner has considered this in his ecclesiology.

A. The Church and the Parousia of Christ

In terms of his eschatological principles Rahner argues
that all we can say about the parousia is that it is the completion of Christ's real history. And this means we can speak
of the "last things" as really yet to come. But what is the
church's relation to the parousia? Rahner answers in a
series of theses.

(1) The church is the community of those summoned
together into community with Jesus Christ in hope and
love and belief in the parousia as still to come. So belief in
a second coming of Christ is not just something the church
teaches but is a vital constitutive element of the community. The church must understand itself in its basic self-
performance as a community of pilgrims still in search of
their true home.

(2) The church has a different relation to the completion of created reality and history (and so for the parousia) from that of everything else, because the church itself
is eschatological.

(a) The church is eschatological in the same sense
that it is the church filled with the Holy Spirit in its
members. The church is not just a religious association.
Instead, it is the body of Christ, since its members are
given grace, and since the possession of the Spirit is essential to the church. This grace of Christ is the real presence
of the future. As a gift it carries man's history of accepting
his future.

(b) This eschatological self-communication of the
three-personal God is not only unsurpassable as a communication but also includes a belief in this grace precisely as
victorious element of the church. As a community the

church continually proclaims this victory. And if such proclamation is an historical constitutive moment on the church, the historical presence of God can never be removed. It is because of this that the church can claim an infallibility.

(c) The hiddenness of grace as that of an already given immortality, and the possession of this eternal life as faith and hope (as separated from a revealed possession), condition one another and in their unity form the unique situation of the eschatological church. Faith and hope are not human attitudes regarding the future but are personal self-performances made possible by God's grace.[20]

(3) The official church participates in the infallibility of the eschatological church. The church could only disappear if its teaching office were to make such use of its supreme power as to oppose the truth to such an extent that Christ's salvific will would be so distorted that following it would lead to error and not to truth. And this would mean God's promise was insincere, an impossibility for God. Rahner stresses that where it is not a question of a definitive and irreversible act of the total church, the supreme leadership does not enjoy the prerogative of indefectability. Thus, in so far as the church is a pilgrim church, most of its acts belong to this phase of pilgrimage and must share in the uncertainty of the journey.

Rahner thinks that an approach of this kind clarifies many problems surrounding infallibility. He observes that according to a Catholic interpretation, an *infallible* definition of pope or council does not necessarily mean that it is opportune from every point of view, that is, that its content as far as the historical situation of the mass of the faithful are concerned is not easily assimilable and so not necessarily obligatory as a whole. A definition—even an infallible one—does not necessarily imply that its real understanding, whatever the clarity and precision of its formulation in a definite historical context, involves an interpretation (factually incongruent with the schemata

and development) which does not participate in the infallibility. So an interpretation might be given a definition
which would make its obligatory acceptance difficult or
perhaps make subjective guilt on the part of some of the
faithful impossible. Often, only a later situation can clarify
earlier situations and statements and make them reflexively understandable.[21]

B. *The Theology of Death*

A cardinal application of Rahner's eschatological principles is found in his theology of death. He stresses the
importance of a proper appreciation of the theological
meaning of death. He belongs to the increasing circle of
thinkers who are aware that in the domain of human
experience death is not just an impersonal problem but a
mystery which engages man's entire being. Heidegger considered the dimension of death as the very situation of
life, constitutive of man's very being.[22] Rahner stresses the
fact that death is an event which engages the entire man,
nature and person. Its theological foundation rests on the
certainty that every man must die. The usual description of
death as a separation of body and soul is wholly inadequate.

By means of man's corporeality his soul is open to the
totality of his world. Hence life does not include the picture of the soul as a kind of windowless monad. And in
death the soul moves into an even greater degree of nearness, a closer relation to the ground of all the unity of the
world. Such a cosmic relationship to the world implies that
the moment of death involves the task of self-completion.
A number of psychological factors as well as the doctrine
of purgatory points up this fact that the soul takes on in
death a self-determination defined more sharply in terms
of its harmony or disharmony with the objective structure
of the world of which the soul is in a sense a co-
determining principle.

Rahner sees death as neither the end of man's being nor

as a simple transition from one kind of existence into another which would have something in common with the previous existence, a kind of incomplete temporality. Death is the beginning of eternity (in so far as it is possible to speak of a beginning of eternity). Death is an interruption, because man's reality is never fully possessed, never rounded off completely. Death is "natural," and even men living in the "last days" will need to undergo some kind of radical change, a real death.

Death should not be thought of as a medical exit coming at the end of a period of life, as a mere biological event. Rather, it is a completely human event. A plant or animal is finished when the process of biological life is complete. It passively undergoes total change. Only man "dies." Death has an active as well as a passive moment. Rahner notes how it participates in the same kind of act that every "passion" of man involves. A favorite example is the case of a man who is struck a blow by another. The man suffers the blow "passively" but because of the tension between person and nature he reacts actively in anger which he may have a hard time controlling. This double aspect of human passion is found most clearly in death. The end of man as a spiritual person involves an active perfecting from within, the result of a life-long effort to take complete possession of self. And at the same time it is an interruption from without, an attack which implies man's most radical physical suffering. Death, then, is simultaneously man's most active and most passive moment. And given man's substantial unity, these two aspects cannot simply be assigned one to body and the other to soul.

Since this double aspect exists, death can never be fully clarified existentially. A question always remains whether the achieved fullness of life is not also just a veiled emptiness of man or whether in death this seeming emptiness is but the appearance of true completeness in a real liberation of the person. Because of the hidden side of death, it can be both expression of and penalty for sin. In this sense it is the most real expression of "mortal sin."

Rahner follows Heidegger in observing that man is a creature made for death. We live our death every day to the extent that we engage our freedom in a repeated effort at launching ourselves in self-disposal. Whereas Heidegger prescinds from the question of life after death, Rahner answers on the basis of scripture affirmatively. Because Christ assumed the "flesh of sin," He underwent death in its active and passive sense. So Christ assumed immortality in death. Christ underwent this "death" as satisfaction for sin. He assumed the expression of sin to satisfy for sin, and He did this in absolute freedom. Hence death has become something wholly other than what it would be for man who had no potency at all for divine life. It is in death's aura of mystery and hiddenness that the death of Christ receives expression. For what was before the *appearance* of sin has now become the *appearance* of that affirmation which overcomes sin. Through the death of Christ the meaning of the world has become life in Christ. Christ's death ratified the supernatural destiny of the world.

The inevitability of death determines life. It is the most visible expression of man's limitedness. By making death present consciously, by facing up to that natural anxiety in the face of death, man can see that death points beyond itself. It is the spring for positing man's real question about himself. And in death man's basic decision regarding himself, the world, and God experiences a finality which man hopes brings his salvation. Man is robbed in death of his power of integrating his world, so his personal life is threatened with emptiness. This is the consequence of original sin. And every decision a man makes throughout his life is essentially a preparation for the final definitive decision when man is both most passive and most active at the moment of death.

Considering death as the decisive moment of life is not a new theme in theology. Certain 19th-century theologians defended the theory of a special illumination at the moment of death. Almost half a century ago Glorieux proposed a theory in which the moment of death became the moment of decisive importance since at that moment there was granted the soul a final option which could determine its fate.[23] The last moments of human life must be human in the fullest sense of the word. And this means, Rahner argues, that the final act has been prepared by the exercise of freedom throughout life. In death, man's personal freedom is engaged wholly as never before. The final act of freedom completes and summarizes the series of human free acts in a choice recapitulating, in a sense, all of life's choices.

Dying with Christ in the sacrament of baptism becomes fully realized at the moment of death. Insofar as a Christian life has become a real configuration of the death of Christ, it becomes personally complete in a true act of dying in the Lord. Rahner says that before a complete theology of death can be developed, we must have answers to such questions as the relation between human and animal death, the question of how the "separated" soul is related to the material cosmos before the resurrection, the relation of death as "natural" to death as punishment for sin, the relation of death to mortal sin, and to many other questions.[24]

C. Rahner's Contributions to Ecclesiology

Rahner has made a number of important contributions to the theology of the church. We have observed some aspects of this contribution in his theology of the church as total sacrament and in his eschatology which he structures ecclesiastically and develops as a further moment of theological anthropology and Christology.

His studies in church organization have also been important. Almost certainly his studies on the diaconate influenced the renewed interest in the question and influenced the final restoration of the diaconate as an office *sui generis* by Vatican II. Rahner has helped clarify the nature of the hierarchial church. He says it is of paramount importance to grasp firmly the point that the apostolic college as a genuine corporate body holds the authority in the church, that the apostles as individuals did not first receive their distinct powers from Christ separately and then afterwards join a college with one another. The true ontological and juridical relationship is the other way round: Jesus founds a college of apostles. In this college the apostles have power in so far as they are members and are acting as such. Only in this way can we see how Peter appears from the start as head of the apostolic college.

Rahner's commentary on the twenty-first article of the *Dogmatic Constitution on the Church* [25] clarifies his latest thinking on such ecclesiological matters. Speaking of the episcopal office he says that Christ Himself is present and effective in the bishops as His ministers. He understands the phrase, *"spiritu sancto organicam structuram eiusque concordiam continenter roborante"* (Article 22) in such a way that even a thoroughly Protestant theology must appreciate the fact that the Catholic affirms that the institutional element in the church does not "function" alone but only by means of the Spirit. The Holy Spirit does not identify Himself with an institution but can be found as a lasting moment of the institutional. This means that in the long run it makes no sense to argue against the papacy and against the limited teaching of the synodal structure of the church. For the Pope *could* autocratically do everything himself and practically ignore the council of bishops. But as guarantee that this does not happen the Catholic can appeal to the guardianship of the Holy Spirit within the church in precisely the same way that a Protestant can regarding the possibility that his "free" theology could lead to the absolute subversion of the basic teachings of Christianity.

Rahner thinks that the church displays the double relationship between the ἐκκλησία as local community of the word and the liturgy. It is possible to start from the community in which Christ's word is preached and arrive at an understanding of the church as a whole, because the whole church in its entirety is present in the local parish community. Rahner thinks that a new possibility for developing ecclesiology starting with the word and the altar community has been opened up by the Constitution on the Church.[26] This fact has a tremendous ecumenical significance.

Today when for understandable reasons the bishop's cathedral is no longer identifiable with the parish community—as was the case in the early church—the priest is no longer just a part of the bishop's presbytery. Instead, he is a relatively independent leader of a parish community. Rahner thinks that despite this fact there is need to preserve and make more evident the episcopal structure of the church. This fact has obvious implications for answering the question how large a diocese should be and still preserve the basic picture of the church, so that the bishop does not merely become the highest administrator of an entire ecclesiastical regiment, a commander having nothing directly to do with his faithful troops.

Again, Rahner thinks that the Christian religion has to be understood from the fact that it is the complete revelation of God in Christ. And preaching the word both in the liturgy and on the missions is the act wherein the church speaks this revelation to believer and non-believer. But just as Christ sealed His own preaching by giving Himself on the cross, so the central service of the liturgy, the eucharist, must remain as the seal on the life of the church. In this connection Rahner brings home the fact that the priest should not so much be seen as a "father" of the laity but more as a "brother in Christ." Article 9 of the new Constitution emphasizes this notion of the brotherhood of the faithful. And between church officials and laymen a genuine brotherhood must prevail. "As the laity out of God's providence have Christ for a brother . . . , so also they have the ordained officials as brothers" (Article 32).[27]

Rahner's contributions to ecclesiology both theoretical and practical have been numerous. What we have summarized in this chapter are simply approaches to some of his later speculation on the church. The new series of pastoral-theology books now being partially edited by Rahner will embody many of these contributions in a practical way for the help of both priest and layman. Perhaps Rahner's chief contribution in this area has been a careful restatement of the fundamental problems in modern ecclesiology. He has indicated directions for answering some of them. His restoration of the concept of real symbol to its rightful place in the church has a tidal-wave significance. The church is the symbol of both transcendent and cosmic love in the world, most clearly expressed in the unity of the one church, the strongest argument we have for ecumenism. If we recall his thought on the importance of love of neighbor in the achievement of personality and of being at least an "anonymous Christian" (which we will examine in the next chapter), the importance of this unity of people who "love one another" begins to make better sense than has been allowed to appear in past ecclesiology.

The church is the sacramental visibility of the eschatological presence of God's salvation in the world. Accordingly, God wills that it re-present (bring to appearance, symbolize as a real sign) the eschatological transcendence of love, the inner life of the church. *Sacramentally,* this takes place in the sacraments, particularly those of baptism and the eucharist, where man is baptized into the death of Christ and proclaims that death until Christ comes in the parousia. *Existentially,* this happens in the habit of Christian self-denial. To the extent that this self-denial receives expression as an element of the real symbol of the church it is called living the evangelical counsels. A life of the evangelical counsels symbolizes externally what the church always lives internally, the divine love of God's self-communication which transcends the world eschatologically. The religious life has its meaning in the modern world in the sense of manifesting this transcendence as a real symbol.

APPENDIX TO CHAPTER SEVEN

1. See *Studies in Theology*, pp. 40–45.

2. This is so even if the race were not so called in Adam (or not summoned in Adam because called in Christ) as first willed by God. God maintains this vocation of humanity in spite of sin because of Christ, who by what He is and does is a member of the one human race. See *The Church and the Sacraments*, p. 13.

3. Rightly to appreciate Rahner's notion of belonging to the πόλις means we must have a deeper understanding of what πολιτεύμα means in *Philippians* 3, 20. The basic understanding is one given by Aristotle in the *Politics* (1374b) wherein the totality of active membership is the actual constitution of the whole (ἡ γὰρ πόλς πολιτῶν τὸ πλῆθός ἐστιν).

4. "The Church is the abiding presence of the primal sacramental word of definitive grace, which Christ is in the world, effecting what is uttered by uttering it in sign." *The Church and the Sacraments*, p. 18.

5. See *Schriften*, vol. VI, p. 114.

6. Note that this is a theological interpretation of the inerrancy of Scripture. In this light scripture is the *norma non normata*, and must be so in order to be the work of God as such. It must be as God's work simply inerrant. See *ibid.*, p. 112.

7. In the case of a human act the subject's concomitant self-consciousness cannot be replaced by this same consciousness seen as an object in an act of reflexion. It would be wrong, however, to argue on this basis that there must be other cases which fall outside the range of such consciousness. Similarly, the scriptures taken as the church's self-consciousness made objective cannot be separated from the concomitant consciousness of the church (itself incapable of being made completely objective in scripture) that is scripture. This does not prove that there must be other objects of faith

(a consciousness of the church not contained—even implicitly) in the scriptures.

8. See *Schriften,* vol. VI, pp. 126–128.

9. *Ibid.,* p. 129.

10. *Ibid.,* p. 131.

11. *Ibid.,* p. 337; cp. *Schriften,* vol. IV, p. 329.

12. A sacrament is and remains an effective word because considered metaphysically and theologically, sign and word have the same nature. Rahner notes that as far as the relation between matter and form in the sacraments is concerned this fact should not be overlooked. It is not and cannot be the fact that the material element in the sacrament (water, washing, and so on) is wholly determinative. The thesis could be established: for supernatural reality in the strict sense can have a natural efficient cause in creation *ad extra* but cannot have a "symbol" function such that of itself supernatural reality would be achieved. A sign of supernatural reality can only occur through the fact that the transcendental openness of man to God becomes itself a constitutive moment of the sign. And this means that supernatural reality can only manifest itself in the medium of the word. See *Hörer des Wortes,* and *Schriften,* vol. IV, p. 331.

13. *Schriften,* vol. IV, p. 337.

14. *Sendung und Gnade,* p. 156.

15. See *Schriften,* vol. III, pp. 194, 195.

16. For elaboration of this point and for bibliography see *Dogmatic versus Biblical Theology,* ed. by Herbert Vorgrimler, Baltimore and London, 1965.

17. *Schriften,* vol. IV, p. 418.

18. See *ibid.,* p. 423.

19. Rudolf Schnackenburg, "The Dogmatic Evaluation of the New Testament," *Dogmatic versus Biblical Theology,* ed. Vorgrimler, p. 170.

20. A better insight into what Rahner intends is had if one recalls how Rahner understands the theological virtues of faith and hope. See Chapter Three for some indication of this point. In so far as faith and hope have as "inner formal object" that which they hope and believe, God Himself, this hope is more than a concept of something yet to come under the horizon of human desire but is the reality itself that is desired. In this gift the church is given eschatologically, con-

stituted not only factually but experientially. The church is the community of those who possess the gift of God, the disclosure of which constitutes the temporal moments of the church.

21. See *Schriften,* vol. VI, p. 363.

22. *Sein und Zeit,* Tübingen, 1953, p. 233.

23. P. Glorieux, "Endurcissement final et grâces dernières," *Nouvelle Revue Théologique* (1932), pp. 865–892. See *Lexikon für Theologie und Kirche,* vol. 10, cols. 221–226; and James Demske, "La Mort," *Christus,* 9 (1962).

24. See "Zur Theologie des Todes," *Synopsis, Studien aus Medizin und Naturwissenschaft,* 3 (1949), pp. 87–112, and the article "Tod" in *Lexikon für Theologie und Kirche* to appreciate the change in Rahner's own treatment of the theology of death. In the latter treatment his thought is more integrated in the whole of his system as well as having a better theological balance. See also Henri Rondet, *Problèmes sur la réflexion chrétienne,* Paris, 1945, pp. 149 ff.; Robert W. Gleason, "Toward a Theology of Death," *Thought,* 32 (1957), pp. 38–68.

25. See *Lexikon für Theologie und Kirche,* suppl. I, pp. 217 ff.

26. *Ibid.,* cap. 3, art. 26.

27. *Ibid.,* and see especially cap. 4. Article 29 shows a good deal of Rahner's influence. The book *Diaconia in Christo,* ed. by K. Rahner and H. Vorgrimler, Freiburg, 1962, was a basic text in the work of the theological commission.

CHAPTER EIGHT

THE PHENOMENOLOGY
OF RELIGION

This last chapter ties together a number of loosely related questions, most of which are characteristic of Rahner's more recent thought, particularly since leaving Innsbruck in 1964 and coming more into contact with students from faculties other than theology. In a sense, what we do in this chapter is to reflect more abstractly, if that is possible, on some of the material already covered. We consider some select problems from Rahner's philosophy of religion which are truly critical for the world today. The selection is based primarily on a judgment of what issues in Anglo-Saxon countries require greater clarification and a solid intellectual basis.

PLAN OF CHAPTER

After briefly discussing the meaning of religion in the philosophy and phenomenology of religion, we then take up its perversion in the form of heresy for a Catholic. Next we inquire into the problem of Christian existence in a society that is intellectually and religiously pluralist. We specifically ask the question of the relation of Christianity to non-Christian religions and consider some added ecumenical questions involving the Christian denominations.

The chapter concludes with some of Rahner's insights on the matter of intellectual honesty not only in the church but in the world. Some of the issues discussed in this chapter may in the long run prove to be among Rahner's more significant contributions to the real theological future.

I. MEANING OF "RELIGION" IN THE PHILOSOPHY AND PHENOMENOLOGY OF RELIGION

The term *religion* in general signifies (when seen independent of value judgments) the relation of man to *the holy*. Worship of itself is religion as crystallized in the medium of creed, word and cult—including all elements such as gesture, dance, ritual washing, anointing, blessing, sacrifice, sacrificial meal, and so on) and law. Religion establishes a relation that is only possible in so far as *the holy* appears to man. Religion becomes man's response to this appearance and is open to the corruption which can affect all that is human. Religion can attempt to win a share in the *holy* simply on the basis of man's effort and turn into a matter of self-justification. This possibility, usually realized as intermingled with other false elements in historical religions, shows the need for numinous guidance. In religion, a relation is established which is mutual.

As subjective, religion springs from man's absolute listening, his readiness to receive transcendence. In this, man realizes his relation to the holy to the extent that he completely opens himself in receptivity. Man must make no reservations. But this same element can become involved in a total self-affirmation which claims man's self-sufficiency. Yet man enters into religious behavior not because of any decision to expect a divine summons but because religion as such is a moment of humanity and its ultimate ground. Cult is the objective form of religion. But cult in its objectivity does not solve the problem of religion. When faith weakens and still needs to be received, various formalizations of cult and concept can become so isolated that they actually oppose that which for the sake of whose mediation they exist. A careful examination of the concept of religion shows that the first impulses to culture spring from religion. And the religious significance of things is that a deeper meaning can follow upon them, that they are essentially symbolic. Rahner finds the key to this whole problem in interpreting all things Christocentrically.[1]

Rahner thinks that for the great majority of men today a profound erosion in the terrain of religious faith has occurred. This is not something which confronts the Christian externally alone, since because he breathes the atmosphere of the age he is himself a secular man. For this reason, many theologians of the contemporary period, Protestants like Paul Tillich and Dietrich Bonhoeffer—both deceased—and Friedrich Gogarten, Catholics like Rahner, Hans Urs von Balthasar, Anglicans like John Robinson and Paul Van Buren, and many others in one way or another are brooding upon the "eclipse" of God or the "absence" of God. It is indeed something of this sort that constitutes a primary datum for the religious imagination of our time. For men whose standards of intelligibility derive from a world of electronic computers and nuclear fission are not quite certain how we can still talk about God and transcendence. Just where is the *place* in which God may be said to be? And this question will become more and more significant for theology as greater interest in theology as a science is displayed on university campuses. Rahner's answer deserves serious consideration.

A tendency in current thinking is to overlook the fact that no philosophical or theological system is presuppositionless. And Rahner wants to drive to the heart of these presuppositions. His method forces him to this logical conclusion, since transcendental philosophy insists on justification of knowledge. If no understanding of "justification"—within a Kantian framework—can be assumed at the start, it cannot be built up from "facts."

Just as *a priori* objects of a science like geometry and its assertions about them are claimed as *a priori* bases of objects of experience—bases in the spatial continuum—so transcendental philosophy accepts an *a priori* contribution on the part of thought, a dynamism which is the spring of every question. As a method, a way of doing philosophy, it exercises a specific appeal to men of today.

A. Phenomenology of Religion

Transcendental philosophy plays its greatest role regarding religion as phenomenology. Phenomenology is the systematic discussion of what appears. The concept of *appearance* comes up in Rahner's thought in connection with the real symbol. And to this extent he can be called a "phenomenologist." Religion is an ultimate experience. It evades observation and is a revelation which is and remains hidden. How can man deal with what is so completely hidden? How can phenomenology be pursued where there are no phenomena? This antinomy belongs to all religions. Yet this same problem is true of all understanding. Consequently, a phenomenology of religion is possible in the same way that a phenomenology of the understanding exists. Phenomenology is really a hermeneutics. Because it works in terms of an "intellectual suspense," an *epoche,* faith and this suspense are not mutually exclusive. It is not possible to confront an event which on the one hand is an ultimate experience and on the other hand is manifested in an attitude of intellectual restraint. Rahner thinks that the more deeply comprehension penetrates an event, the better the event is understood, becoming clearer to the understanding which sees that the ultimate ground is not itself but an *other* in terms of which the event is comprehended.

This is the very condition of all understanding. And so all understanding is ultimately religious.

If we recall the outlines of Rahner's metaphysics of knowledge, we can see how it can be translated phenomenologically. The structure of knowledge involves that universal and permanent dynamic tendency of man's spirit driving toward the Absolute. The dynamism of the understanding can only be finalized, only respected in its real meaning, when we admit the reality of the infinite divine understanding. Thus transcendence of the finite order and of limited objects presented by the phantasm is the ultimate implication of man's dynamism. Phenomenologically, all understanding, since it is structured descriptively in this way, must be ultimately religious. And in terms of will, all love is only a response to the love of God bestowed on man. And all understanding must rest on the self-abandonment of love. If this were not the case, then not only all discussion of *appearances* in religion but all discussion of *appearance* in general would be impossible. Given Rahner's hermeneutics, it is not enough to let theology simply follow on "phenomenology" in virtue of its content, since the fundamental problem is methodological. Przywara blazed a frontier trail for Rahner in his search for the intimate relationship existing between faith and the obviously given data, in the fact that the evidence the data provide is essentially a "preparedness for revelation." [2]

The phenomenology of religion is not the history of religion. Both disciplines, however, are subject to correction by the evidence. History cannot proceed without adopting a phenomenological viewpoint on religion. Not even a religious text can be edited without adopting a hermeneutics. Phenomenology may be regarded as a forerunner of the philosophy of religion. For it is systematic and builds a bridge between the special sciences concerned with the history of religion and philosophical speculation.

Rahner defines the philosophy of religion as that knowledge available to man of the real relationship of man to

God as absolute. Philosophy of religion should be grounded scientifically by means of metaphysics, but the object of the philosphy of religion is nothing other than metaphysics itself. Rahner solves this antinomy by observing that the foundations of the philosophy of religion must be the actual self-grounding of metaphysics. In the long run, the question about the philosophy of religion becomes the question why man must study metaphysics, what metaphysics is, and how a human metaphysics arrives necessarily at God.

In asking about the relation of the philosophy of religion to theology Rahner points to the difficulty of knowing theology as revelation. He says the ultimate resolution of this difficulty lies in a proper understanding of man. So the solution of the relationship between the two disciplines may be found within theological anthropology.

B. Phenomenology of Heresy

To a large extent the history of theology mirrors in reverse the history of heresy. For in a panoramic view we can distinguish three periods: (1) prior to the Reformation the chief issue was whether this or that particular doctrine was revealed, and consequently creeds of differing complexity were framed; (2) in the 16th century the focus shifted to the problem of the norms of revelation; (3) and in the past century it has become fashionable to question the existence of supernatural revelation.

Rahner notes that all religions which have some kind of definite doctrine, that is, all the higher religions, have their heresies. Differences of opinion about the doctrine lead to conflicts and even to attacks on the socially organized forms of the religion. To this extent all religions exemplify the concept of heresy. But what is peculiar to Christianity is that religious wars are fought *within* Christendom. Only Christianity adopts a definite, radical attitude to truth. Christianity has an awareness of the revelation of God's truth. This revelation is an event happening in space and time, and its truth is important for salvation.

1. POSSIBILITY OF ERROR

Where it is only a matter of different opinions regarding the actual contents of a message, one interpretation cannot be seen as simply true and another simply false. "Only where in principle both sides have the will to take this occurrence and the authority manifesting itself in it as their point of reference can each party look upon the other as heretical, that is, as persons who in their differences of opinion regarding matters of factual content, destroy in spite of themselves the authentic and direct relationship to that authoritative event, though in itself this latter is maintained." [3] So heresy is not just a matter of error. It involves a doctrine which despite itself threatens the whole of spiritual existence of the individual. Where a heretic no longer attempts explanation in terms of reference to the one complete revelation event, there can be no question of heresy.

Rahner states this in more theological terms. The content of the act of intellectual knowledge is no longer important for salvation with the necessity of means but only has the moral quality of something that should be had and is of vital importance. This means that God has so ordered creation that nothing happens ultimately because of error as such. Rahner points up the danger in such an attitude of coming to think that *thoughts* which after all are "within" really have no effect in the reality "outside." Actually thinking about things means that we enter into a definite relationship with them, so that things themselves take on meaning for us according to how we think about them. Rahner regrets that this basic truth has largely been lost to the contemporary mind. And the current view of the ultimate indifference of truth is precisely what Christianity rejects. The nucleus of Christianity builds out from the teaching that there is a truth which it is impossible to fail to attain without guilt. And the truth is both subjective and objective and so not just a question of propositional knowledge.

Attaining this truth is not simply a matter of good will or of decent attitude but of whether we have in fact laid hold of reality itself, "because in such a grasp, which is essentially though not exclusively an act of cognition, salvation itself consists." [4] Christianity teaches that the absolute truth in which salvation consists is communicated in Christ. The teaching authority of the church can give this truth definition. For this reason Christianity is most sensitive to heresy which arises among Christians. Heresy is the failure to attain authentic existence at that point where—as the truth of God—it is already present absolutely.

Rahner distinguishes heresy from apostasy in the sense that heretics retain the name of Christian. Since the virtue of faith is produced divinely, it can never be found only half present. So Rahner believes that it is better to call the modern world heretical rather than apostate, since given the state of communication and the extent of missionary activity, it is difficult to contradict Christianity and expressly dissociate oneself from it. In a way, all non-Christians assume a role of hostility and thereby stand in a permanent relation to Christianity.

It is further important to recognize, Rahner says, that historically effective heresies are not rooted in stupidity or lack of information. Rather, they are founded on an authentic and original experience and molded by reality and truth. It is possible and probable that the reality any heresy contains was not yet seen and experienced in orthodox Christianity with the same degree of explicitness and intensity. "Just as evil lives by the power of God and can only be willed in virtue of the will to the residual good which still persists in the evil, and without which it could not even be evil, but simply nothing, which cannot be the object of the will, so it is too in the relation between the truth affirmed and experienced and the error actually brought to expression." [5]

2. HERESY IN THE CHURCH

It is never possible to say with certainty whether the heretic is in the truth in spite of his heresy by reason of the Christian truths to which he adheres or whether despite living by these truths he is really in error because of the heretical doctrines which he holds. It is an ambiguity that cannot be removed. The same thing is true of the orthodox believer. Neither the baptized Catholic nor anyone else can say whether a "heresy" is in him really just an opinion and so not the sort of thing which would annul his radical decision for the truth of the faith.

a. Cryptic Heresy

Rahner thinks that today more than in earlier times cryptic, latent heresy exists in the church. Such tacit heresy exists alongside explicit orthodoxy. This kind of heresy has a tendency to remain implicit, that is, unrecognized where the real danger lies. The characteristically Christian attitude of anxiety about heresy needs to be directed against this cryptic heresy. But this is difficult because it is found within the church and is difficult to distinguish from legitimate trends, especially the developing paracanonical styles of life. Rahner thinks that such cryptic heresy finds a strange ally in men of today who in their distaste for conceptual precision become lax in religious truth. Rahner observes how the man of today is much more willing to talk about his sexual life in detail with a psychiatrist than to hold even the briefest theoretical discussion on religion. Such contemporary movements as philosophical relativism and "death of God" theology tend to make modern man uneasy in the area of conceptual religious thought.

Furthermore, and Rahner gives just weight to this, there is the feeling of the immense disproportion between a religious statement framed in human language and the reality intended. Consequently, trying to achieve precision in religious language may strike modern man as irreverent. The paradox involved in this is that people are willing to live heresy but are averse to expressing it as a doctrinal system.[6] But the truth of God is intended for a vital encounter. It calls for a ceaselessly renewed assimilation by the individual in his real situation. A will to harden the form within which the gospel truth is expressed is a dangerous symptom of indifference to truth. It is also a symptom of the inability or lack of strength to assimilate this truth and make it one's own. People who suffer from this deficiency are sometimes called "traditionalists" in the pejorative sense.

According to his method, Rahner observes that men, because of their finitude and complexity, are forced to act on the basis of a plurality of principles, the positive contents of which they cannot synthesize into a unity. The problem of proportions then has a tendency of taking over, the problem of simultaneously respecting a number of requirements which cannot be reduced theoretically to a single higher criterion, whether of principle or of authority. Because of this difficulty, cryptic heresy always tends to be a heresy of improper proportions. Hence it is often impossible to demonstrate theoretically.

C. The Uncatholic and Heresy

The concept of the "Uncatholic" is not Rahner's. However, it expresses the real fruit of cryptic heresy. As long as Catholics are simply ignorant, there is no question of formal heretical opinion. But there is a growing tendency for not just those poorly instructed in the faith but for the educated also when confronted by the manifold problems of our pluralist world to interpret truth in their own way.

Thus an Uncatholic arrives at a "private" opinion that, say, the Trinitarian doctrine could not really be true because it is logically inconsistent (in terms of his "private" logic). So such an Uncatholic privately rejects this doctrine and lives a life of public Catholicism. His heresy is cryptic but he is an Uncatholic. This sort of thing can be very dangerous for the church. Paradoxically, if most Uncatholics would take the time and effort needed to learn the truth about the doctrines they tend to reject, they might learn that what they hold is but an imperfect and incomplete expression of the real theological truth. Rahner's contribution to this problem lies in his presentation of many traditional doctrines in new conceptual dress which better clothes and displays their contemporary relevance.

Basically, Rahner is as serenely unimpressed by this kind of modern unbelief as is Karl Barth, and for much the same reasons. For theology, as we have seen, is primarily dogmatics, a science built on the data of revelation and not on problems springing from the human predicament, the sort of things which trouble the Uncatholic. From the viewpoint of revelation the present crisis of faith is, so to speak, normal. Faith is always a miracle of election and grace. "Anyone who seriously believes in our Lord's second coming must by the very fact of his belief take into account the possibility . . . that we now see the signs of the end of time given us so that we shall not go astray even when the elect are in danger." [7] All things considered, it is not the increasingly diasporic situation of the church that is abnormal, but the 1500 years when Christianity was the majority religion of a whole culture.

Nor should we regret the return to the normal state of affairs. It enables people to see more clearly that faith involves a risk, a decision, and a personal relationship with God in Christ obligating the individual to responsibilities going far beyond passive acceptance of the directives of the church. It is the glory of the present age that it gives the church its chance to become more rather than less

religious, a "summoned community" engaged in the consecration of the world. Rahner says, "We Christians want to
accept boldly the situation of our diaspora in a pluralist
society and take care not to flee into the ghetto of a
reactionary defense of tradition or the comfortable cow-
ardice of a refusal to remake public life." [8]

D. Problems of Pluralism

Rahner argues that the real problem of the church in a
pluralist society consists in how it is to face the change
from a geographical unit form of organization at the parish
level to being a moment in the power structure. This is
critical for the practical structuring of the hierarchical
church. For the bishop should not become simply an administrator of a power faction.

A Christian must allow another on the basis of his own
principles the same space of freedom which the Christian
claims for himself, even when the other uses this freedom
for non-Christian decisions. But Rahner adds that we must
admit honestly that the formal rules of play in the game of
democracy alone are not enough to make possible a common life in peace and freedom. A society and a state
having a common material basis cannot abandon ultimate
moral convictions, whether these are called the "natural
law" or something else.

The heart of this problem is that of intellectual pluralism. It has recently been approached by Rahner [9] who
writes that it is becoming more and more obvious that
today's expert in one field really knows nothing of another
field. He cites the case of a priest who is a paleontologist
and a rather good one but who is a layman, even if he
does not recognize and admit the fact, in the field of real
theology and philosophy. This is true even if he is a priest
who has studied philosophy and theology in the seminary.
The same situation applies to most clergy who have completed their seminary studies. It is a bitter pill but a

necessary one, given the exploding state of these sciences today. Rahner specifically cites the case of Teilhard de Chardin whom he says theologians tend to think of as a scientist, and scientists think of as a theologian!

The same problematic situation obtains among philosophers and theologians themselves. The real problems of contemporary philosophy cannot be mastered in the normal two- or three-year course of philosophy in the seminary. The same thing is true of all the historical sciences. Questions which are pertinent to the faith raised by philosophy and the historical sciences, including philology, simply cannot be mastered in a few years. They require the specialist. Rahner asks, for example, what a typical Catholic pastor could really tell a good Protestant biblical exegete? Rahner compares the present situation with the 16th century to illustrate the difference and the magnitude of today's problem. The sum of relevant problems today has grown so in relation to the situation of four hundred years ago that they cannot be grasped and handled in a whole lifetime, let alone be integrated into a single philosophical system. Rahner implies that we can no longer hope to find a Cusanus or a Bellarmine to synthesize the faith for our day as such men did in the past. The sheer amount of material is too vast.

Just as in earlier times the simple folk (*rudi*) did not know even the basic elements of fundamental theology and were still good Catholics objectively, so this kind of situation has now expanded to include even more educated people and even the official representatives of the hierarchical church. Just as the *rudi,* the simple folk, did not harm the church earlier, so in the present situation will an increase in their factual number be no danger—provided they recognize their lack of specialization. A hypocritical pretense of knowledge in the face of specialized learning could do great damage. This fact has implications for the position of the clergy in the modern world.

The pluralism represented by these specialities has a greater importance for the church in terms of the pluralism of philosophies, of world theories, that they come to represent.[10] Since it is an intellectual problem it must seek resolution in a dialogue. And the dialogue today must from the start forego coercion and its manifold express or anonymous forms in society. The dialogue must be open and honest and conducted on a truly intellectual level. There were dialogues in the earlier church (for example, *Dialogus cum Tryphone*) but, Rahner says, up until now there was no real *time* of dialogue. In earlier periods homogeneous societies were formed in which only one viewpoint was allowed to rule and which forced different viewpoints either out of public scrutiny and society or forced them into relatively unimportant, narrow minority ghetto opinions.

Fortunately, this is no longer a possible option. A situation of dialogue is the only thinkable position for genuine co-existence, a manner of existence which has never existed previously and which will last now a long time, because those holding divergent world philosophies cannot hope to emigrate to different social spaces nor may they attempt to remove contrary opinion by force—despite what followers of certain Marxist systems maintain. But a world philosophy which sees itself ready to co-exist in this way is ready and open for the future and ready for dialogue.

Rahner thinks that it is possible in the dialogue to appropriate slowly (and perhaps only asymptotically) that historical experience in which the partner arrived at his attitude, even if in the judgment of the dialogue partner this has been interpreted falsely or inadequately. The contemporary dialogue is not only characterized through the fact that the partners share different viewpoints, represent wholly opposite opinions, but also by the fact that no one any longer knows everything nor can one know everything even that the dialogue partner knows. The advantage of this is in the fact that there is now for the first time a real possibility of learning from one another.

The moment that we ask in earnest whether Christianity

has a chance in this dialogue we have already left the ground of faith. We are demanding to appear before God as a people already justified, instead of abandoning ourselves to Him as a people in need of justification.

III. CHRISTIANITY AND NON-CHRISTIAN RELIGIONS

Rahner approaches the problem of the real pluralism of religions, the existence of non-Christian religions, hermeneutically. He sees that the church must take into account the fact that the existence of these religions is important. In overcoming the scandal of contradiction they represent, the church so structures itself that it can comprehend this pluralism by understanding itself as their higher unity. This requires an attitude of "open Catholicism" to the pluralism of different world outlooks. This pluralism must be seen from the unity of Christianity, and one of the most difficult tasks of Christianity is to order the various moments of this pluralism. And the pluralism of religions has more meaning for the church than merely the pluralism of philosophies.

In previous ages, other religions were identified with different cultures. Christians had no or little contact for the most part with these cultures, and different histories ran parallel, touching only at isolated moments of belligerence in missionary activity. Today the problem of the relations with non-Christian pluralist society and cultures has entered a new age. Rahner offers some basic principles of a "Catholic-dogmatic" interpretation of this religious pluralism. He proposes them in several theses.

His first thesis builds on a theological interpretation of Christian belief: Christianity proclaims itself as the religion determined absolutely for all men and recognizes no equal beside itself. Although Christianity has a prehistory which carries significance for this problem, its real beginning came within history. This means that Christianity was not always *the* way of salvation. So this absolute religion encounters men, even in its genesis, historically. And the temporal moment of its encounter is not the same for all men, for all cultures and historical spaces. This fact has a number of consequences. For example, on the basis that Pentecost marked the moment when all men were obliged to become Christians, theologians have been tempted to assume that all children since then who died unbaptized lost supernatural salvation.

On the positive side, Rahner affirms that Christianity is truly the religion of all mankind, but he leaves the question open as to the exact temporal moment that this obligation becomes real for an individual. And this would include the question of unbaptized infants. A second consequence of his first thesis is that a socially constituted religion belongs to man's existence. Man can only be himself, in one sense, when his religion has a social structure. This implies that man is obliged to seek religion in a social expression. Thirdly, the present tendency toward one world culture in which the pagan gradually enters a new age has great importance. For we now have the *one* world history in which both Christian and pagan live as *one* in the situation of the dialogue.

Rahner's second thesis states that up to the precise moment in which the gospel really enters the individual, historical situation, a non-Christian religion contains not only real elements of a natural knowledge of God mixed in with false elements, but also wholly supernatural moments of grace. Hence a non-Christian religion can be recognized as a *legitimate* religion without denying at the same time its errors and depravations. Rahner reminds us that we have to remember the universality of God's saving will and that salvation is the salvation of Christ. It would be absurd to imagine that those standing outside the walls of official Christianity were all so evil and blind that they must always reject God's summons. Furthermore, we have seen how it is wrong to consider nature and grace as two successive phases in the life of an individual. Nor can we imagine that God's self-communication remains ineffectual because of personal guilt. The gospel offers no real grounds for thinking so pessimistically about men, and we have many reasons for being optimistic about God's saving will which rules more powerfully than man's shortsighted view. Whenever an individual performs a moral act (and except for pathological instances this could happen anywhere), such a moral decision can realize the "supernatural." Given the nature of man's supernatural existential, any free self-disposal is more than just an exercise of "natural morality." This thesis implies that the form of pre-Christian religions should not be thought of as illegitimate but as having a real meaning within salvation history. Different religions would have greater or less claim to such consideration, since a legitimate religion is one whose practice establishes a positive relationship with God at a definite period of history and so can be a means of individual salvation. Men must have the possibility of being saved within the culture in which they live and whose task it is to integrate this culture.

Rahner's third thesis follows upon the second. Christianity encounters the pagan not as a non-Christian but as a man who must be considered an *anonymous Christian*. If any man has experienced grace, has accepted the final entelechy of his being, then revelation in the true sense has already taken place within him before he hears its formal expression in the word of a missionary. We recall that hearing the gospel is not the same kind of learning that we have when a child hears for the first time that Atlanta is the capital of Georgia. Hearing the gospel is but the reflex conceptual statement of what man has already necessarily performed in the depths of his spiritual being. And this performance necessarily involves the grace of Christ, because there exists no other salvation than that of Christ. Hence any non-Christian must be considered not simply an anonymous theist but an anonymous Christian.

The fourth thesis argues that if we cannot hope on the one hand that the situation of religious pluralism will vanish in the near future, and if on the other hand we should understand the non-Christian as an anonymous Christian, then the church today will not consider itself so smugly as the exclusive community of guardians of salvation. Rather, the church will better recognize itself as the historical expression of what exists outside the visible church also. The covenant of universal salvation history is valid for all men. It is only superseded among those for whom special saving history becomes actually experienced through faith in the community of God's people, a representative people who symbolize mankind as a whole.

A. The Anonymous Christian

The concept of anonymous Christianity is not some questionable novelty smuggled recently into Catholic thinking by Rahner and a small group of "arm-chair theologians" in Germany.[11] Nor is the concept equated co-extensively with the whole of the non-Christian world. Rahner has tried to explain the concept more clearly.[12] He says that if we truly mean that God became man, then we must admit that man is that which becomes when God expresses Himself. Man in his most basic definition is that which becomes God when God undertakes to appear in the realm of creation. Turned around and formulated of man, man is that which comes to himself when he gives himself away to absolute mystery. In other words, man has an obediential potency for the hypostatic union, as we saw in Chapter Three. And we have seen a number of times in Rahner's thought emphasis on the fact that grace and the Incarnation are the two ways of God's self-communication and that these can be called the most radical possible transcendence.

God's word effects what it expresses. Man's nature, prior to his free self-determination, has a supernatural existential. In experiencing transcendence man experiences the actual offer of grace, not necessarily reflexively but really and unthematically. All grace is grace of Christ, so that in accepting himself man accepts Christ. The acceptance of the faith is not man's work but the action of the grace of Christ. This means that the grace of the church of Christ—the extension in time of the mystery of Christ—is found potentially in every man. However, we cannot simply call every man an anonymous Christian. For whoever denies and rejects his orientation to an Absolute and in so doing places himself in opposition to what he really is as a person, cannot even be called a theist. But whoever believes in a holy mystery and allows such belief to penetrate his existence, that man has the grace of Christ and can be called an anonymous Christian.

Rahner calls attention to the fact that he is not attempting to salvage something for Christianity out of a world in which the Christian message is slowly disappearing. The Christian is not dispensed in his diaspora situation from the responsibility of bringing the gospel to express recognition. So it is important that we not situate this teaching falsely.

Rahner's concept of anonymous Christianity is not a hermeneutical principle whereby the corpus of previous theology could be reduced like the theses of Bishop Robinson's *Honest to God* in a futile attempt to make Christianity more acceptable. Rahner's teaching considered from the dogmatic point of view is a border phenomenon, a theologoumenon, the necessity and aptness of which result from separate data of the faith. But many teachings of the faith are such theologoumena. This one can be situated historically-existentially at the heart of the contemporary situation without coming into conflict with other teachings. So it would be foolish to think that a discussion of anonymous Christianity could lessen the importance of the missions, of preaching, and of the sacraments.[13] Rahner says that we need consider only two facts in order to understand anonymous Christianity. First, we must really think again the different and often sterile data of traditional theology, and second, we must review in an unprejudiced manner the real situation of mankind, of Christianity, and of the church in the modern world.

So what Rahner understands by the phrase "anonymous Christianity" is really what Vatican II teaches in the Constitution on the Church (Article 16). According to this constitution, the possibility of being saved exists for all who without guilt have not yet heard the gospel. Presupposed is only what comes from the side of God, *influxus gratiae*.[14] Atheism is viewed simply as opposition to express recognition of God. Such an atheism, then, could be truly unthematic and really be an essentially performed theism. Given certain conditions, such a theism could last a long time without our being able to say anything about attainment of salvation. The Vatican II Decree on the Missions states that God in unknown ways gives His grace without which there is no salvation to men who have not heard the gospel. In the light of this teaching of Vatican II there can be no good reason for questioning what Rahner means by "anonymous Christianity."

B. Christianity and Israel

In a public exchange of correspondence [15] between Rahner and F. G. Friedmann, Rahner takes his clearest position to date on the problem of Christian and Jew. He agrees with Friedmann that a state of open respect for one another must be sought after more ardently. Both Christian and Jew must recognize their obligation to live in love of one another. And to do this both sides must meet openly, honestly, and publicly. Differences can be met and really overcome in love. Rahner admits that all Christian denominations have much to do in establishing a state of true religious freedom regarding the Jew.

Rahner confesses to a feeling of sadness which is part and parcel of the real problem of establishing a dialogue between Catholic and Jew. The centuries piling up the burden of evil which Christians have inflicted on Jews, the fact that the recent decree of Vatican II on the Jews had to wait for nearly 2000 years before being published, the thought of just how un-Christian Christians can be, all these things make Rahner sad. And he asks whether Christians might not even now have other blind spots without noticing them. In the matter of Christian-Jewish relations the situation is doubly sad because the power of grace was helpless in a question involving the stock from which Incarnate grace comes. Rahner says that there is a mystery in this. It is the mystery of love which conquers precisely in being despised and rejected. He asks whether even now we can be certain that we are not failing in real love for the Jewish people, even though we no longer discriminate and physically punish them. (We recall that Rahner is writing in Germany.)

In the second place, Karl Rahner feels helpless before the growing awareness that the Jews are slowly giving up their view of having a special messianic purpose and are reinterpreting this as simply a call to an exemplary way of living. They no longer want to be "different from others." It is important that the Jewish people not lose their religious identity. He illustrates this by pointing out how a Christian and a Jew can meet on the ground of nationality like anyone else, but because they are more than just fellow countrymen, they have a great deal more in common than their citizenship. The Christian thinks, "Here is a man from the people of my Redeemer." It would be tragic if this fact were to come to have no more significance than, say, the reminiscence of a physicist who recalls that Einstein was a Jew. Christians and Jews are related quite differently than are other peoples. Today both live in a state of diaspora. They have an improved chance of meeting one another. Neither side dare think of themselves as just two among many different groups in a pluralist society.

C. Christianity and Ideology

Rahner first defines ideology negatively as a false system to be rejected by a proper interpretation of reality. An ideology may involve more of what is an attitude than a philosophical system. Positively, an ideology is a door closed to the whole of reality. It turns a partial bit of reality into absolute reality. Rahner divides ideologies into those of immanence, transmanence, and transcendence. All are wrong.

The ideology of immanence tends to make absolute limited regions of the experiential world and turns the laws of the limited region into laws of reality in general. This group of ideologies encompasses what we customarily regard as ideologies, for example nationalism, racism, sociologism, materialism, scientism. A reaction to these ideologies of immanence is the ideology of transmanence. This includes such ideologies as supranaturalism, quietism, and utopianism. This form of ideology makes an ultimate region of reality absolute and so defines the real in terms of the ultimate alone. It is a typical danger for the continental philosopher and the religious. A third form of ideology, that of transcendence, wants to overcome the other two and in so doing hypostatizes itself by claiming that it alone has validity. It claims a so-called *openness* for everything and is careful to avoid engaging the self in anything. Rahner observes that it is attachment to such an ideology which makes some intellectuals so vulnerable to the attractions of Marxism.

Christianity is accused of being an ideology. From the purely scientific or empirical viewpoint such a complaint might appear to be justified. For Christianity has often been misused for ideological purposes. The greatest danger lies in a categorial objectivization of the essence of Christianity, particularly in terms of its institutional or sacramental orders. Such an understanding of God's self-communication is necessary in a sense, because historical man must become present to himself in space and time and cannot do this within a pure mysticism. The spirit performs itself in the body. But the body of Christianity, its visible aspects as institution, veil the real meaning and make it liable to misuse, so that it becomes an ideology of immanence or transmanence or transcendence. Any or all of these aspects can be confused with the real nature of Christianity and make Christianity vulnerable to the criticism of being an ideology. Yet another reason for suspecting Christianity lurks in the pluralism of world philosophies which form the basis of a contemporary relativism.

Rahner argues that in reality Christianity is not an ideology of any kind. This is the case first because Christianity makes statements that are true absolutely in the clearest sense of the word, that is, it makes statements which are "metaphysical." For they are expressed with a claim to absolute truth which cannot be demonstrated as valid by the methods of empirical science. Consequently, whoever cannot appreciate metaphysics or any truth not empirically established must consider Christianity an ideology.[16] In the light of this kind of objection, we can see how important a true metaphysics becomes for the life of theology today and how important it is that we understand the real brunt of what Rahner is trying to accomplish. For he argues that men must come to see how a true metaphysics is inevitably given with their existence as men. The horizon of metaphysical statements cannot be identified with the experience of every day or with empirical science. A true attitude to the pluralism of world philosophies cannot honestly consist in a bluff suspicion of all world philosophies and metaphysics as various forms of mythology. An honest and "scientific" attitude must test critically and hold itself open for further knowledge and modification. It truly attempts to discover the common experience found within all "systems." It also has the courage to decide and confess with certainty that in an historically conditioned but open proposition absolute truth can be achieved, even if it remains a mystery that cannot be phrased within the concepts available in any system known to man. We shall have more to say on this shortly.

Again Christianity is not an ideology because its real *place* is in the knowledge and freedom of transcendental experience, the unthematic ground and condition of the possibility and horizon of every day experience. Because such experience as a drive into absolute mystery necessarily transcends every ideology to the extent that ideology makes a part of experience absolute, and because Christianity actually means a true transcendence, Christianity cannot be identified with any particular form of ideology. This aspect of genuine transcendence Rahner thinks is a good starting point for understanding the theology of Rudolf Bultmann and others of his school. For if the reality of Christianity is genuine transcendence and freedom, that is, grace, then man is carried by God at the very foundation of his personal nature. In other words, Christianity is the experience of absolute nearness to God. And this supersedes every form of ideology.

At the same time, Christianity is the history of man's turning to spatio-temporal events as events of salvation. And this is another reason why Christianity must reject all ideologies of transmanence and transcendence. Christianity must display ever more clearly the fact that real transcendence and real historicity mutually condition one another. Man cannot clarify this mutuality in an *a priori* reflexion. For within man's real history there is need for genuine engagement and commitment, which can even be of obligation where what is at stake may be purely contingent. We have observed several times how for Rahner man's historicity as the mediation of his transcendental nature attains its climax in Jesus Christ, so that a historical, eschatological mediation of the divine is given the world in the history of grace. This fact in no way identifies the historical mediation of God with Himself in a kind of monophysitism. Man can accept this "mediation by immediacy" as ultimate, and inasmuch as man does accept it in his own transcendence he does so historically and contingently. This fact tells the Christian that he must take history seriously, but must not make an ideology out of it. If we recall that metaphysics is to be the mediation of the immediate, we can gain both further insight into why Christianity is not an ideology and a further appreciation

for Rahner's hermeneutics and use of the transcendental method in theology.

Lastly, ideologies tend to exclude non-conformists.
Christianity recognizes even the anonymous Christian. It
comprehends under God's saving will a possibility of salvation for all. The fact that the church is not an ideology
has many consequences for the current scene. First, it
means that there are no imperatives that Christianity can
hand down about ordering society, no basic lines for developing real history. The refusal of the church to become an
ideology, however, does not release the individual from his
obligation to act for himself in trying to structure the
world in accordance with his belief as best he can. This is
the specific task of the layman.

There must be tolerance of others as well as avoidance
of particular ideologies within the church. There must be
tolerance because one cannot expect that in the choice of
imperatives each individual choice will always be the right
one. Tolerance is simply an honest understanding for the
position of another, a fairness in competition, and a genuine readiness to yield if one sees that one's own position
is not really the best one. Christianity's rejection of ideology as such has obvious implications for the structuring of
academic freedom in American Catholic colleges and universities. Indeed, it has even real meaning in developing a
"catholic" philosophy of education.

D. Ecumenism in Rahner's Thinking

Practically every theme that Rahner has touched upon has
some interest for Protestant theologians. This is true of his
Christology, anthropology, ecclesiology, and eschatology.
Even such "traditionally" scholastic theories as the "supernatural existential" and the relation between sin and concupiscence are of interest to non-Catholics. His insistence
that the understanding of revelation and the form of the
church change radically and unpredictably in time is so

strong that most Protestants would be surprised at it. His use of philosophy is subordinated to scripture. "Not even a Barth, it seems to me, could find plausible objections to this kind of natural theology, to this modest and circumspect use of human reason to communicate to the unbeliever and half-believer within each one of us." [17] George Lindbeck goes on to say that this is only one of the merits of Rahner who alone among contemporary Catholics can be ranged alongside of Barth and Tillich. Lindbeck calls Rahner the most balanced of the three. Such praise from a Protestant theologian illuminates better than anything else the real source of Rahner's ecumenical contribution. So although Rahner has not been active ecumenically, though he has many contacts with the Lutheran church in Germany, his theological work has been of immense ecumenical value and might indicate where more stress is really needed on the part of those more actively engaged.

It was not many years ago that Protestant scholars tended to identify the intellectual life of the church with a rather musty medieval museum. In the effort to shake off this image, Rahner can be of great service as a model. Paradoxically, much of Rahner's thought is more comprehensible to Protestants, who for several years have been aware of developments in continental theology. For Catholics still tend sometimes to view with a jaundiced look anything that seems to smack of Kant or transcendental philosophy.

As a practical illustration of how Rahner contributes ecumenically, we can take up his interpretation of the phrase *"simul justus et peccator."* All Christians must confess that man is a sinner and is only justified by the grace of God. So all Christians have to ask themselves how they can live as Christians confronted by the un-Christian spirit of the modern age. In the light of this fact the old inner confessional struggle about the nature of justification assumes a new significance, that of finding the right way of preaching.

The Protestant views man as both just and sinner (*simul*

justus et peccator) in the sight of God. He does not shrink
before the paradox. He knows he is justified by the unmerited grace of God. For the Catholic, justification means an
event of salvation history in which something new is
created which is inconsistent with the previous human
condition. For salvation history is not just total history as
objectively saved but includes individual salvation history
in which something new happens which was not given
previously. Since justification involves the act of God and
is decidedly His, the reality and experience of justification
are not necessarily identical. Catholic doctrine teaches that
God's action is the decisive moment. Man's action is
wholly borne by this.[18] The problem cannot be answered
from the point of view of experience. So in order to give
God's power and grace its due, Catholic teaching stresses
that we *are* by the grace of God sons of God in whom the
Spirit dwells. This reality is not fiction, an "as if we were
sons of God," but is the true reality of man.

From the time of Augustine, however, the church has
affirmed boldly that man is and remains a sinner. He has
been justified and yet still commits sin. The recent English
translation of Küng's work on Barth and the Barthian
justification theory will doubtless arouse more interest in
this question. Rahner's strictures on this theory may well
be useful.

Rahner begins by observing that ecumenical theology
demands that in order to have the right to live in separate
churches, we must know for certain that we are not agreed
on the truth. Both groups have the same authority, however, that of scripture. Rahner believes that the Küng
presentation is in general good and quite acceptable from
the Catholic side, even though not always witnessed in the
magisterium. Rahner cites as an example the question how
man should make intelligible the teaching on original sin
without stressing the theologoumenon of the strictly analogous character of this sin with personal sin. Barth has
explained that Küng's representation of his position is
correct and that he could accept Küng's "Catholic" posi-

tion. The problem, as Rahner points it out, is that Barth's position is not *the* Protestant position.

In this question of justification, Rahner shows how his own position regards objective justification as "preceding" the subjective acceptance of salvation. Hence in the question of whether justification comes through faith or baptism, justification and sanctification can only be considered two aspects of one process. Insofar as justification happens in the acceptance of the knowledge of being redeemed by Christ, it can rightly be said to take place in *faith*. This is the terminology of scripture, and if justification and sanctification are but two sides of a single process, then *caritas* cannot be less present than faith. So we are referred back to Rahner's understanding of grace and the theological virtues for an answer to his position on justification.

Another ecumenical contribution comes in Rahner's positive evaluation of the Lutheran *theologia crucis*. He admits that theology itself is crucified theology and can speak only from the cross. This is the case because the theory of theology is itself practice. Just as all Christian performance of existence is determined by the cross of Christ, so is theology. The *habitus fidei* and *theologiae* is carried by the grace of the Crucified, and this gives theology a definite form. As long as man is still on the way (in saving history), this crucified situation obtains. Theology must remain conscious that it is carried on in the minds of sinful men who can misuse even theological truth and that all positive expressions ultimately must empty into the mystery that is God. On the other hand, Rahner notes that given the present order and eschatological situation, the *theologia crucis* and *theologia gloriae* are ordered to one another as moments of one theology which preaches the crucified and resurrected Christ and only so receives its whole measure and meaning.[19]

Protestants tend to view the church as the place where the word of God is preached effectively. The Catholic, at least from the time of Berengarius, has seen the church as a place of silence, of the sacramental presence of the Lord. Rahner's emphasis on understanding the eucharist as the supreme word overcomes this division between Catholic and Protestant. The two-table theory (pulpit and altar) with the scripture on one table and the bread of life on the other has not been laid to rest. But these cannot remain separated, especially once the choice between a church of the word and a church of the sacraments is seen as a false choice.

IV. INTELLECTUAL HONESTY IN THE CHURCH

A. Faith and Intellectual Honesty

Rahner's work at the University of Munich has forced him to answer a perpetual question of the serious student in a secular university, that of the problem of intellectual honesty and its relation to belief. His position may rank as one of the soundest to be put forward in recent years and has much to recommend it. Hence a rather detailed consideration may not be out of place as a conclusion to this study of his thought.

1. INTELLECTUAL HONESTY AND SPIRITUAL DECISION

Intellectual honesty does not mean freedom from the burden of spiritual decision, not even the condition in which one may believe himself to be free from having to decide about such existence. There is a popular temptation to think the man intellectually honest who trudges through life wearing a shield of skeptical reserve, who never makes any absolute statements. What is unrecognized is that such an attitude involves the absolute decision that this is what one should do—and on what basis is one to make this decision? Is it possible to be honest in such a case when one has really tried to find the answers to basic questions such as why man exists and has failed? This condition can be quite prevalent, and many who seek and are then tempted to view existence as absurd or who are only exposed to the view through Sartre's nihilism or Kafka's glasses represent such "atheists." But even such men would have to admit that theirs is not the only possible attitude of intellectual honesty, if they are truly honest.

Rahner argues that there are no ultimate beliefs or attitudes (of belief or unbelief) which can be given without the effort of thought and the risk of responsible freedom. The will to remain skeptical, to refuse to commit oneself, because this involves the risk of possibly being wrong, does not produce freedom but is really to enter into the worst kind of engagement. It is an attitude of total commitment to non-commitment. Such a man tries to live without decision, to live an impossible neutrality. But as indicated, this in itself implies an absolute decision, and it is not at all clear that this is any more justified than an option for any other position.

Furthermore, such an attitude fails to maintain perspective before the area of decision-making. An attempt to remain neutral is factually the refusal to see that such a decision is already made in deciding to remain neutral. In short, intellectual honesty demands as a condition of its possibility the courage to face spiritual decision, even when this courage bears a load of uncertainty and risk. Whoever then feels himself obliged to remain uncertain regarding his ultimate understanding of truth, in order to remain true to this obligation, in order to hold every question truly open, must be certain about this attitude at least. And he must then be able to give absolute reasons for it. And in doing so comes closest to the best possible position about intellectual honesty. A believer has only a few things to say about this attitude. Where it is a question of true openness to the meaning of existence, the journey to the Absolute has already begun.

Where this involves an inability to decide, the Christian can only say that no one really knows about another individual where in the history of that individual a stand might have been taken in opposition to that individual's existence. This fact does not give one an automatic right, however, to honor this notion just because the individual in question must. Secondly, the believer will call to the attention of the man who is unable to decide "because of intellectual honesty" that his decision in this regard is already an affirmation of what the believer calls the mystery of existence. The believer says that courage has not yet been given the skeptic to confess expressly what his life already silently confesses.

2. INTELLECTUAL HONESTY, FAITH, AND THEORETICAL REFLEXION

A second misunderstanding is prevalent. It is that in order to believe one must have considered and "scientifically" reflected on all the presuppositions which faith—Christian faith in particular—has as conditions. Yet if this were the case, if everyone had to reflect completely on the content of the faith to be intellectually honest, then no one could ever resolve the problem of intellectual honesty and faith. Considering the shortness of life, how many men could really accomplish this? Not even the theologian, who outside of a narrow slice of his own speciality is in the same state as are all other Christians. The specialist can only hope in a lifetime to reflect adequately on his own speciality and in the end must admit that he will never "know" it all. Perhaps this fact will gradually scare off the prejudice that only the uneducated are excused from a thorough examination of their faith and its fundamental problems.

The problem here is that the educated man, because he really knows the complexity of modern sciences and because he experiences the weaknesses of their methodology, knows that he cannot accomplish an examination of the faith. So he thinks that if he is to be intellectually honest, he is not allowed to believe.

A Catholic understanding of the faith does have an intellectual moment. It concerns historical realities which can be approached rationally. The faith cannot split the logical and existential unity of consciousness. An irrational conception of belief turns the faith into an ideology. So the presupposition that for the sake of intellectual honesty it is necessary to have done fundamental theology adequately in order to believe is false. Man's intellectual existence is so constructed that an evident existential difference obtains between the implications of the act of living and of scientific reflexion. Man cannot construct his existence out of elements he has made his own through scientific reflexion on them. Man knows that the actions of life cannot simply be a consequence of thematic rationality. Man is therefore obliged to accept this difference in intellectual honesty and go on to engage in the decisions of life—in this case, to believe—few of which can be demonstrated scientifically.

Rahner carefully points out that this does not mean that where it is possible a rational demonstration is not a matter of obligation. There exists a necessary zone of reflexion wherein critical proof and trial must continually be exercised. But there must also be enough courage to make a decision even before all the facts are harvested. This is true particularly in the matter of faith. For faith is concerned with an all-inclusive explanation of existence. In this case, the existential difference between what is intended and its demonstration on the one hand, and the theoretical reflexion on the other hand, is unavoidably the greatest possible. Any believer who is intellectually honest knows this and readily confesses it. But every man must give life a chance to justify itself. And this can only be done if man lives according to a trust which in rough outline reads: Because faith gives order and meaning to existence, because faith opens life up to the infinite out of which the mystery of life can be controlled, because moral truth regulates such control, therefore I an individual commit myself to such a trust.

A genuinely critical attitude allows questions to arise which man declares himself incompetent to answer. Not every Christian must be a Qumran specialist in order to be intellectually honest and still believe. Rahner says that it is truly remarkable that today we talk so much about man's historicity and yet do not really believe history as evidence for knowing truth.

B. The Meaning of Christian Faith

1. CHRISTIAN FAITH AS A WHOLE

Faith is just as complex as existence itself. A Christian may not dissolve his faith into individual propositions, each of which requires a demonstration. Yet it is wholly reasonable that Christianity can only be accepted or refused as a whole. Christianity as a whole is fundamental in belief, and the act of accepting it as a whole can stand up to the demands of intellectual honesty.

In what does this fundamental whole of Christianity consist? This question is hard to answer because of the real danger of not seeing the sky because of the clouds. Christianity is the express and socially organized confession that absolute mystery which governs existence shares Himself with man historically in Jesus Christ and appears glorious and victorious. The essential whole of Christian faith is expressed in this proposition, and if properly understood it contains the contents of Christian faith. It presents no real problem for intellectual honesty. Let us examine its contents briefly.

2. GOD AS MYSTERY OF HUMAN EXISTENCE

The first thing Rahner's formula states is that God is that incomprehensible mystery and that He must be known as mystery. Christianity is not a religion which places God within the calculus of human existence as known. It is the religion which instead places man in the incomprehensible, and this includes and penetrates his being. Christianity is not a palace of truth with an infinite number of rooms which man inhabits in order to dwell "in" the truth. Instead, it is the one doorway which leads man out of all individual truths (and even errors) into *the* truth, the one mystery that is the Absolute. This mystery is what makes possible a "return to ourselves" in knowledge and freedom and thus constitutes our "world," but in such a way that we experience ourselves always as limited. This mystery gives Himself in His divine life in a genuine self-communication. This mystery is the grace of our existence. What we call creation appears as the creation of the precondition for this divine self-communication. The relation between creature and Creator is an inevitable structure of reality but is not its content. God creates because He wills to share Himself. This is the answer to the question why anything is. And there is distance in order that there be togetherness in love.

3. HISTORICAL PARTICIPATION IN CHRIST

To the basic whole of Christianity belongs that which gives it its name, Jesus Christ. This is the mystery of the Incarnation, and as such belongs together with the first element. For the mystery of God's self-communication, even though always remaining a mystery, actually entered history, because in an encounter with the world God's word humanly performed Himself. God's self-communication, even though it is the transcendent ground of the world and its history, has its own entelechy which we call salvation history. Where this divine offer and human acceptance reaches its highest instance, where the dialogue between God and man enters into an absolute yes on both sides, there we find the meaning of the Incarnation.

Here the question is whether such a message can be

believed by a man who is intellectually honest. Rahner says that in the first place such a bundle of statements which always intends the whole of human existence is the most difficult complex that can be thought. The whole bundle has no fixed concept to express it. Because in this bundle absolute truth receives approximate expression, what is said is necessarily incomplete and unclear. Every attempt at stating it always points to the one mystery that always remains a mystery. Intellectual honesty actually encourages one because it discourages identifying the whole of reality with the sum total of available truths or statements of truth. Consequently, if mystery is not just a border phenomenon of intellectual existence, not just an undeveloped remnant of psychology, but the very ground of the possibility of knowing, what could forbid the intellectually honest man from assenting to the transcendental experience and the message of revelation which clarifies this experience imperfectly?

Even the concept of the Incarnation can be accepted by the man who is intellectually honest. The only presuppositions are that man really understand himself as a nature transcendent to himself. Given this transcendental understanding of human nature, the *idea* of a God-man, the implied eschatological climax of the mediation of transcendence, can be thought as the asymptotic conceptual goal of this nature. Every kind of mythological understanding must be removed from this idea, so that the God-man be not thought of as a passive instrument, a puppet, a suit of clothes for God. Rightly understood, nearness to God and personal individuality grow in direct and not in inverse proportion. The Incarnation must always remain a mystery, but if approached from the right direction, no mythological elements are tacked onto it which would make it unworthy of belief by the intellectually honest man.

What can be a scandal for the uncritical man can be critically interpreted by one who is intellectually honest and who sees that real history cannot be replaced by means of theories about historicity and that the never adequately reflected history of mankind is the necessary mediation of man's transcendental intellect and freedom. The honest individual sees that man has to trust himself to the spatio-temporal order not only in order to have an abstract concept but even to possess himself at all. The courage to abandon oneself to this fact cannot be substituted for. And Rahner admits that the exegetical demonstration that Jesus understood Himself as the metaphysical Son of God in the sense of Christian doctrine is not easy. Still, we may not expect that Jesus uttered any developed metaphysical formulas theologically to say what is really the case.

Finally, Rahner says, when we experience man as one, whole, and indivisible, when we can really hold on to the performance of existence, so that we believe in the resurrection of the body in such a way that we understand this as a formula expressing our absolute future (without falling victim to Neoplatonism), when we look historically at the life and death of Jesus, what real ground of intellectual sobriety might be given that would assist belief in the experience of the disciples about the resurrection? Both believer and skeptic know that the experience of the disciples of the risen Lord is incommensurable with other kinds of spatio-temporal experience. On the basis of this fact we realize that it has to be so, because this was not an experience of reality ordered to space and time. But to order it in a different way is not at all to deny it.

Rahner's answer to the problem of intellectual honesty is simply a condensation of his own thought-out position. He shows how a position of neutrality is basically intellectually dishonest, that skepticism has no better rational grounds than faith, that materialism becomes an ideology contradicted by experience, and that within Christianity as a whole there is nothing unworthy of intellectually honest belief. Such a contribution is not the whole answer. Rahner would be the first to admit this. But his explorations push the frontier a little further back, giving the church a little more intellectual breathing room. In his position on faith as in many other positions he is incomplete. His intention is really to ask the important questions. It requires the courage of faith to ask such questions. The future of theology in the West cannot be the same once these questions have been asked by Karl Rahner. It is to be hoped that he will supply more materials for answering some of them and that future theologians will build upon the directions of his blueprint.

In this book we have examined a part of this blueprint in terms of Rahner's transcendental method, the hermeneutics that orders his theological reasoning. It should be clear that such a tight system of thought cannot be clarified in a summary of eight short chapters. If Karl Rahner can be more easily understood with the aid of this book, we have accomplished our purpose.

APPENDIX TO CHAPTER EIGHT

1. For a brief account of the philosophy and phenomenology of religion as understood on the continent, see G. Van der Leeuw, *Religion in Essence and Manifestation*, vol. II, New York, 1963, pp. 680 ff.

2. See E. Przywara, "Die Problematik der Neuscholastik," *Kantstudien*, 33 (1928), pp. 92 ff.

3. "The Christian Attitude Towards Heresy," *Studies in Modern Theology*, London, 1964, p. 405. In general, see "Was ist Häresie?", *Schriften*, vol. V, pp. 527–576.

4. "The Christian Attitude Towards Heresy," p. 410.

5. *Ibid.*, p. 434.

6. "For example, someone will actually live a religious and metaphysical agnosticism but will be very careful indeed not to assert that the First Vatican Council was incorrect in teaching that men can know the existence of God by the light of reason. They prefer not to inquire what this affirmation of the Vatican Council really means and what it does not." *Ibid.*, p. 452.

7. "The Prospect for Christianity," *Free Speech in the Church*, New York, 1964, p. 65.

8. "Der Christ in seiner Umwelt," *Stimmen der Zeit*, 176 (October 1965), p. 484.

9. See "Zum heutigen Pluralismus in der geistigen Situation der Katholiken und der Kirche," *Stimmen der Zeit*, 176 (June 1965), pp. 191–199.

10. See "Ueber den Dialog in der pluralistischen Gesellschaft," *Stimmen der Zeit*, 176 (August, 1965), pp. 321–331.

11. Representative of those who argue against Rahner's concept of "anonymous Christianity" is H. Van Straelen, *Our Attitude Towards Other Religions*, Tokyo, 1965.

12. The most complete English study on "anonymous Christianity" is Anita Röper, *The Anonymous Christian*, New York and London, 1966. An essay that clarifies Rahner's

position by Klaus Riesenhuber, S.J. has been added to this book which is most helpful. See also Eugene Hillman, C.S.Sp., "Anonymous Christianity and the Missions," *Downside Review*, 85 (1966), pp. 361–380.

13. Particularly helpful in this regard is L. Elders, "Die Taufe der Weltreligionen. Bemerkungen zu einer Theorie Karl Rahners," *Theologie und Glaube*, 55 (1965), pp. 124–131. See also K. Rahner, *Handbuch der Pastoraltheologie*, vol. II, Freiburg, 1966, Chapter VII, paras. 3 ff.

14. From the side of man: *Deum sincero corde quaerere eiusque voluntatem per conscientiae dictamen agnitam operibus adimplere.* This task of obeying conscience is made express in those who have not yet come to an express recognition of God.

15. The literary exchange is published in *Stimmen der Zeit* (August 1966), pp. 81–98.

16. This point gets at what is perhaps the major difficulty in Anglo-American philosophical analysis of the problem of God. Even though the verifiability principle has been restructured, most analytical philosophers in the tradition of Frege, Russell, and G. H. Meade consider metaphysical statements of this kind nonsense. Most of these philosophers tend to identify all transcendental philosophy as just another form of the idealism against which they personally reacted.

17. See George Lindbeck, *op. cit.*, pp. 214 f.

18. *Schriften*, vol. VI, p. 266.

19. See *Lexikon für Theologie und Kirche*, vol. 10, col. 61.

For more recent articles on the subjects treated in this chapter see *Schriften*, vol. VI, esp. "Der Mensch von heute und die Religion," pp. 13–33; "Ideologie und Christentum," pp. 59–76; "Marxistische Utopie und christliche Zukunft des Menschen," pp. 77–90; "Gerecht und Sünder Zugleich," pp. 262–276; "Pastoraltheologische Bemerkungen über den Episkopat in der Lehre des II. Vaticanum," pp. 423–431; "Ueber Bischofskonferenzen," pp. 434–454. For "intellectual honesty" see "Glaube und intellektuelle Redlichkeit," *Stimmen der Zeit*, 177 (June 1966), pp. 401–418.

NAME INDEX

SUBJECT INDEX